Bicycle Guide
to the
Lewis & Clark Trail

Happy riding!

Ted Rodger

Bicycle Guide
to the
Lewis & Clark Trail

Tod Rodger

DEERFOOT PUBLICATIONS
Harvard, MA

Bicycle Guide to the Lewis & Clark Trail

Disclaimers

The author and publisher of this book, and the government agencies on whose roads you bicycle, are not responsible for your riding habits, bicycle condition, and any accidents which might occur while following this route. They urge users of this Guide to wear a certified bicycle helmet, wear highly visible clothing, use reflectors and lights, obey all traffic laws, watch for pedestrians and motorists, and generally use good common sense and courtesy.

Road and trail conditions change. The routes suggested in this book may be altered due to road and trail maintenance, changes in state and local roads, and road and trail surface conditions. Surface conditions of roads and trails may change due to weather, construction, and other local factors. Every effort has been made to provide accurate information in this book at the time of publication.

Updates will be posted on the author's website at www.deerfootpublications.com as they are received and verified. Readers are invited to send suggested updates to Tod@deerfootpublications.com.

ISBN 0-9704027-0-8

Design and Composition by Lyn Rodger, Deerfoot Studios.
Cover design by Lyn Rodger, Deerfoot Studios.

Dedicated to:

Doug Rodger (1971–1991)
my first and best touring partner

Contents

Acknowledgments

I love bicycle touring. I am grateful to all those who have tolerated, supported, and encouraged me in this passion—especially my friends, riding partners, extended family, and daughter Chris, who nursed me back to health after an accident, and still urged me to, "Go for it, Dad."

Although my early academic strengths and interests were in math and science, I have come to appreciate and love the beauty and history of our United States as I have aged and travelled. And as I gradually became the one who documents family and group travels, I have also realized how much I enjoy writing.

I was on a sabbatical from teaching high school math in 1998 when I first saw Ken Burns' public television series on Lewis and Clark, and saw the light. I could combine all these things I love. Stephen Ambrose's *Undaunted Courage* further inspired me and provided the final kick I needed to get going. After a year of trying to convince Adventure Cycling to work together on a map and book description of the Lewis and Clark Trail, I was discouraged when they decided to proceed without my help. However, Harvey Botzman of Cyclotours and many friends encouraged me to proceed anyway.

Many people helped along the way. The Lauritzens, Aikens, Hales, and Bells were generous with accommodations, hospitality, and ideas. Visitor centers, chambers of commerce, B&Bs, National and State Park informations centers, and Lewis and Clark interpretive centers have been very interested, helpful, friendly, generous, and patient; and many have read and critiqued sections of the book. Rex Garrelts and Mark Viets (Captain Lew and Captain Bill) have road tested parts of the book on their bicycle tour. The Ankers and staff at Anker Publishing and the Dufurs at Pebble Publishing have been most helpful with publishing issues.

I thank Mary Wilson at the Harvard Library, who has provided so much cheerful help with research. I am grateful to my sister, Jean Preis, who has steadfastly encouraged me and has proven to be a masterful editor—challenging me to tighten, rewrite, tighten, and rewrite to make this book more readable and useful. And above all, my wife and touring partner in the journey of life, Lyn, has devoted countless hours from her business as a professional graphic artist to travel with me, take photographs, navigate, and document mileage, elevation, and directions. At home she has edited, proofread, drawn maps, and comprehensively prepared this book for publication. She has also helped me with innumerable computer problems and generally been a beacon of hope and encouragement throughout the entire process.

The quotations from the journals of Lewis and Clark are all from the Moulton edition, and I am grateful to the University of Nebraska Press for permission to use them. For the most part, the quotations are referenced by date, because that is the easiest way to locate them in the journals. I thank the National Park Service for permission to use the familiar silhouette of Lewis and Clark on the cover of this book. All photographs are by Lyn and Tod Rodger, except the cover photograph of the author by Roy Moffa.

WHY BIKE THE LEWIS & CLARK TRAIL?

ORGANIZATION OF THIS BOOK

The author looking up to his heroes, who are looking west.
Explorers at the Portage by Robert M. Scriver,
is at the Great Falls Visitor Center.

WHO WERE LEWIS AND CLARK?

WHAT DID THEY DO?

WHY IS THEIR TRIP SIGNIFICANT?

When the fledgling United States was only 26 years old in 1803, the Mississippi River formed its western boundary. The vast continent beyond the Mississippi was legally administered by Spain; but it was populated only by "Indian" tribes that could be either friendly or dangerous, a few French trappers and traders who had ventured beyond the French settlement of St. Louis, and a few American pioneers who had illegally homesteaded fertile farmland.

The Pacific coast was sparsely inhabited by Spanish missionaries, and ownership was claimed and disputed by Spain, Britain, and Russia. The American explorer Grey had discovered the mouth of the Columbia River, and the British explorer Vancouver had ventured 100 miles up the Columbia River; but no European had seen the vast area between the Dakotas and the Pacific Ocean.

Where others saw conflict, confusion, and desert wasteland, Thomas Jefferson, our nation's third president, saw opportunity. Some historians have pointed out that America was an empire before it was a nation—struggling with the British, French, and Spanish to find the "northwest passage" to the rich Orient and to establish a nation on the American continent. In what many saw as folly, but history later confirmed was brilliance, Jefferson convinced Congress to purchase the Louisiana Territory for three cents an acre, thereby doubling the size of the United States.

On June 20, 1803 Jefferson charged Meriwether Lewis and William Clark with leading a U.S. Army expedition of 30 men to explore this new land. His instructions to Lewis stated, *"The object of your mission is to explore the Missouri river, & such principal stream of it, as, by it's course & communication with the waters of the Pacific Ocean, may offer the most direct & practicable water communication across this continent, for the purposes of commerce."* Even with the inconsistent spelling and stilted grammar of the times, the instructions are still very clear.

Over the next two years the "Corps of Discovery" travelled 7,000 miles from St. Louis, up the Missouri River, over the Rocky Mountains, down the Columbia River to Astoria, Oregon, and back again. In this epic American exploration of unknown territory they lived off the country, made maps, acted as ambassadors to many curious and mostly friendly Native American tribes, and documented many new species of plants and animals. Although their intentions were to find new routes, learn about the land, develop friends and trading partners—not to conquer or convert—in hindsight the eventual outcomes seem obvious.

By the time of the expedition's return in 1806, traders and settlers were already pushing westward into the new territory—a process which in many ways defined the United States for the next 100 years. Even today, the phrase "go west, young man," still rings with adventure and opportunity.

This was very much the age of exploration and empire building. Individuals were moving west for free land, better beaver trapping, and new trade with native people. Governments were encouraging and supporting this movement, both to reap commercial benefits and to expand their empires.

Trade with the Orient was already very profitable, but the sea voyage around either South America or Africa was long, dangerous, and expensive. The strategic importance of a water route across the North American continent had been clearly recognized for many years, and the race to discover this was well underway. In 1793 Jefferson had tried to send a private expedition to cross the continent, but it was aborted when the leader was found out to be a secret French agent. In the same year, the British explorer Mackenzie was the first to cross the North American continent over the Canadian Rockies, but his route offered no hope for either commercial use or future settlement. The race languished for almost ten years as other events claimed more attention.

The common knowledge of the time assumed there was a geographical divide somewhere between the Mississippi River and the Pacific Ocean. Since the Missouri River was the largest river flowing eastward from the plains, it seemed logical that you could travel up the Missouri River, portage over the divide, pick up the "River of the West" (generally assumed to be the Columbia River), and float down to the Pacific. Everyone thought "the divide" was similar to the Appalachian Divide—not very high or steep, and easy to portage in a day or so.

The surprises of the expedition would be both daunting and awesome. No one could imagine how high, dramatic, and complex the Rockies would be, or what kind of weather could be expected there. No one knew the Rockies are not a single mountain range, but a confusing puzzle of interlocking ranges. No one knew the length of the Missouri River, or that it included a series of five "great falls" cut between steep cliffs. These are only a few of the things Lewis and Clark discovered, and these and many other adventures are still there for you to discover on your own epic journey.

WHAT IS THE LEWIS & CLARK *TRAIL*?

In 1978 Congress established the Lewis & Clark National Historic Trail as part of the National Trails System. The National Park Service administers this trail in partnership with many federal, state, and local agencies, private organizations, and private landowners. These groups are also involved in many recreational and interpretive sites and activities along the Trail. See Appendix E for additional resources and information.

Although the Lewis and Clark expedition travelled mostly on rivers, Lewis often explored the adjacent land, and hunting parties walked to search for game. Today some roads that follow the rivers have been marked with the familiar silhouettes (on the cover of this book) of Lewis and Clark pointing the way. Sometimes roads on both sides of the river display these signs. Sometimes the expedition split up and took multiple routes. Sometimes the exact route is unknown. And many times the exact route and campsites have been wiped out by the changing course of the rivers over the last 200 years.

So the words "Lewis & Clark Trail" have come to signify the general and approximate route followed by the Corps of Discovery. Although this book follows many of these roads, it also uses some different roads and trails that are more suitable for bicycle travel.

WHY *BIKE* THE LEWIS & CLARK TRAIL ?

In 1804 Lewis and Clark's two-year expedition grabbed the imagination and attention of the whole country—as it still does today. The PBS television program first caught my interest and sparked the idea of bicycling this route. Reading Stephen Ambrose's *Undaunted Courage* immediately confirmed my decision.

When I first read about the Corps of Discovery sailing, rowing, poling, and pulling their boats up the Missouri River and then crossing the Rocky Mountains and riding down the wild Columbia River, I was impressed and amazed. What hardships! What joys! What accomplishment! After riding this route, my sense of amazement, respect, and admiration have grown even greater.

I will also proudly admit my own feeling of accomplishment. As usual, I have forgotten most of the hardships and remembered most of the joys. This is a challenging bicycle tour, and the feeling of accomplishment is proportional to the challenge and the effort.

First, it's a great ride. Even without any association with Lewis and Clark, it provides a panorama of beautiful scenery, good roads with light traffic, a variety of accommodations and food, and exposure to wonderful people. On this basis alone, it's as good as any long distance bicycle tour.

Second, it's a great way to see, feel, and fully experience our vast and varied country. Passing through nine states from St. Louis, Missouri, to Astoria, Oregon, it provides a comprehensive sampling of these "united states." For myself, having grown up on the east coast and having lived on both coasts, it was an awakening to the vast middle of our country. Although technically not a "transcontinental" ride, at 3,000 miles it's almost as long. If you really need to accomplish a true transcontinental ride, it's easy enough to find a route between St. Louis and the east coast—perhaps following Meriwether Lewis's path from Philadelphia to Pittsburgh and down the Ohio River to St. Louis.

Third, this route has great historical meaning and significance for our country. By 1804, both France and Spain were in trouble in North America, and opportunity was ripe for the new United States. Jefferson's purchase of the Louisiana Territory doubled the size of our country, and Lewis and Clark's exploration described the new land and opened it for future settlement. It's interesting to ponder what the current United States might be like if it still ended at the Mississippi River.

Fourth, bicycling this route is a way to make history come alive. There are many historical sites and exhibits along the way which are both fun and educational to visit. This book describes most of them briefly, and the route was devised to include as many as possible directly on or near the route. Appendix D describes other books that tell more about the Lewis and Clark expedition and will help prepare you for a bicycle trip on the Trail.

Finally, the years 2003–2006 mark the bicentennial of the Lewis and Clark expedition. Renewed attention is being focussed on this heroic and significant event in our country's history, and many towns and states along the route are adding to their repertoire of services, activities, and celebrations.

ORGANIZATION OF THIS BOOK

Bicycle Guide to the Lewis & Clark Trail is intended for dreaming, planning, and executing your trip. It is large enough to contain all the information you will need, and small enough to carry with you.

Chapter 2 describes my **philosophy** of flexibility and trade-offs, and some questions that will help you plan a successful tour.

Chapter 3 is an **overview** of the entire Lewis & Clark Trail. It is intended to help you understand the big picture and create a "Master Plan" for an overall trip or series of trips. A table summarizes all possible places for overnight stops and the services they provide.

Chapter 4 contains **descriptions and maps** for **towns** along the route. In my touring experience—especially in the western United States—it's relatively easy to get from town to town. The problems come when you reach a town: where can you find camping, motels, supermarkets, bike store, etc. This section is intended to help you on a daily basis as you travel the Trail.

Chapter 5 provides **detailed cue sheets** (directions) and **maps** for riding between towns. This chapter is separate, so you can tear out pages and put them in your handlebar bag or pocket as you ride from town to town. For your convenience, there are separate sets of cue sheets for both westbound and eastbound travellers; so you can tear out and discard unnecessary pages to lighten the book.

Appendix A makes suggestions about **preparing your bicycle**.

Appendix B is a suggested **equipment list**.

Appendix C provides tables summarizing **weather** for different areas on the Trail.

Appendix D lists and briefly describes **other books** about the Lewis and Clark expedition and route. These provide both fun reading and helpful information as you prepare for your bike tour.

Appendix E provides sources for state highway maps and other **additional information**.

Appendix F shows **public transportation**—a list of airports and a map of major train and bus routes.

Although this book contains sufficient maps and information to plan and execute a bicycle tour of the Lewis & Clark Trail, many people will want to acquire state highway maps to see how the route fits into the big picture. After planning a trip, I like to cut up state maps and carry only the essential parts. Western states offer these maps free, along with lots of general information about interesting things to see and do in their states.

You will note that cumulative miles have been placed sideways in the righthand page margins in Chapters 4 and 5. These are to aid you in cross-referencing and moving among Chapters 3, 4, and 5. They will also help you thumb through the book and quickly find the page you want.

PHILOSOPHY

Miles of corn in Iowa

This chapter is intended to give you a feel for my philosophy—and therefore the philosophy of this book and this tour. Even though I think I know a lot about bicycle touring, I usually learn something new and worthwhile from every book I read and every experienced cyclist I meet. Hopefully, you too will learn something from this section.

PERSONAL

Although I played with a bike as a child, I was in my late 20s when I dug out my old Rudge 3-speed and started commuting to graduate school at Stanford as a way to save money and get some exercise. I enjoyed riding so much that I started exploring the nearby countryside on weekends. At that point I invested $30 in a used Schwinn Varsity with 10 different gears!

After graduate school I upgraded to a new 10-speed Peugot UO-8 for $110. Two years later it was stolen from my office, and I splurged $250 on an Atala Competizione with Campagnolo components. This was light, fast day touring at its best—until I got my first flat on a tubular tire. Never able to patch tubulars successfully, I replaced the whole tire. After a few of these expensive experiences, I switched to the light clincher wheels and tires that were becoming more available.

In my early 40s I started fantasizing about longer bicycle trips, and I bought a set of rear panniers. My wife couldn't understand why I needed panniers to carry my lunch to work. Her suspicions and fears increased when I bought a Specialized Expedition—a long-wheelbase heavy-duty touring bicycle with 40-spoke wheels and lots of braze-ons.

When my son was fifteen, we took a three-day bicycle trip through the White Mountains of New Hampshire in early September. We enjoyed it so much that we immediately started planning a longer tour to Nova Scotia for the next summer. We wanted to go for the whole summer, but agreed with my wife to a three-week compromise. She wasn't crazy about the whole idea, but she figured she'd put up with it and we'd "get it out of our systems."

Ha! The next summer it was five weeks on the West Coast, justified as "a once-in-a-lifetime father-son opportunity." It certainly was, because after age seventeen my son lost interest in touring with his slower and duller old man. Although my ego was hurt, as a rational father I understood both the physiological and social forces at work.

My wife came to accept that I was not going to "get this out of my system" anytime soon, and I have since led more than a dozen major tours with friends, groups of high school students, and alone. I have toured in many areas of the United States, Canada, and Europe. My ideal tour used to be about five weeks and 2,000 miles—long enough to lose track of time and really "live" the tour, but short enough to hang onto my happy marriage. More recently, I have preferred many different tours of 2–14 days with less camping and more motels and B&Bs. We also bought a tandem, and my wife now enjoys joining me on day trips. A few years ago, I passed Mile 100,000 since I started keeping a log twenty years ago. I peaked at 10,000 miles/year, and now do a more reasonable 6,000–8,000.

FLEXIBILITY

I believe flexibility is critically important for a successful bicycle tour—and for life in general! The more flexible you are, the happier you will be. Although you don't need to be flexible in *every* way, it's important to understand your priorities—and the priorities of your travelling companions.

The *ideal* bicycle tour has small to medium towns at intervals of 25 miles. Each town has a beautiful campground with private grassy sites, shade trees, covered picnic tables, clean restrooms with showers, and a sandy beach. Near the campground is a large supermarket with deli and salad bar, a variety of restaurants for different tastes and budgets, a bicycle shop, a hospital with a walk-in clinic, a hostel, a classy B&B, an inexpensive motel with basic amenities, and a more expensive motel with pool, sauna, and hot tub.

In this environment you can choose a daily ride of 25, 50, 75, etc. miles. You can fill water bottles and buy snacks or meals every 25 miles. Since nobody knows about this perfect route, you don't need any reservations, and you can make last minute decisions based on the weather and how tired you are. But of course the weather would always be perfect on this ideal tour.

The bad news is that the Lewis & Clark Trail falls short of this ideal. The good news is that it's still a great route, and this book will give you information to make the best possible choices to match up with your priorities. The more flexible you are, the easier it will be for you. For example, on a particular day you might have to choose among riding 40 miles and camping at a campground next to the river with no showers, riding 65 miles and staying at a basic motel with a restaurant next door, or riding 80 miles and camping in a pleasant state park with all amenities. Answer the questions below for yourself (and for each member of your group), and then use this book to try a "virtual tour" to see what impact your choices will have.

ROUTE

Since most of the Lewis and Clark journey was on rivers, any land tour can only be an approximation of their route. I have travelled most of the Trail on both sides of the rivers and tried to choose the best side for bicycle touring. There are many places where one side is clearly better. However, in other areas where it is less clear, this book offers a recommended route and mentions alternatives with the trade-offs. For example, the recommended route might offer more hills and less traffic, while an alternative offers fewer hills and more traffic.

Although I tried to stay close to the rivers, there are a few places where I found compelling reasons to stray from them in order to provide a better bicycle tour. I try to justify these situations in the book. Although I wanted to include all the states that border the Missouri River, this was not a high priority. Kansas and Nebraska are left out, because I felt the east side was so much better for bicycle touring. However, I do offer a couple of alternatives for forays into interesting parts of both states.

The biggest dilemma I faced was which route to take in western Montana—where Lewis and Clark explored three different routes—one westbound and two on their return trip. In this case I offer all three routes, along with the pros and cons of each, so you can tailor the route to fit your own interests.

East to West vs. West to East
Although historical purists will probably want to follow Lewis and Clark's actual progress from east to west, it is possible to enjoy the route in either direction. Wind is often used as a (questionable) argument for riding west to east (see below). Other considerations may include what time of year you ride, when you want to tackle the mountains, whether you do the trip in sections, where you live, and how you arrange supplemental transportation to and from this tour. With all this in mind, I prioritized history over the windy Columbia River Gorge and chose to orient this book from east to west. However, Chapter 5 includes detailed directions both eastbound and westbound, and it's easy to use this book to go either direction. Lewis and Clark, of course, went both ways!

Wind Direction
The argument for going west to east is often related to wind. North of the equator weather systems move from west to east. Many people believe this means the wind also blows from west to east, but wind actually moves in circles around high- and low-pressure areas. This means it can blow in almost any direction, and wind direction changes as weather systems move.

Wind direction is also determined by local conditions. For example, wind usually blows hard from the west in the Columbia River Gorge during the summer; that's why Hood River, Oregon, is the wind-surfing capital of the west. However, in the spring and fall it sometimes howls from the east. Keep in perspective that this stretch involves perhaps 40 miles of the whole Lewis and Clark route, and some of this is on heavily wooded roads that are somewhat protected from wind.

My own experience is more in line with that of people who live along the route: "The wind blows from all different directions with differing intensities." When I asked one farmer if the wind always blew this hard, he responded, "Well, it'll blow like this for a few days, and then it'll change direction and really blow."

ONE LONG TOUR VS. SEVERAL SHORTER TOURS
Although this book is written as a single 3,000-mile tour from St. Louis, Missouri, to Astoria, Oregon, many people may not want a tour this long. There are many opportunities to access this bicycle route by public transportation at various cities and towns along the way. Appendix F includes a list of airports and an overview map of the entire route, highlighting railroads and bus routes, to help you understand the available public transportation. Appendix F also includes contacts for major rail and bus lines. If your time is limited and/or you have preferences about riding certain sections, you may also want to consider using public transportation to skip over parts of your tour.

WEATHER

There are reams of data available on the Internet about weather. How much is useful is another matter. Appendix C includes a brief summary of temperature and precipitation data for those who would like some quantitative data.

Common sense helps a lot. For example, it can be very hot during the summer, especially from St. Louis to Great Falls. In most of the plains states there are few trees and very little shade. Use heavy-duty sunscreen, apply it several times a day, and drink lots of fluids.

Late spring and early fall are often pleasant from St. Louis to Great Falls and from Lewiston to Astoria, although nights can be chilly. On April 26 in eastern Montana Clark wrote, *"last night was verry Cold. the Thermometer Stood at 32 abov 0 this morning."*

The mountains have always made their own weather, and a useful rule of thumb is that 1,000 feet of elevation equals 300 miles of latitude—i.e. climbing 1,000 feet results in a weather change equivalent to travelling 300 miles north. In the mountains between Great Falls and Lewiston I have ridden in short sleeves during the day and had water bottles freeze overnight in the middle of summer. On August 2, near Cardwell, Montana, Lewis wrote, *"the tops of these mountains were yet partially covered with snow while we in the valley were suffocated nearly with the intense heat of the midday sun. the nights are so could that two blankets are not more than sufficient covering."*

The plains area, especially in the Dakotas, can spawn severe thunderstorms and occasional tornadoes during summer months. It's a good idea to keep an eye on the weather, both literally and figuratively. One day in Selby, SD, with threatening dark clouds approaching, I stopped in a bar to get some weather information. They were watching the weather channel, whose map looked exactly like the sky outside. Since severe thunderstorms and possible tornado touchdowns were predicted in about two hours, I decided to stay in a small hotel in Selby. It was a smart move; high winds and heavy rain came through right on schedule. Fifty miles north a tornado touched down briefly. If you can't occasionally monitor TV and radio weather forecasts, ask local people. They understand their weather pretty well, since their lives and businesses often depend on it.

Although you should certainly respect tornadoes, you shouldn't let them frighten you away from this beautiful part of the country. As a former high school math teacher, I have occasionally spent riding time thinking about the probability of getting caught by a tornado. Although I haven't proved it yet, I'm absolutely convinced that you're safer riding in the Dakotas during summer months than you are driving around home, flying in an airplane, stepping in and out of the bathtub, etc.

TIME OF YEAR

Although you can ride this route in much less than the eighteen months that Lewis and Clark took to travel west, it's still important to plan around the seasons, just as they did. Primarily, you have a window during July and August (and probably June and September) to tackle the mountains of Montana and Idaho. It pretty much boils down to when you can make the time available, how far you can ride per day, and how you want to trade off potentially hot summer days on the plains with potentially cold spring and fall days in the mountains.

My reasoning for an ideal westbound ride goes like this: Hit the Continental Divide (Mile 2070) June 15—about the earliest you can count on its being free from snow. Averaging 60 miles/day, this means leaving St. Louis about May 10, gaining both latitude and elevation while enjoying the longer days as early summer arrives, and arriving in Astoria (Mile 2930) about July 1.

Notice the words "about." Although I make an overall plan for a tour like this, I make detailed daily plans only a few days in advance. Stay flexible! Travelling eastbound, I might want to hit the Divide as late in the season as possible—about September 1. At 50 miles/day because of the shorter days, this means leaving Astoria about August 12, enjoying the advent of early fall while losing both latitude and elevation, and arriving in St. Louis to a hero's welcome about October 12.

Give some thought to the length of days during June vs. September and the impact this has on how many miles per day you can comfortably ride. If you plan to ride short days of 40–50 miles, this won't be a problem; although you'll need to be more flexible about where you're willing to spend your nights. If you plan to ride longer days and/or do a lot of camping, the length of days can make a real difference. For example, at 45° latitude on much of this route, there are almost 16 hours of daylight on June 15, but only 12 hours on September 15.

MILES/DAY

How many miles you want to ride each day is a good question for you and your partners to ponder as part of your tour planning. Maybe you know from experience how many miles per day you like to do. If not, think about how many hours per day you want to ride and multiply by 10 miles/hour. Although this seems excessively simpleminded, it works quite well. 10 miles/hour may seem slow, but this method includes all the time you spend stopping for snacks, lunch, breaks, etc. All the groups I have toured with have only varied between 8 and 12 miles/hour for overall planning purposes. If you can keep track of what you do the first few days, you can adjust your number. But you'll find it doesn't make that much difference for planning.

For example, if you want to camp, get up at 7:30 am, leave at 9:30, and get to your next campground by 3:30 in order to set up camp and enjoy your destination, that means 6 hours elapsed time and 60 miles. If you use 11 miles/hour instead, it means 66 miles instead of 60 for the day. You can reverse this planning process if you know you have to ride 95 miles. You have to either leave earlier in the morning and/or arrive later in the afternoon. DON'T count on riding faster! You may want to treat yourself to a restaurant and/or a motel if you have to ride a long day.

The next section can help you refine this process based on the hills you can expect each day.

Hills

Valuable information about hills can be found in three places in this book. First, the Master Plan in Chapter 3 has a column on hills and a legend to help you understand hills in various ways. This provides data on "average hilliness" between towns and is most useful when planning how far you want to ride each day. Second, each overview section in Chapter 4 has a general description that includes hills. This is useful when planning which sections of the Trail you might like to ride. Finally, there is a brief description of hills below each detailed cue map in Chapter 5. This is most helpful when you are riding each section and want to know what to expect in more detail.

When planning my daily riding distance, I use an average of 10 miles/hour for planning, as described above. If I know a section is going to be "flat," I may use 12 miles/hour. If I know there will be "significant hills," I may use 8 miles/hour.

I use an altimeter (built into my cyclecomputer) while touring and for gathering data for this book. You don't need an altimeter, because the planning data in Chapter 2 includes hill information for sections of the route. However, they are lots of fun for gadget people!

Wind Speed

Wind can be as important as (and sometimes more important than) hills in planning your speed, but it's almost impossible to predict. If you knew you were going to have a strong tailwind, you could easily add 2 miles/hour to your speed. Conversely, if you knew you were going to have a strong headwind, you could easily lose 2 miles/hour. It's possible to carefully monitor weather forecasts each day, but I've found wind forecasts to be generally unavailable and inaccurate. I've also found wind to vary with location and time of day, and I usually ignore it in planning. However, I also try to schedule things loosely enough so a headwind doesn't ruin my day.

PAVED VS. DIRT ROADS

This tour is designed as a "road" tour on paved roads. Since traffic generally varies from moderate to none, and the scenery is mostly great wide open vistas, there is little incentive to avoid comfortable paved roads. However, I don't think I've ever taken a road tour without at least one construction site or campground access road that required a few miles on dirt or gravel. There are also times when you pick up local information about a fantastic shortcut or scenic road that includes some dirt.

There are a few short sections of dirt on our route that are recommended for various reasons. These can be ridden on touring bikes with strong tires, or they can be avoided by choosing alternate routes. The pros and cons of each alternative are outlined for you. Once again, it's helpful if you have the flexibility to consider both options.

ROAD VS. MOUNTAIN BIKE

Either will do fine; this is *not* the key question. The key questions you want to ask yourself are: Is the bike comfortable, is it reliable, can I fix things that break, will it carry what I want to carry, can I ride it on a dirt road if I have to or want to? Mountain bikes are very popular for touring these days because they meet many of these criteria. If I weren't so tall (6'6"), I would probably use one for touring. Reasonably good ones are comfortable, strong, rugged, reliable, and they can carry more than you can. Relatively smooth tire treads with high pressure will provide a comfortable and efficient ride on paved roads. Bar ends (or other curved handlebars) provide multiple hand configurations for comfort, variety, and aerodynamic riding.

If you want to use a road bike, test it with more weight than you intend to carry on a bumpy dirt road before your tour. A bicycle that is strong enough for dirt roads will also require less maintenance and cause you fewer problems. Flat tires, broken spokes, and other equipment failures are not much fun on a tour; they rarely occur at convenient times and places!

BICYCLE PREPARATION

Mechanical problems with your bicycle and your equipment are no fun on a long tour, especially in remote areas. Although the laws of probability suggest that you will have some problems on a 3,000-mile tour, the same laws of probability can reduce the problems if you are smart before you leave. There are many things you can do to minimize the probability of problems. Appendix A offers suggestions on preparing your bicycle. Whatever you do, NEVER make any changes just before you leave; always check out any changes for a few hundred miles while you are still close to home and help. Don't assume that a brand new bicycle or a new repair is reliable.

BODY PREPARATION

I know people who hop on a bicycle and ride 50 miles with negligible preparation, but they're often not so happy the next morning when they have to get back on the bike and ride another 50 miles. Lots of experience and common sense suggest that you will be happier if you prepare your body for a tour.

Although bicycling magazines have articles and formulas every year for getting in shape, here are some basic guidelines I use: Ride 1,200 miles (or 20 times your planned daily mileage) during the few months before your tour, building up as you go. Make sure you can do a single ride of your planned daily mileage two months before you leave, and do two consecutive days of your planned daily mileage one month before you leave. You may also want to plan your tour so the first week or two are shorter and easier than later weeks.

EQUIPMENT LIST

Appendix B is the equipment list I have developed over years of touring. People who tour with me have found it useful, although they usually make modifications to suit personal tastes and whims.

Some things I emphasize: Use a good rear rack with a four-point (vs. three-point) attachment. Use a good "low rider" front rack to keep weight low in the front (improves stability and safety). Keep weight balanced between front and rear, and between left and right. Pack larger, lighter things in the larger rear panniers; smaller, heavier things in the smaller front panniers. Use wide (preferably 1.375 inch or 38 mm width) tires with Kevlar belts. If you are heavy, consider 40-spoke wheels, especially on the rear. Using this strategy, I average one flat tire about every 5,000 miles, and I have broken only one spoke in over 125,000 miles.

A triple chainwheel is mandatory for me, although I know younger and stronger riders who claim they don't need one. Spinning faster in lower gears is much easier on your knees and muscles. The number of gears is less important than having a wide range—especially at the low end; 20 gear inches to 100 gear inches (an indication of how far the bike travels per pedal revolution) is much better than 30 to 100.

Experienced bicycle tourers have strong and varied opinions about how many tools and spare parts to carry. My philosophy leans toward better bicycle preparation and fewer tools, as shown in the Equipment List in Appendix B. However, larger groups of people allow you to share both tools and spare parts, and therefore carry more without adding much weight.

Of course, you must be able to fix a flat tire. I carry a spare tube, so I can change it quickly on the road and then patch the tube leisurely at the end of the day. I do not carry a spare tire; if in doubt about your tires, buy new ones before you go—preferably strong wide ones with Kevlar belts. I do carry a five-inch piece of old tire that I can insert inside a severely cut tire; this will work for several hundred miles until you can buy a new tire.

A chain tool is also essential. If you break a chain, just remove a link. Otherwise, a broken chain is a stopper. I don't carry spare spokes, because I use very strong 40-spoke wheels with high quality 14-gauge spokes. It's also possible to ride for many miles with a broken spoke if you adjust the tension on the neighboring spokes. If you do carry spare spokes, you probably also need different length spokes, a special freewheel remover, and a large wrench.

SAG WAGON VS. UNSUPPORTED

Although Lewis and Clark would roll over in their graves, consider including a sag vehicle if you are touring with a group. You don't have to carry gear on your bike, and you can carry more "stuff." If you have four people, each person can drive every fourth day, rest, shop, find a campground or motel, etc. It can balance unequal abilities and/or desires to ride. You can visit places farther off the route. You have a vehicle in bad weather. It can be an ambulance. It solves problems getting to and from a tour.

Having cited all these advantages, I have never used a sag wagon. I prefer the freedom and sense of accomplishment of a pure bicycle tour.

MOTELS AND B&Bs

Do you prefer to stay indoors at night and eat at restaurants? Use the Master Plan to find towns with motels and/or B&Bs, and use the Town Descriptions to find specific motels and B&Bs. If you prefer to lighten your load by not carrying any camping gear, it's possible to ride this entire 3,000-mile tour and stay indoors every night. The longest single stretch between motels is 84 miles in eastern Oregon; generally you can choose daily rides from 20 to 60 miles.

If you are primarily a budget camper, are you willing and able to spend some nights in motels and B&Bs, or does your budget or personal philosophy require camping every night? Although there are many good campgrounds along this route, there are some places where campgrounds are either far apart or inconvenient distances from the Trail. This book provides the information to help you make these trade-offs.

Planning and Reservations

At one end of the spectrum, some people plan every day of their tour in advance and make reservations for every night. At the other extreme, some people make no reservations and take their chances every night. Of course there are many options in between, and you need to think about what suits you.

I resist making reservations; it takes time and effort to research them in advance, make the phone calls, and then lose flexibility because I feel forced every day to make it to a certain town no matter what the weather, how I feel, or what better options I might discover at the last minute. Campgrounds can almost always fit in tenters arriving on bicycles. The only time I've been turned away from a campground was near Aspen, Colorado, on the 4th of July. Although we were tired, inconvenienced, and annoyed, we ended up spending a memorable night camping at a nearby shooting range recommended by the local police. I occasionally pay a premium for not making reservations, like the time I arrived in Pierre during the annual bass fishing tournament. But even there, several phone calls turned up a room in a more expensive motel—with a hot tub for compensation!

Over the years I have learned to modify my "no reservations" philosophy to suit my personality. Each day I try to make a detailed plan for the next couple of days. I try to consider projected weather, how my companions and I are feeling, weekday vs. weekend, number and type of accommodation options at daily destinations, and any special events. I stop at *every* visitor information center, Ranger Station, etc. and often pick up valuable local information that I would have been sorry to miss. Sometimes I make a reservation. I was very glad I called Prairie Knights Casino and Hotel a day in advance—halfway between Mobridge, South

Dakota, and Bismarck, North Dakota; the alternatives were a 115-mile day into a fierce headwind or camping by the side of the road.

CAMPING

Will you carry a tent, sleeping bag, etc. to camp? I often do, and I recommend it. Although it means carrying extra weight, it allows more flexibility in the length of your riding day, saves money (some town parks and campgrounds are free!), helps you make contact with other campers, and takes advantage of many excellent (and some not so excellent!) parks along the route. I love to camp when the weather is good, I enjoy hearing a brief shower on my tent while I sleep, and I'm willing to occasionally pack up a wet tent on a rainy morning, but I will *not* camp when the weather is bad or threatening in the late afternoon. When I tour with others and can share the load, we often carry a parabolic rain fly to make camping more comfortable in "iffy" weather.

Primitive Camping

Do you require a campground, or are you comfortable with "primitive camping?" I have a strong preference for camping in established campgrounds for comfort, convenience, and safety; although I have occasionally camped in some strange and interesting places in emergencies. This book includes only established campgrounds and describes their amenities. If you are comfortable with "primitive camping" or asking people for permission to camp on their lawns or fields, you already know how to do it, and you will find many opportunities along this route.

Cooking and Food

Will you take a stove, cooking gear, and some bulk food to allow you to eat on your own—sometimes without shopping for a day or two? Although it means extra weight, I recommend it for the flexibility it provides. There are many campgrounds with food shopping nearby, but there are also some away from towns that require planning where you will shop and eat. I prefer to shop every day as late in the day as possible, but I also carry at least one emergency dinner of rice, onions, and lentils, and one breakfast of hot cereal, brown sugar, and raisins.

Mosquitoes

Lewis and Clark often complained about mosquitoes in their journals. Even in 1804 they used mosquito netting for sleeping, and one day Lewis recorded that he had to spend a night away from the main camp without his netting and couldn't sleep at all. The bad news is that mosquitoes like warm weather and wet areas, and that's where some of the best camping is located. The good news is that mosquitoes seem to be largely a local and temporary phenomenon. Sometimes there aren't any near the river where you expect them—perhaps because of dry weather or local spraying. Other times they're in places that seem high and dry where you wouldn't expect them. After a period of heavy rain, they can be annoying. After several dry weeks, they may be only a minor nuisance. I have never been bothered while riding, and only occasionally while camping. You probably already know they are worst around dusk and daybreak. The best thing is to be prepared. Experiment with different insect repellents and types of clothing before you go—elastic bands around your slacks at the ankles, a light windbreaker, a hat with netting. Also ask local people. A supermarket checkout clerk once told me mosquitoes were terrible in one local campground but non-existent in another only two miles away.

WATER FILTER

Today's small water filters provide protection from giardia and other impurities. I often carry a water filter when I'm touring with others and can share common equipment, especially in remote areas where it adds a lot of flexibility in obtaining water from streams and other questionable sources. Although it's technically and medically possible, I wouldn't want to drink even filtered water from most of the Missouri and its tributaries. There's a reason why it's called the "Big Muddy," and mud clogs up filters very quickly. Except for "primitive camping" and a few National Forest Service campgrounds, the established campgrounds on this route all have drinking water; and there is not a compelling reason to carry a water filter.

LOCKS

I have heard arguments and seen the whole spectrum on locks—from heavy duty U-bolts to nothing. Personally, I use a medium cable with a combination padlock to protect myself from "joyriders" and spur-of-the-moment opportunists; and I have never had any problem. My wife locks things more carefully than I do, because she feels the hassle of locking is less than the hassle of finding and replacing. You need to handle this to suit your own comfort level.

I also try to use common sense. When in doubt, lock it. If possible, leave your bicycle in sight of a ticket booth, information booth, or at least in a visible public place. I often ask an attendant to keep an eye on it, also explaining that I don't expect them to accept responsibility. I keep my essential valuables in a small fanny pack and *always* take them with me.

INDIANS VS. NATIVE AMERICANS

My experience is that "political correctness" has not updated the vocabulary out west as much as it has in the east when it comes to Indians vs. Native Americans. Since I rarely encountered the name "Native Americans" in either conversations or literature, and there didn't appear to be any disrespect in the word "Indian," I have been flexible in using both names.

SAFETY

Although nothing can *guarantee* safety, there are many things you can do to increase the probability of a safe ride. Wear bright, highly visible clothing, especially when it's rainy and foggy. Neon yellow is best. Reflective tape on clothing (especially on rain gear) helps when cars may have headlights on. Bright yellow pannier covers make your bicycle more visible. When I ride with groups, I try to convince the whole team to wear the same neon yellow shirts. Although it may impinge on individual tastes, it makes a group look both visible and professional—deserving respect.

Obey all vehicle traffic laws, like stopping at stop signs and riding single file when other vehicles are near. Don't antagonize people in larger vehicles, and resist the urge to retaliate—even if you think it's justified. Finally, don't make obscene gestures to pickup trucks with guns in the rear window!

Wear a helmet! All the time you are riding! I'm probably alive today because my helmet split instead of my head.

Carry a first-aid kit. I prefer to make up my own for two reasons. First, I know what's in it because I had to think about it and acquire it. Hopefully, this also means I know how to use the items. Second, it's more specific to the needs of bicyclists. The most common injury involves abrasions, so carry a variety of bandaids, gauze pads, non-adhesive dressings, and adhesive tape. The most critical thing to do in this type of accident is to stop any bleeding. It's helpful if someone in your group knows CPR. It's also helpful to have a cell phone with you. Since almost every part of the country now responds to 911 calls, this book does not include emergency phone numbers.

Every effort has been made to provide accurate information in this book. However, road and trail conditions change. The routes I've suggested may be altered due to maintenance, construction, and weather. Your safety is your responsibility and you need to check conditions locally as you travel.

OVERVIEW: THE MASTER PLAN

Oops! I started too early.

How to Use This Chapter

The table starting on the next page is intended to help you do two things:

1. Develop an overview master plan before you leave home.

2. Update your master plan as you encounter opportunities and surprises during your tour.

When you're first developing your master plan, you need to think about—and maybe trade off:

- how far you want to ride each day (**Cum**ulative miles and **Leg** miles), taking into account how hilly each section is (**Hills**)

- whether you want to **Camp** or stay in a **Motel** or **B&B**

- whether you will eat in a **Restaurant** or shop for food (**Food Shop**)

- your need for a **Bike Shop** or **Hospital**

(See the Philosophy section in Chapter 2 for more discussion about each item.)

You may also want to think about adding in some rest days and/or days to visit special attractions. Each line on the plan includes the page in Chapter 4 where you can find a description, map, and much more information about each town.

I like to add in about one day per week to do some non-biking activity or to be an emergency buffer day for unexpected weather, mechanical, or health problems. Sometimes this is planned for a specific day and town; other times it's there in case I just feel like it!

Once you have a "master plan," it's up to you how much you're willing to deviate from this plan. If you have airline reservations or need to be back to work on a certain day, you either need to achieve your plan exactly or add in a few spare days. If you prefer to make a reservation for every night far in advance, you need to execute your plan exactly. If you're able to be more flexible, you can adjust your plan almost every day depending on weather, how you feel, and what surprises you find along the way. I like to update a 2–3 day detailed plan every day, and I always try to have an alternate plan in mind in case something unexpected happens.

Towns

italics	optional town, off bike route

Camping

C	no showers
C-s	showers
C-p	showers at nearby pool

Food Shopping

*	Convenience Store: Calories, Survival
**	Small Mkt: Canned Goods, Fruit, Bread
***	Large Market: Meat, Frozen Foods
****	Large Supermarket: Full Variety

Restaurants

*	at least a Bar + Grill
**	at least 1 small/full restaurant
***	several restaurants
****	wide variety of restaurants

Hills

Symbol	Overall Description	on Average Climb (feet/mile)	Gradient Individual Hills (% grade)	Gearing Comments
0	flat	0 to 5	0 to 1	don't notice
h	gentle	5 to 20	1 to 3	some shifting
hh	moderate	20 to 40	3 to 5	low gears
hhh	significant	40 to 60	5+	granny gears
hhhh	steep + long	60+	6+	mountain pass

Cum. Miles	Leg Miles	Hills	Town	State	Page	Population	Camp	Food Shop	Motel	B&B	Restau-rant	Bike Shop	Hos-pital
0	0	0	St. Louis	MO	39	350,000			M		****		H
27	27	0	St. Charles	MO	42	55,000		***	M	B	****	**	H
35	8	0	Augusta	MO	44	300				B	***		
		0	Dutzow	MO		230					**	*	
38	3	0	*Washington*	*MO*	*45*	*12,000*		*****	*M*	*B*	****		*H*
		0	Marthasville	MO		675				B	**	*	
61	23	0	Hermann	MO	46	3,000	C-s	***	M	B	***		H
71	10	0	Bluffton	MO	48		C-s			B	**		
104	32	0	N. Jefferson	MO									

Cum. Miles	Leg Miles	Hills	Town	State	Page	Population	Camp	Food Shop	Motel	B&B	Restaurant	Bike Shop	Hospital
			Jefferson City	MO	48	*36,000*		****	M	B	****		*H*
114	10	0	Hartsburg	MO	49	130	C			B	**	*	
130	16	0	McBaine	MO		30		*					
		0	*Columbia*	MO	50	*90,000*		****	M	B	****		*H*
139	9	0	Rocheport	MO	50	260	C-s	*		B	***	*	
149	10	0	New Franklin	MO	52	1,100					**		
152	3	0	Boonville	MO	53	7,500		***	M	B	***		H
171	19	hh	Arrow Rock	MO	56	80	C-s			B	***		
186	15	hh	Marshall	MO	58	13,000		****	M		***		H
225	39	hh	Lexington	MO	59	5,000		****	M	B	***		H
262	37	hh	Liberty	MO	60	25,000		****	M	B	****	**	H
			Independence	MO	62	*110,000*		****	M	B	****		*H*
			Kansas City	MO	62	*450,000*		****	M	B	****		*H*
283	21	hh	KC Airport	MO			C-s		M		**		
288	5	hh	Platte City	MO	66	3,000	C-s	****	M		***		
296	8	hh	Weston	MO	67	1,600	C-s	***		B	****		
328	32	h	St. Joseph	MO	69	72,000	C-s	****	M		****	**	H
370	42	h	Big Lake SP	MO	72		C-s	**	M		**		
400	30	0	Rock Port	MO	72	1,500	C-s	***	M		***		
			Brownville	NE	73	*150*	C			B	**		
408	8	hhh	Tarkio	MO	74	2,200		***	M		**		
427	19	hhh	Blanchard	IA	74								
444	17	h	Shenandoah	IA	74	6,000	C-s	****	M		***		H
490	46	h	Council Bluffs	IA	76	55,000	C-s	****	M		****	*	H

Cum. Miles	Leg Miles	Hills	Town	State	Page	Population	Camp	Food Shop	Motel	B&B	Restaurant	Bike Shop	Hospital
			Omaha	*NE*	*81*	*355,000*		****	*M*	*	***		*H*
513	23	h	Missouri Valley	IA	82	3,000	C-s	***	M	B	***		H
553	40	0	Onawa	IA	83	3,000	C-s	****	M		***		H
594	41	h	Sioux City	IA	85	85,000	C-s	****	M		****	*	H
619	25	0	Elk Point	SD	88	1,400	C-s	**	M		**		
633	14	0	Vermillion	SD	88	10,000	C-p	****	M	B	***	*	H
662	29	0	Yankton	SD	90	14,000	C-s	****	M	B	***	*	H
694	32	hh	Springfield	SD	95	900	C-s	**	M		**		
740	46	hhh	Pickstown	SD	96	100		*	M		**		
746	6	hh	Lake Andes	SD	97	850	C-s	**	M		**		
776	30	hh	Platte	SD	98	1,300		***	M	B	***		
829	53	hh	Chamberlain	SD	98	2,500	C-s	***	M	B	***		
851	22	hhh	Fort Thompson	SD	100	1,100		**	M		**		
910	59	hh	Pierre	SD	100	13,000	C-s	****	M		***	*	H
956	46	hh	Onida	SD	103	760		**	M		**		
983	27	hh	Gettysburg	SD	104	1,500	C-s	***	M		***		
1023	40	hh	Selby	SD	105	700	C-s	**	M		**		
1043	20	hh	Mobridge	SD	106	3,800	C-s	***	M		***		H
1100	57	hh	Prairie Knights	ND	108				M		***		
1141	41	hh	Ft. Abe Lincoln	ND	111		C-s	*			*		
1146	5	hh	Mandan	ND	109	15,000	C-s	****	M		****		
1149	3	0	Bismarck	ND	109	55,000	C-s	****	M		****	*	H
1186	37	hh	Washburn	ND	114	1,500	C	***	M		**		
1206	20	h	Stanton	ND	117	500	C	**			**		

Cum. Miles	Leg Miles	Hills	Town	State	Page	Population	Camp	Food Shop	Motel	B&B	Restau- rant	Bike Shop	Hos- pital
1217	11	hh	Hazen	ND	117	2,800	C-s	***	M		***		H
1224	7	hh	Beulah	ND	118	3,400	C-s	***	M		***		
1252	28	hh	Halliday	ND	119	300		**	M		**		
1272	20	hh	Killdeer	ND	119	725	C-s	***	M		***		
1311	39	hhh	Roosevelt NP	ND	120		C						
1326	15	hhh	Watford City	ND	121	1,800	C-s	***	M		***		H
1346	20	hh	Alexander	ND	122	220	C	**	M		**		
1366	21	hh	Fairview	MT	122	900	C-p	**	M		**		
1378	11	0	Fort Union	MT	125								
1413	35	hh	Culbertson	MT	127	1,000	C-p	***	M		**		
1446	33	hh	Poplar	MT	127	900		**	M		**		
1467	21	h	Wolf Point	MT	128	2,900	C-s	****	M		***		
1516	49	h	Glasgow	MT	129	3,600	C-s	****	M		****		
1558	42	h	Saco	MT	131	225		**	M		**		
1568	10	h	Sleeping Buffalo	MT	131		C-s	*	M		**		
1586	18	hh	Malta	MT	132	2,400	C-s	****	M		***		
1631	45	h	Harlem	MT	133	900		***	M		**		
1652	21	0	Chinook	MT	133	1,600	C-s	***	M		***		
1673	21	h	Havre	MT	135	11,000	C-s	****	M		***	*	H
1708	35	hh	Big Sandy	MT	136	750	C	***			**		
1747	39	hh	Fort Benton	MT	137	1,700	C-p	***	M	B	***		
1786	39	hh	Great Falls	MT	139	60,000	C-s	****	M	B	****	**	H

Cum. Miles	Leg Miles	Hills	Town	State	Page	Population	Camp	Food Shop	Motel	B&B	Restau- rant	Bike Shop	Hos- pital
Lemhi Pass Route													
0			Great Falls	MT	139								
26	26	hh	Cascade	MT	146	730	C-p	***	M		**		
58	32	hhh	Wolf Creek	MT	147	150	C	**	M		**		
92	34	hhhh	Helena	MT	147	30,000	C-s	****	M	B	****	**	H
124	32	hh	Townsend	MT	150	1,650	C	***	M		***		
156	32	hh	3 Forks	MT	151	1,200	C-s	***	M		****		
178	22	hhh	Cardwell	MT	153	35	C-s	**					
186	8	h	Whitehall	MT	153	1,100		***	M		***		
202	16	hh	Silver Star	MT	153	50	C-s		M		**		
213	11	hh	Twin Bridges	MT	153	375	C-s	**	M		**		
241	28	hh	Dillon	MT	155	4,000	C-s	****	M	B	***	*	H
261	20	hh	Clark Canyon	MT	157	0	C-s	*			**		
273	12	hhh	Grant	MT	158	35	C-s			B	**		
327	54	hhhh	Salmon	MT	160	3,000	C-s	****	M	B	***		H
348	21	h	North Fork	MT	162	250	C-s	**	M		**		
385	37	hhhh	Sula	MT	165	10	C-s	**	M		**		
403	18	0	Darby	MT	166	800	C-s	***	M		***		
420	17	h	Hamilton	MT	167	3,000	C-s	****	M		***	*	H
460	40	h	Lolo	MT	168	2,800	C-s	**	M		***		
467	7	h	Missoula	MT	169	52,000	C-s	****	M		****	**	H

Cum. Miles	Leg Miles	Hills	Town	State	Page	Population	Camp	Food Shop	Motel	B&B	Restau- rant	Bike Shop	Hos- pital
Big Hole Route													
0			Great Falls	MT	139								
26	26	hh	Cascade	MT	146	730	C-p	***	M		**	**	
58	32	hhh	Wolf Creek	MT	147	150	C	**	M		**		
92	34	hhhh	Helena	MT	147	30,000	C-s	****	M	B	****	**	H
124	32	hh	Townsend	MT	150	1,650	C	***	M		***		
156	32	hh	Three Forks	MT	151	1,200	C-s	***	M		****		
178	22	hhh	Cardwell	MT	153	35	C-s	**					
186	8	h	Whitehall	MT	153	1,100		***	M		***		
202	16	hh	Silver Star	MT	153	50	C-s		M		**		
213	11	hh	Twin Bridges	MT	153	375	C-s	**	M		**		
241	28	hh	Dillon	MT	155	4,000	C-s	****	M	B	***	*	H
288	47	hhhh	Jackson	MT	163	75	C	**	M		**		
306	18	h	Wisdom	MT	164	135	C-s	**	M		**		
345	39	hhhh	Sula	MT	165	10	C-s	**	M		**		
363	18	0	Darby	MT	166	800	C-s	***	M		***		
380	17	h	Hamilton	MT	167	3,000	C-s	****	M		***	*	H
420	40	h	Lolo	MT	168	2,800	C-s	**	M		***		
427	7	h	Missoula	MT	169	52,000	C-s	****	M		****	**	H

Cum. Miles	Leg Miles	Hills	Town	State	Page	Population	Camp	Food Shop	Motel	B&B	Restaurant	Bike Shop	Hospital
Route 200 Shortcut													
0			Great Falls	MT	139							**	
87	87	0	Augusta	MT	172				M		**		
113	26	hhhh	Lincoln	MT	172	530	C	***	M		***		
		h	Ovando	MT	173	100	C		M		**		
165	52	h	Missoula	MT	169	52,000	C-s	****	M		****	**	
Resume Main Route													
2253			Missoula	MT	169							**	
2260	7	h	Lolo	MT	168	2,800	C-s	**	M		***		
2285	25	hhh	Lolo Hot Spg.	MT	176	20	C-s	*	M		**		
2292	7	hhhh	Lolo Pass	MT									
2305	13	0	Powell	ID	177		C	**	M		**		
2370	65	0	Lowell	ID	178	25	C-s	**	M		**		
2392	22	0	Kooskia	ID	179	700	C	***	M		**		
2401	9	0	Kamiah	ID	180	1,200	C-s	****	M		***		
2423	22	0	Orofino	ID	181	3,000	C-s	****	M		***		
2465	42	0	Lewiston	ID	183	31,000	C-s	****	M		****	**	
2467	2	0	Clarkston	WA	183	7,000	C	****	M		****		
2533	66	hhhh	Dayton	WA	187	2,600	C	***	M	B	****		
2543	10	hhh	Waitsburg	WA	188	1,000		**	M		**		
2565	22	hh	Walla Walla	WA	188	30,000		****	M	B	****	*	H
2619	54	h	Umatilla	OR	190	3,000	C-s		M		***		
2647	28	hh	Crow Butte SP	WA	191	3,000	C-s	****	M				

Cum. Miles	Leg Miles	Hills	Town	State	Page	Population	Camp	Food Shop	Motel	B&B	Restau- rant	Bike Shop	Hos- pital
2703	56	hhh	Biggs Junction	OR	194		C-s	**	M		***		
2723	20	0	The Dalles	OR	195	11,000		****	M		***	*	
2748	25	hhh	Hood River	OR	197	4,600	C-s	****	M		****	*	
2768	20	hh	Cascade Locks	OR	199		C-s	***	M		***		
2800	32	hhh	Troutdale	OR	199				M		**		
2819	19	h	Vancouver	WA	202	135,000		****	M	B	****	*	H
			Portland	*OR*	*204*	*500,000*		****	*M*	*B*	****		*H*
2867	48	hh	Rainier	OR	205	1,700		***	M		**		
2872	5	hh	Longview	WA	205	32,000		****	M	B	****	**	H
2897	25	hh	Cathlamet	WA	207	550	C-s	***		B	**		
		h	*Skamokawa*	*WA*	*209*		*C-s*	**		*B*	**		
2901	4	0	Westport	OR	209	250		**	M		**		
2927	26	hhh	Astoria	OR	209	10,000	C-s	****	M	B	****	*	H

DETAILED ROUTE:
TOWN MAPS AND DESCRIPTIONS

St. Louis: Gateway to the West and
eastern end of Lewis & Clark Trail

MAP SYMBOLS

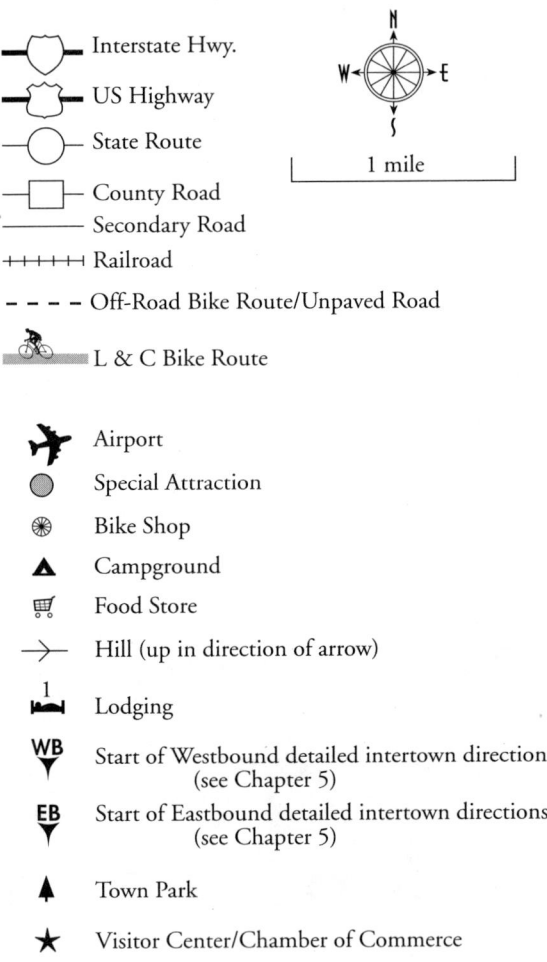

Interstate Hwy.

US Highway

State Route

County Road

Secondary Road

Railroad

Off-Road Bike Route/Unpaved Road

L & C Bike Route

1 mile

Airport

Special Attraction

Bike Shop

Campground

Food Store

Hill (up in direction of arrow)

Lodging

WB Start of Westbound detailed intertown directions
(see Chapter 5)

EB Start of Eastbound detailed intertown directions
(see Chapter 5)

Town Park

Visitor Center/Chamber of Commerce

How to Use This Chapter

This chapter is the heart of the book, providing the next level of detail below the Master Plan. It includes descriptions of all towns listed in the Master Plan that offer services, including maps of the larger towns.

When you are planning your tour, you can read about towns and highlight things that make you want to visit (or skip) particular towns. What services are available? What museums, special sites, or special activities are available? What's the history of the town and what did Lewis and Clark do there?

When you actually arrive in a town, this chapter will again be valuable by directing you to the key things you need. Keep in mind that all businesses, including tourist services, open, close, change names, change owners and philosophies, etc. Some may also close temporarily for certain seasons, holidays, or personal vacations. Many change their operating hours from season to season or year to year. When in doubt, especially if you are really counting on something being open, call ahead. If you call ahead for a motel or B&B reservation, remember to ask about restaurants and other services you may need in the area.

Lodging

If a town has only a few lodging options, all are listed. If there are more than a few, I have tried to include a few convenient options in different price categories, and a reference to the local visitor center or chamber of commerce. My experience is that motels sometimes change ownership and name, but they usually keep the same telephone number for obvious reasons. B&Bs tend to be more stable, but owners often close down for certain seasons; occasionally they retire or sell their business.

Although lodging prices in a single establishment often fluctuate for many reasons (weekends, special events, seasons, changes in competition or owners, etc.), I have tried to offer a general indication of price for two people as follows:

$	less than $50
$$	$50 – $100
$$$	over $100

Some lodging establishments have indicated a special interest in serving cyclists and have paid a small fee for a "preferred listing" with additional information about them. I have personally visited all these places, and I am comfortable recommending them.

Restaurants

The Master Plan (Chapter 3) offers a quick summary of restaurant availability in each town, and in this chapter I try to add a sentence or two about restaurants. I have hesitated to recommend specific ones, because owners, chefs, managers, and employees tend to change; and the quality is sometimes inconsistent. However, there are some instances where I could not resist mentioning a specific restaurant—especially when I felt it offered something special.

Special Events

Special events are included with the towns for two reasons. First, they may be of special interest to cyclists or followers of Lewis and Clark. Second, they are big enough to cause motels and campgrounds to fill up.

Sections

This chapter is divided into eleven sections, each with a general overview map and description. Sections and towns are sequenced for a westbound traveller, but it's easy enough to read this chapter backwards if you want to travel eastbound.

Detailed directions for travelling between towns can be found in Chapter 5, where there are separate sets for westbound and eastbound riders.

🚲 A. THE KATY TRAIL

ST. LOUIS TO BOONVILLE, MO

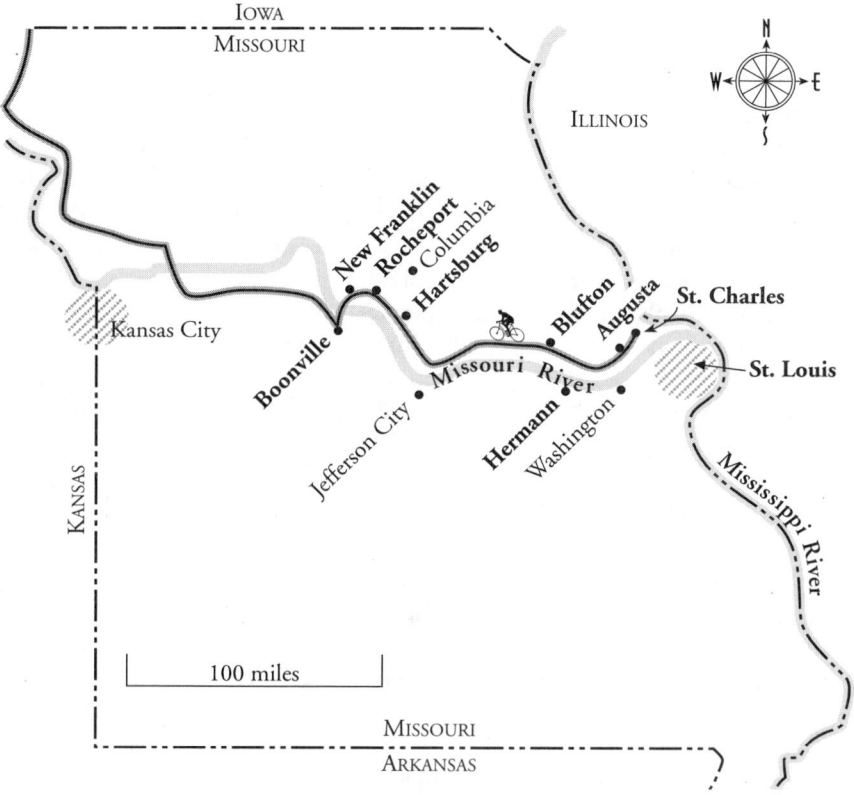

Why did Lewis and Clark start in St. Louis? First, because it was located on the Mississippi River—the western boundary of the United States in 1803. Second, because it was located on the Missouri River—the route of entry into the vast western lands. Third, because it was the last major U.S. city heading west—the last place to obtain equipment and provisions, and the best place to gather current information. For all these reasons, St. Louis was—and to some degree still is—*the* gateway to the West.

In 1803 St. Louis was a bustling trading town of 1,000 built on a bluff above the flood plain on the western bank of the Mississippi River. Although American pioneers were already pushing westward into Ohio, Kentucky, and other frontier states, the pressure to move beyond the Mississippi was still slight. However, farsighted people could see this was inevitable. Manufactured goods from Europe were carried overland, or up the Mississippi River, to St. Louis. From there small groups of traders carried them farther up the Mississippi, the Missouri, and their tributaries to trade for beaver furs. A load of furs worth $1,000 in St. Louis could be worth $10,000 in New

York and $100,000 in China—an indication of where the profit was and why there was so much interest in finding a direct water route to the Pacific Ocean.

Lewis spent the first half of 1803 studying in Washington, gathering rifles in Harper's Ferry, and studying with scientific experts in Philadelphia in preparation for the expedition. In July he left Philadelphia and travelled to Pittsburgh to pick up a keelboat built specifically for the journey up the Missouri River. Even in those days schedules were not always met, and Lewis had to wait impatiently for the boat to be completed.

In October Lewis picked up his co-commander, William Clark, at his farm in Indiana Territory, and together they floated down the Ohio River to St. Louis. Clark was a knowledgeable frontiersman and experienced army officer, personally known by both Lewis and President Jefferson. As Lewis and Clark visited army forts and frontier towns along the way, they selected skilled soldiers, hunters, and boatmen who volunteered for this special assignment.

In December 1803, Lewis and Clark established Camp Dubois at the mouth of the Wood River, about 15 miles north of St. Louis and opposite the mouth of the Missouri River. While Lewis and Clark spent time in St. Louis gathering equipment and provisions for the trip, their soldiers spent a relatively boring winter in their remote camp—doing some drilling and a lot of sitting around, drinking, and fighting.

Two things held up their departure from St. Louis—winter and waiting for the transfer of the Louisiana Territory from Spain to France and then to the United States. The official transfer took place in St. Louis on March 9, 1804. Unfortunately, Lewis still felt the need for additional supplies, and the expedition didn't get started until May 21—pretty late in the Spring.

Arriving in St. Louis, it's hard to miss the magnificent Gateway Arch. Although I've been aware of the arch for years as the symbol of St. Louis, I had always missed the obvious symbolism of the arch as the "gateway to the West." Designed by Eero Saarinen in shining stainless steel, it strikes me as the ultimate in elegant simplicity. Many people think it is a parabola, but it is actually a catenary arch—an upside down version of the curve formed by a chain hanging from two points. The construction story (told at its base) is fascinating, and the view from the top is excellent. We could hardly feel it swaying in the moderate wind the day we took the tram to the top. Located appropriately below the arch is the Museum of Westward Expansion.

Along both sides of the river, where dozens of huge riverboats used to nose in to shore like cars parking diagonally, there are now several riverboat casinos. At first gambling was allowed only on boats actually sailing on the river. After Illinois allowed them to stay tied up, Missouri felt forced to follow suit or lose all that revenue. For some reason, gambling is still allowed only on the river. We saw one new "riverboat casino" that looked as if it had been built on a very solid foundation, and then a moat was dug around it to allow water to flow in from the Missouri River.

Lewis and Clark actually started their journey together from the smaller town of St. Charles—on the north side of the Missouri River about 20 miles from St.

Louis on Interstate 70. Easy by car, but people told us it was easier for Lewis and Clark to get there in 1804 than it would be for us today on bicycles. Visitor centers and local bike shops suggested we find some other starting point for our ride. In addition to railroads, stockyards, and industrial areas, the real problem is crossing the Missouri River. The ferries are gone, and the only bridges carry trains and interstate highways—very dangerous and usually illegal for bicycles.

But we found a way! One trick is to use the new, clean, efficient MetroLink light rail system between downtown St. Louis and the airport. Since it is new, it provides easy access for both wheelchairs and bicycles. They use the same honor system we found in France, where tickets are only checked randomly, and there are no fences, gates, or turnstiles. Although tickets are not checked often, the fines are large if you don't have one.

We also found an easy bicycle route from the airport to St. Charles. We learned from the police that bicycles are allowed on only one bridge over the Missouri, and we searched out an excellent bike route using the "370 bridge." The Detailed Directions in Chapter 5 include this route.

The Corps of Discovery progressed only three miles up river on their first day—mostly due to a late start from St. Charles after lunch. While it's still possible to camp in several "primitive" campgrounds next to the river, we spent our first night at the Hermann City Park Campground. Camped next to us were three gentlemen in their 70s who had come from Illinois to bike across Missouri on the Katy Trail. Each summer they ride across a different state; they are on their 8th state and hope to do them all. Good luck! They were great neighbors—our first introduction to many friendly people in the Midwest, a quality we had often heard about, but never experienced first hand.

Along the Katy Trail

Although the Lewis and Clark expedition travelled by boat up the Missouri River, one or more of the party usually walked along the shore to hunt, explore, or just get away from the other men. We travelled the first 150 miles up river on the new Katy "Rail Trail." When the Missouri–Kansas–Texas (MKT or "The Katy") Railroad closed down operations on the north side of the Missouri River in 1986, several groups worked together to turn it into Katy Trail State Park.

This beautiful bike trail runs through cool woods, rich river bottomland farms, and small towns making a comeback with tourist facilities after being abandoned by the railroad. There are old railroad trestles, new bridges, a tunnel, and many views of the river and limestone cliffs. The surface is hard packed cinder dust, which is no problem for a touring bike—even with a load. And it's *flat* for the first 150 miles—a good way to warm up.

Just a few miles away from the river the land provides a dramatic contrast. Although the limestone bluffs are only about 100 feet higher than the river, they have been cut by many rivers and streams to form a very hilly landscape. This is a land of small farms and orchards—many settled by Germans who came to this area in groups and brought their culture with them. Known as "Missouri's Rhineland," there are several wineries along the Trail and in the nearby hills.

We were always disappointed not to see more traffic on the river—at least a few tugs and barges, if not romantic sternwheelers. Long unit freight trains on the south shore of the river reminded us how coal and other bulk freight moves today, and anyone who has driven the interstate highways knows how the rest of the freight moves.

Lewis and Clark wrote very little in their journals about their trip through what is now the state of Missouri. Perhaps they were too busy coping with all the little problems on their shakedown cruise, or perhaps they felt this part of the river had already been pretty well explored and didn't require their documentation.

Since this guide is primarily about the Lewis & Clark Trail, it does not do full justice to all the attractions available along the Katy Trail. Most people will want to spend 2–3 days riding the Katy Trail (50–75 miles per day), and this guide will offer and describe several options. However, you could easily spend a week exploring the Katy Trail at a more leisurely pace. For more information I recommend Brett Dufur's *Katy Trail Guide Book* (Appendix D) and the Interactive Katy Trail web site, www.katytrail.showmestate.com (Appendix E).

State Champion Great Burr Oak Tree, 350 years old, half mile south of Katy Trail in Huntsdale (mile marker 170)

St. Louis, MO

Population: 350,000

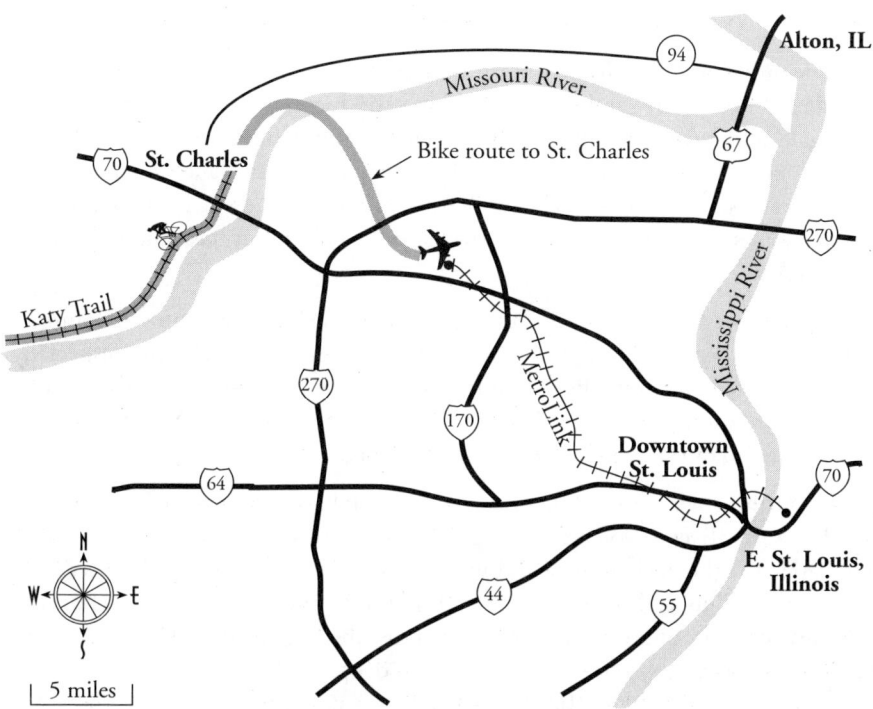

St. Louis Overview — Zip: 63102

St. Louis is the focal point for the eastern terminus of the Lewis & Clark Trail. Although our bicycle route really starts across the Missouri River in St. Charles, St. Louis is a more convenient and obvious transportation hub—with a major airport, train station, bus station, and intersection of interstate highways.

If you want to rest and/or explore this area for a day or two, there is lots to do and several options for lodging. Although there is no camping in the metropolitan area, inexpensive lodging can be found in St. Louis at the hostel about two miles south of downtown. The best deals on motels for both price and convenience can be found right across the highway from the St. Louis airport. If you want to start riding as soon as possible and/or prefer a B&B in a smaller town, get to St. Charles as soon as possible.

There are three **key geographical areas** in greater St. Louis, as shown on the overview map:

1. Downtown — train station, bus station, hostel, hotels, restaurants, museums, visitor center, casinos, entertainment, sports events

2. Airport — motels, restaurants

3. St. Charles — start of the Trail, B&Bs, motels, restaurants, museums, visitor center, casino, bike shop

There are two key **modes of transportation** between these key areas:

1. Downtown and the airport are connected by the excellent, new, inexpensive **MetroLink train**—and it is designed to carry bicycles! Although bicycles are legally allowed at any hour, common sense recommends avoiding commuting rush hours. A single ticket is $1, and a $3 day pass is also valid on all buses. It takes about 30 minutes between the airport and downtown. There is also frequent bus service between downtown and the hostel, but these buses don't carry bicycles.

2. The airport and St. Charles are connected by an eleven-mile bicycle route described below. Although the major rivers create a natural barrier (especially since bicycles are not allowed on interstate highways), there is a relatively easy and pleasant bicycle route. Public transportation connecting St. Charles to downtown or the airport means expensive taxis.

If you are arriving by bicycle from the east, you have three choices for crossing the Mississippi River. If you are coming from the north and/or want to go directly to St. Charles, use the new bridge with bike lane from Alton, Illinois, or the ferry from Golden Eagle, Illinois. If you are coming from the southeast, go to East St. Louis, Illinois, and take your bike on the MetroLink across the Eads Bridge. All other bridges are interstate highways—closed to bicycles and dangerous!

St. Louis is a *big* city (350,000). If you have some time and money, there is lots to do in both St. Louis and St. Charles, and you should contact the visitor centers below to request information. A small sample of the 96 suggestions in the St. Louis Visitor's Guide:

1. Gateway Arch — symbol of St. Louis, fascinating architecture and construction story, ride to top for view (www.stlouisarch.com)

2. Museum of Westward Expansion — below arch, broad overview of westward expansion, free (314-655-1700)

3. Union Station — huge refurbished train station and hotel with 100 shops and restaurants, free

4. Old Courthouse — scene of Dred Scott trial, exhibits, free

5. Riverboat rides and casinos

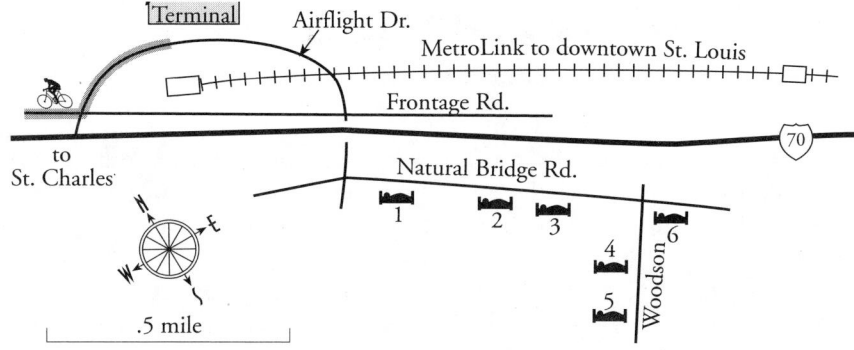

St. Louis Airport Area

★ **St. Louis Visitor Center:** 330 No. 4th St., St. Louis, MO, 63102, 800-916-0092, www.st-louis-cvc.com, tourism@st-louis-cvc.com

Missouri Tourism: Box 1055, Jefferson City, MO, 65102, 800-877-1234, www.missouritourism.org, tourism@mail.state.mo.us

🛏 **Downtown**

1) Huck Finn Hostel ($), 314-241-0076, (2 mi. south of downtown on bus routes; old, pleasant, and friendly; but hot and crowded during summer)

2) Holiday Inn ($$), 200 N 4th, 800-925-1395

3) Hampton Inn ($$), 2211 Market, 314-241-3200

🛏 **Airport:** (These motels are within 1 mile of the main airport entrance and MetroLink station. Near restaurants.)

1) Drury Inn ($$), 800-DRURYINN

2) Hilton ($$$), 800-345-5500

3) Best Western ($$), 800-872-0070

4) Days Inn ($$), 800-325-2525

5) Holiday Inn ($$), 800-446-4656

6) Motel 6 ($), 800-4MOTEL6

St. Charles, MO (Katy Mile 39)

Population: 55,000

Originally founded in 1769 by French Canadian trader, Louis Blanchette, as Les Petite Cotes (the little hills), the town later changed its name to honor the king of France. While St. Louis served the larger and more established traffic on the Mississippi River, St. Charles served traders heading up the Missouri River into the vast unknown territory to the west.

On May 16, 1804, Clark wrote, *"we arrived at St. Charles at 12 oClock a number of Spectators french & Indians flocked to the bank to See the party. This Village is about one mile in length, Situated on the North Side of the Missourie at the foot of a hill from which it takes its name Petiete Coete or the Little hill. This village Contns. about 100 houses, the most of them Small and indefferent and about 450 inhabitents Chiefly French, those people appear pore, polite & harmonious."*

On May 21 *"we Set out at half passed three oClock under three Cheers from the gentlemen on the bank and proceeded on."* The expedition was finally underway.

Main Street, St. Charles, MO

Although St. Charles is a large town of 55,000, it feels smaller because it is divided into two areas. The downtown area along Main Street near the riverfront has been beautifully restored with brick streets, gas lights, pleasant shops, and restaurants; and it's easy to get around by bicycle or on foot. A half mile up the hill is the newer part of town with shopping malls and modern motels along Interstate 70.

St. Charles is currently the eastern end of the Katy Trail State Park, a wonderful new rail trail that crosses most of the state and makes up the first 150 miles of our bicycle route. It starts parallel to Main Street next to Frontier Park down by the river. Stop by the Visitor Information Center to pick up more information about the Trail and things to do in this area. A few highlights:

1. National Register Historic District on Main Street

2. Lewis and Clark Center — small museum with diorama (fee), book store 701 Riverside Dr., 636-947-3199, www.lewisandclarkcenter.org

3. Frontier Park — replicas of Lewis and Clark boats

4. Goldenrod Showboat Dinner Theater — historic showboat

5. Station Casino, St. Charles — gambling

6. Missouri's First State Capitol — restored historic building

Two days after leaving St. Charles, Lewis and Clark stopped at Boone's Settlement near Defiance. This land had been granted to Daniel Boone seven years earlier by the Spanish. On May 24 Clark wrote, *"Crossed to the Settlemt. and took in R & Jo: Fields who had been Sent to purchase Corn & Butter &c. many people Came to See us."* It's interesting that Clark does not mention the great frontiersman; perhaps he was not in residence at the time, or perhaps Clark was too preoccupied with his own agenda to think much about Daniel Boone. It is possible to visit Boone's home and a reconstructed village five hilly miles north of Defiance on County Road F (636-798-2005 for more information).

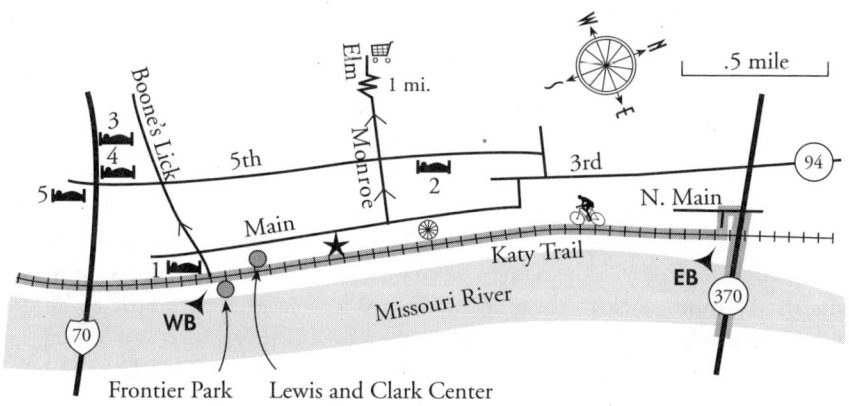

St. Charles, MO — Zip: 83467

★   **St. Charles Convention and Visitors Bureau**
230 S Main St., 800-366-2427, www.historicstcharles.com

1) Boone's Lick Trail Inn ($$–$$$), 1000 South Main Street, 636-947-7000, www.booneslick.com; in a colonial village setting an authentic 1840 inn next to Katy Trail and Missouri River, on Main Street next to shops and restaurants; private baths, mid-week rates, bike storage, full breakfast.

2) Mueller House B&B ($$–$$$), 710 N 5th, 636-947-1228, www.bbhost.com/muellerhouse; 5 blocks from downtown and Katy Trail; suite with private bath; 2 rooms share bath with jacuzzi; all queen beds; full breakfast; mid-week rates; bike storage.

3) Ramada Inn ($$–$$$), 636-947-5900

4) Baymont Inn ($$–$$$), 636-946-6936

5) Day's Inn ($$), 636-946-1000

⊛   Touring Cyclist, 100 S Main, 636-949-9630

Special Events

> Lewis & Clark Heritage Days, 3rd weekend in May
>
> Festival of the Little Hills, 3rd weekend in Aug

Augusta, MO (Katy Mile 66)

Population: 300

Only 27 miles from St. Charles, Augusta makes a good overnight stop if you want an easy first day or decide to spend the morning in St. Charles. After all, the Corps of Discovery didn't get away from St. Charles until 3:30 in the afternoon.

Although the town is up a small hill from the Katy Trail, it's worth the climb to explore this hidden gem. Many of the 300 residents are devoted to offering services to visitors, and you will find several B&Bs, restaurants, wineries, and shops on the quiet streets. It's also a good town for walking.

Like many towns in this area, Augusta was settled by Germans in the mid-1800s. It couldn't have been easy farming in these hills, but for many it was better than their situation in Germany.

Augusta was founded in 1836 as Mt. Pleasant by Leonard Harold, a follower of Daniel Boone. In 1855 the name was changed to Augusta, as German immigrants arrived in response to the glowing descriptions written by Gottfried Duden. This area prospered with farming, grapes, and wine. At this time it was a port right on the Missouri River. After the river changed its course in the 1870s, the railroad builders took advantage of the flat land left behind, and Augusta thrived as a railroad depot. The town was later hurt when rail traffic moved to the other side of the river, but in the 1960s the region again started growing grapes and producing fine wines. Today two wineries have shops right in town.

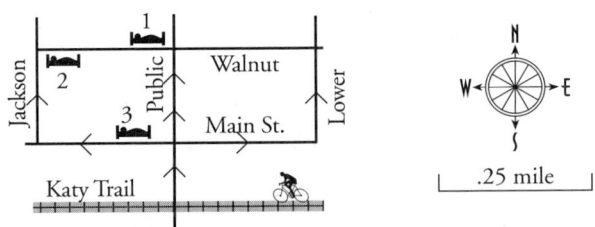

Augusta, MO — Zip: 63332

★ **Augusta Visitors Association:** 636-228-4005, www.augusta-missouri.com

🛏 1) H.S. Clay House ($$$), Public and Walnut (Box 184), 888-309-7334; www.hsclayhouse.com; restored 1885 doctor's home; walking distance to restaurants, wineries, and antiques; pool; rooms and suites with queen beds and private baths; gourmet breakfast and luxury.

2) Lindenhof B&B ($$–$$$), 5596 Walnut (Box 52), 636-228-4617, www.lindenhof-augusta.com; restored 1857/1907 Victorian home; walking distance to restaurants, wineries, and antiques; outdoor jacuzzi; rooms and suites with queen beds and private baths; bountiful breakfast.

3) Old Town Augusta Inn ($$–$$$), Public and Main (Box 172), 636-482-4654; restored 1863 home near Katy Trail; for individuals, couples, families, and groups; tepee, room, and 3 spacious suites with private bath and entrance; sauna, hot tub, whirlpool tub, massage; hearty breakfast.

✳ Touring Cyclist, 5533 Water, 636-482-4038

Washington, MO (Katy Mile 74)
Population: 12,000

Although Washington has many services, it has several problems that make it less attractive to bicycle tourers. First, the bridge over the Missouri River is long, narrow, and dangerous. Second, the town is about 3.5 miles south of the Katy Trail. Third, the town is geographically spread out with the motels at the highway intersection about two miles from the downtown area. In summary, there are better alternatives.

Just east of Washington, across the river from Matson, Lewis and Clark stopped on their second day to explore Tavern Cave. Lewis must have been feeling rambunctious, because he climbed the cliff face on his own and fell, just barely catching himself and preventing serious injury. In retrospect, it must have seemed like a foolish and unnecessary risk; he never mentioned the incident in his journal.

On May 25 the expedition *"camped at the mouth of a Creek called River a Chauritte above a Small french Village of 7 houses and as many families . . . The people at this Village is pore, houses Small, they Sent us milk and eggs to eat."*

Zip: 63090

★ **Washington Visitor Center:** 301 Front St., 888-792-7466, www.washmo.org

✳ Scenic Cycles, on Katy Trail at Marthasville (Mile 78), 636-433-2909

Hermann, MO (Katy Mile 101)

Population: 3,000

About 65 miles from St. Charles, Hermann is a good stopping point for the first night, and the first town with good camping. Although there are other camping sites along the Katy Trail both before and after Hermann, none offer the variety of shopping and services that can be found here. Hermann also offers a large selection of B&Bs and restaurants, as well as a motel.

The town is located directly on the Missouri River just three miles south of the Katy Trail at McKittrick (a parking lot at Mile 101 on the Trail). Be aware that the old bridge across the Missouri is narrow and slopes up going toward Hermann. The three B&Bs listed below all offer shuttle service across this bridge.

Hermann was founded in the mid-1800s by Philadelphia Germans who wanted to maintain their old-world culture. Inexpensive land grants were offered to people who would grow grapes, and the wine business thrived. In the 1870s the Stone Hill Winery was the second largest in the United States and the third largest in the world. Although Prohibition dealt Hermann a severe blow in the 1920s, the people have rebounded. Today the town still maintains its German heritage with a historic downtown of stores, wineries, restaurants, B&Bs, and tidy homes.

The Visitor Information Center and Museum in the old German School can provide lots of information about both the past and present. A walk through the downtown area can be both fun and educational, and the Hermanoff Winery downtown offers excellent sausage and cheese—as well as wine. Be aware that Hermann is a popular getaway spot for people from St. Louis, and the town can be crowded for weekends and special festivals.

*Festhalle,
Hermann, MO*

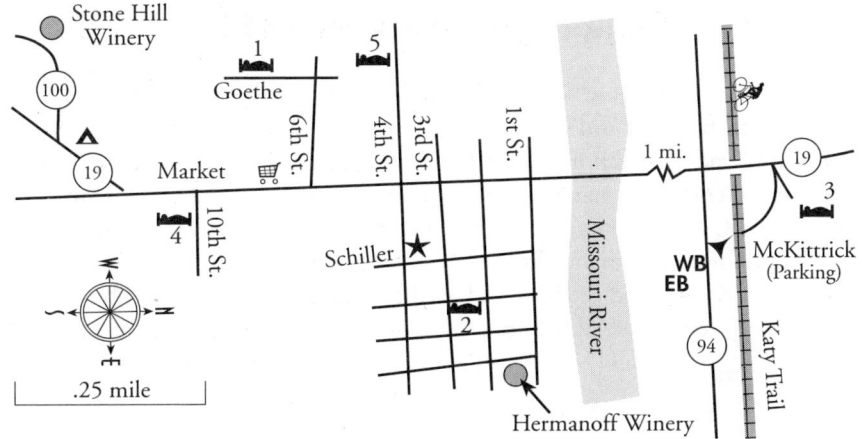

Hermann, MO — Zip: 65041

★   **Visitor Information Center** and German School Museum,
Schiller and 4th St., 800-932-8687

⊫   There are more than 30 B&Bs in Herman. Below is a small sample that are
convenient and that have expressed special interest in serving cyclists:

1) Birk's Gasthaus ($$), 700 Goethe, 573-486-2911, www.birksgasthaus.com;
restored 1886 Victorian mansion, walking distance to downtown;
king/queen beds and private baths available; full breakfast; bike storage and
shuttle service to Katy Trail; reduced weekday rates.

2) Captain Wohlt Inn ($$), 123 E Third, 573-486-3357; historic buildings in
historic downtown; suites with queen bed, sitting room, private bath, kitch-
enette, and cable TV; rooms with various beds and private bath; full breakfast; bike storage and shuttle service to Katy Trail.

3) Meyer's Hilltop Farm B&B ($$), 20 Maggie's Lane, McKittrick,
573-486-5778; mmeyer@ktis.net; quiet farm on hill above Katy Trail; TVs
and private baths; private suite with whirlpool; hearty breakfast;
transportation to Hermann for dinner.

4) Hermann Motel ($), 110 E 10th, 573-486-3131

5) Acorn Bunk n' Bagel ($), 236 W 4th, 877-486-4003

▲   City Park, 0.8 mi. south of bridge on Route 19, 573-486-5400; good grass
and shade, covered pavilion nearby, some covered tables, little privacy, near
road, satisfactory restroom with shower

Blufton, MO (Katy Mile 111)

There is no longer any town here, but it's still a good overnight stop on the Katy Trail. The Benz brothers and their wives purchased a historic farmhouse right on the Katy Trail and turned it into a B&B and campground.

In 1866 George Husmann started a winery here that flourished for many years. In the 1870s the winery failed, but the carpenter William Heckmann decided to stay and build a home for his family. After purchasing the wreck of the steamboat Clara, he dismantled the boat and used the parts to build a home. Now restored with several nautical features, that home is today the Steamboat Junction B&B.

Zip: 65069

🛏 Steamboat Junction B&B ($–$$), 199 Hwy. 94, 573-236-4664, www.steamboatjunction.com; home built from old steamboat on Katy Trail; rooms and cottage; dinner available with advance notice; full country breakfast; laundry.

▲ Steamboat Junction Campground, 314-831-4807

Jefferson City, MO (Katy Mile 143)

Population: 36,000

The state capital offers a wide range of services and is a great city to visit—but not necessarily by bicycle. Jeff City offers the Capitol (including fascinating murals depicting Missouri history by Thomas Hart Benton), the Governor's Mansion, and all the associated government activities. The problem is getting across the Missouri River, and then getting around the geographically spread-out city. Although it is legal to walk—or even ride—your bike across the bridge on the three-foot shoulder of the northbound bridge span, it is still dirty, dangerous, and very stressful. There is only a thin white line between you and three lanes of traffic moving at interstate speed. A taxi shuttle is strongly recommended, and there is a free phone for this purpose at the North Jefferson trailhead.

Once you get across the river, the motels are a mile south of downtown. The city claims to offer camping, but the campgrounds are well outside the city and inconvenient for bicycle tourers. If you still want to pursue this city, you're on your own!

Zip: 65102

★ **Jefferson City Convention and Visitor's Bureau**
213 Adams St., Jefferson City, MO, 800-769-4183

Hartsburg, MO (Katy Mile 153)

Population: 130

Don't let the small population fool you. This tiny town makes a great overnight stop right on the Katy Trail if you prefer to skip both the attractions and hassles of Jefferson City and Columbia. Even if there isn't as much choice of services, the ones available are both good and convenient. There is a restaurant, tavern, winery, and weekend entertainment during the summer. No map is needed; you can see the whole town from wherever you stand.

Zip: 65039

🛏 Globe Hotel B&B ($$), 573-657-4529

🔺 American Legion Park, water, restrooms with no showers, covered picnic pavilion, reservations needed, 573-657-2396

Volunteer Park, port-a-potty, reservations encouraged, 573-657-2396

✸ Hartsburg Cycle Depot, 30 S Second St., Hartsburg, MO 65039, 573-657-9599; www.hartsburg-cycledepot.com; restored historic building on Katy Trail; bicycle sales, rentals, and repairs; cycling accessories, refreshments, shuttle service; seasonal, so always call ahead.

Missouri State Capitol, rising from the bottomland along the Katy Trail, Jefferson City, MO

Cycle Depot, Hartsburg, MO

mile 114

Columbia, MO (Katy Mile 169)

Pop: 90,000

Columbia is primarily the home of the University of Missouri, and it has all the typical attractions of a college town—a wide variety of lodging and restaurants, music, entertainment, sports, etc. Like Jefferson City, it's a great city to visit, but not necessarily by bicycle. There are several motels near the I-70 interchanges just north of downtown, and a couple of B&Bs on the southeast edge of the university. The city claims to have camping, but the nearest one is an RV Park about five miles northeast of downtown.

Columbia is easy to reach on a pleasant eight-mile spur trail from the Katy Trail at McBaine, although this means adding about 20 miles to your riding. At the end of the eight-mile spur trail the city is quite spread out, and you will end up doing several more miles of urban riding in traffic.

Zip: 65201

★   **Columbia Convention and Visitor's Bureau:** 300 S Providence, Columbia, MO, 573-875-1231, 800-652-0987; http://chamber.columbia.mo.us; www.visitcolumbiamo.com

Rocheport, MO (Katy Mile 179)

Population: 260

Rocheport offers an excellent overnight stop directly on the Katy Trail. This gracious small town, listed on the National Register of Historic Places, offers beautiful homes, antique shops, and several B&Bs and restaurants—all within walking distance.

There are two restaurants and cafés right in town. On a bluff (big hill for cyclists!) one mile east, Les Bourgeois Winegarden and Bistro offers good food and a fantastic view of the valley below. Although Rocheport may seem a long distance from anywhere by bicycle, it's very popular with car people, and reservations are a good idea for both lodging and dining.

Lewis and Clark passed by Rocheport in June of 1804 and visited the pictographs on the nearby cliffs. With a good natural harbor, Rocheport was an important steamboat landing and ferry crossing during the 19th century. Later the river changed course, and the railroad came through town and built the only tunnel nearby on the Katy Trail. Although two bad fires destroyed some buildings, many historic homes have been restored. The 1993 flood also clobbered Rocheport, but the community once again pulled together to both rescue and restore itself.

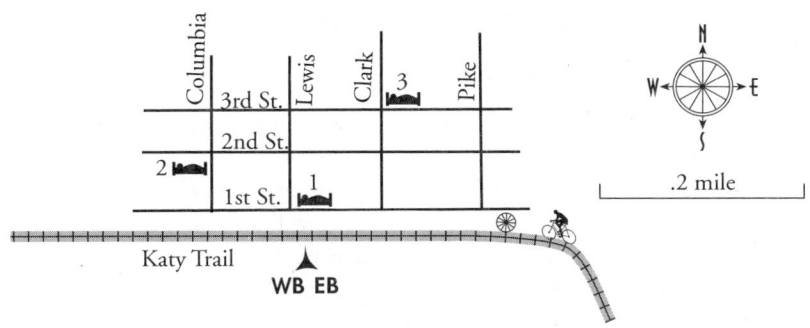

Rocheport, MO — Zip: 65279

★ **Friends of Rocheport:** 573-698-2041, http://rocheport.missouri.org

🛏 1) Katy O'Neil Bed & Bikefest ($–$$), 101 Lewis, 573-698-BIKE, http://rocheport.missouri.org/bike; run by an experienced bicycle tourer on Katy Trail; accommodations range from bunk room to private room or boxcar with bath; hot tub and laundry; generous breakfast.

2) Yates House B&B ($$$), 305 2nd, 573-698-2129

3) Schoolhouse B&B Inn ($$$), 504 3rd, 573-698-2022

⊛ Trailside Café and Bikes, Pike and 1st, 573-698-2702; snacks and lunches for hungry cyclists, outdoor tables; extensive parts inventory, quick repairs for touring cyclists, shuttle service by prior arrangement.

Rodney O'Neil at his B&B in Rocheport, MO

New Franklin, MO (Katy Mile 188)

Population: 1,100

The original town of Franklin is still located about a mile southwest of New Franklin in the river bottom. It was a busy river port and a crossroads on the old Boon's Lick Road between St. Charles and the Boone's salt works just north of here. The first trading expeditions to Santa Fe started from Franklin in 1821; at that time it was the last major town and gateway to the southwest.

A series of disastrous floods wiped out the town in the 1820s, and people rebuilt up on the bluff and called the new town New Franklin. Today it is the crossroads of four trails: Lewis and Clark, Boon's Lick, Santa Fe, and Katy.

If you like camping, Katy Roundhouse, right on the Trail in Franklin, specializes in cyclists. On the north side of the Trail they offer a wine and beer garden, a weekend restaurant specializing in fine meats and fresh ingredients, live entertainment, and showers. Reservations are necessary for meals. Across the tracks there is a large area for camping near the old railroad roundhouse. On weekdays, or if you want to save money, there is pizza and limited food shopping a mile east in New Franklin. Or Boonville is only three miles farther west on the trail with full services.

Zip: 65250

★   **South Howard County Historical Society,** 101 E Broadway

▲   KATY Roundhouse, Mile 189, 800-477-6605, katy.roundhouse@undata.com

Rivercene Bed and Breakfast, Boonville, MO

Boonville, MO (Katy Mile 192)

Pop: 7,500

mile 152

Boonville is a regional center offering all services except good camping. The downtown area is small enough for walking, and it offers B&Bs, restaurants, food shopping, and other shops and galleries. There are over 400 buildings on the National Register of Historic Places, and a walk or ride around High Street near the river is especially pleasant. Several motels are located three moderately hilly miles south of town near I-70. If you want to camp, New Franklin to the east or Arrow Rock to the west is better than the Bobber Campground three miles south at I-70.

Boonville, named for Daniel Boone, was first settled in 1810—only four years after Lewis and Clark returned to St. Louis. Located on fertile ground near the point where the Missouri River turns north, it was a natural intersection of both Indian trails and later settler trails heading west and southwest. The most famous of these trails was the Santa Fe Trail. Unlike other towns that disappeared over time, Boonville prospered as the railroad builders chose to cross the river here in the late 1800s. When I-70 chose a route three miles below town, it took a lot of traffic out of the town center without taking business away.

The Chamber of Commerce, located in the restored Katy railroad depot, is especially friendly and helpful. In addition to all the standard information, they also offer walking tours and descriptions of historic buildings. Music festivals are popular here, and there are performances in the restored Thespian Hall downtown.

Boonville is bicycle friendly—big enough to have lots of services and small enough to get around easily without too much traffic. The new bridge across the Missouri River has a wide separate lane for cyclists and pedestrians. Every new bridge should be built like this. Boonville also marks the end of the Katy Trail for travellers on the Lewis & Clark Trail, as we break off to head northwest.

Chamber of Commerce, Boonville, MO

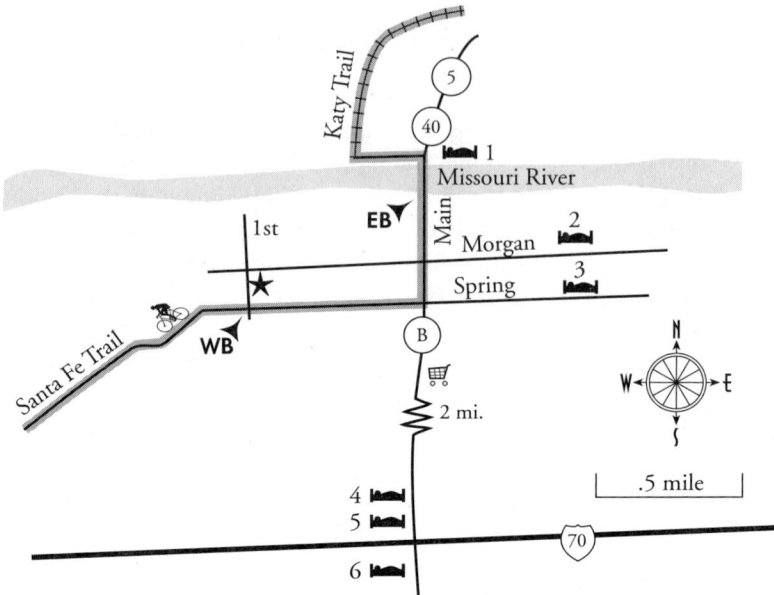

Boonville, MO — Zip: 65233

★ **Boonville Area Chamber of Commerce:** 320 1st, 660-882-2721, www.mo-river.net, boonchamb@c-magic.com

1) Rivercene B&B ($$–$$$), 127 CR 463, www.rivercene.com, 800-531-0862; restored brick captain's home, copied for governor's mansion; half-mile pleasant walk or ride to Boonville; 8 large rooms and suites with queen beds, private baths, and various special amenities; full breakfast.

2) Morgan Street Repose ($$), 611 Morgan, 800-248-5061

3) Lady Goldenrod Inn ($$), 629 E Spring, 660-882-5764

4) Day's Inn ($$), I-70 at Route B, 660-882-8624

5) Super 8 Motel ($$), I-70 and Route B, 660-882-2900

6) QT Inn ($), I-70 and Route B, 660-882-3467

B. Gently Rolling Missouri

Boonville, MO to Kansas City, MO

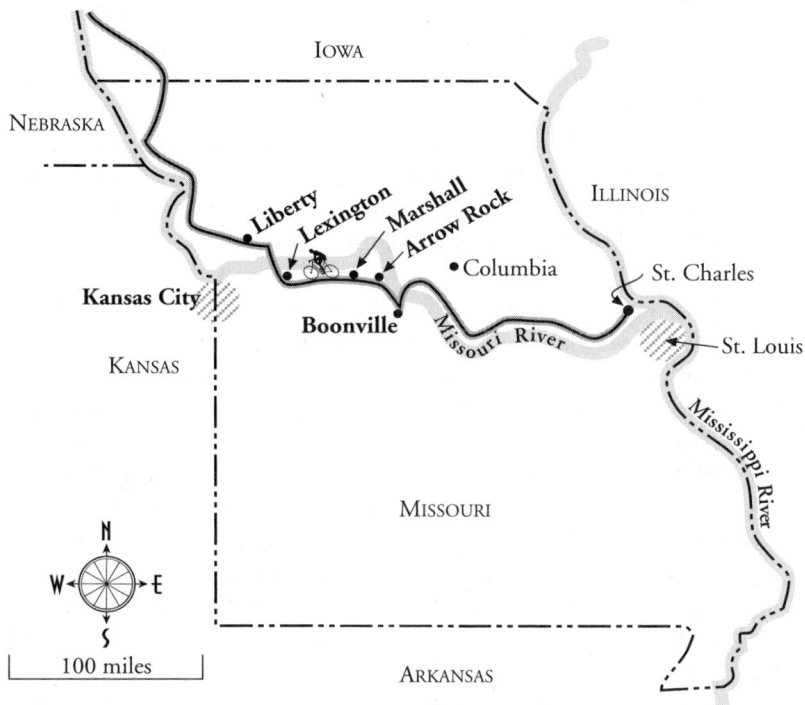

Although Boonville was not a camping spot for Lewis and Clark, it is a significant spot for bicycle tourers. It marks the end of the Katy Trail and the beginning of normal roads. It is also the end of the flat riding, as our route leaves the
river for 75 miles of gently rolling farmland. At Lexington the route crosses the
river and continues in the mostly flat flood plain for 37 miles to Liberty. Traffic is
generally light.

You may also notice a change in surroundings. Leaving the river means leaving
abundant water for trees and fields. The land is drier farmland with fewer trees and
less shade. Towns are farther apart with just a hint of the open feeling of the prairies
far ahead.

Arrow Rock, MO

Population: 80

Arrow Rock is a small historic town that has been delightfully restored and is now home to the Lyceum Summer Theatre (660-837-3311; www.arrowrock.org). The 80 permanent residents operate a number of B&Bs, restaurants, and antique shops. Reservations are strongly recommended, especially on weekends.

There is excellent camping at the Arrow Rock State Historic Site nearby, with 23 "improved" sites for RVs and 22 "basic" sites for tenting. These basic sites are on beautiful lawn with lots of shade, some privacy, and excellent restrooms. There are no reservations, but tent sites probably aren't that popular with the theatre and antique crowd. If you plan to camp, stop at the campground first and get a map of the area. Although the town and the historic site are small, the roads wind around, and you can waste a lot of time and effort if you miss the shortcuts.

The free Visitor Center at the Historic Site has excellent exhibits on both Arrow Rock and the whole Boon's Lick region. What the town lacks is food shopping, so stock up in Boonville or Marshall or plan to eat at the upscale restaurants.

The bluff at Arrow Rock was originally a rendezvous place for Native Americans, where they gathered flint for arrowheads. Although Lewis and Clark did not stop here, they knew it as the Prairie of Arrows. Near this spot they encountered the first dangerous situation mentioned in their journals, when their boats were almost capsized by huge trees floating downriver. Clark later recommended this bluff as a good site for a fort and town. It was settled in 1815 as a ferry crossing, and the town grew to more than 1,000 by the mid-1800s. Right across the river was Boon's Lick, a source of salt that was hauled to St. Charles on the Boon's Lick Trail. Later both the railroads and the highways bypassed this area in favor of a river crossing at Boonville, and the town gradually declined and almost died before its recent revival.

Main Street, Arrow Rock, MO

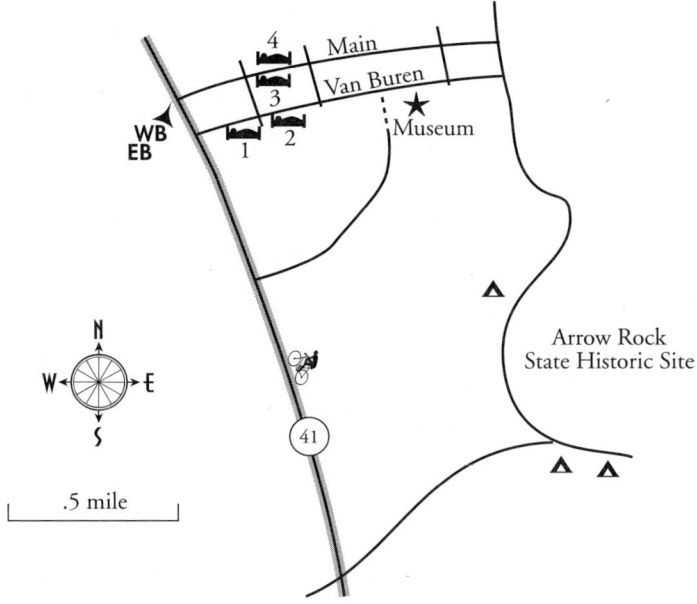

mile 171

Arrow Rock, MO — Zip: 65320

★ **Historic Arrow Rock Council:** Box 147B, 660-837-3335; www.arrowrock.org

🛏 1) Borgman's B&B ($$), Van Buren, 660-837-3350

2) Westward Trails Inn B&B ($$), Van Buren, 660-837-3335

3) Down Over B&B ($$), Main, 660-837-3268

4) Miss Nelle's B&B ($$), Main, 800-795-2797

▲ State Historic Site, Box 1, 660-837-3330; www.arrowrock.org; beautiful grass, shade, excellent restrooms with showers; no reservations.

Marshall, MO

Population: 13,000

Marshall (named after Supreme Court justice Thurgood Marshall) is the county seat of Saline County and a regional center in a hog farming area. There are a couple of motels, good food shopping, and a variety of restaurants; but no camping nearby.

Although Marshall is the home of Missouri Valley College with 1,200 students, this is only a small part of the town. There are a number of attractive historic homes here, and the Chamber of Commerce can provide a brochure with more information and a suggested tour. The town is spread out and flat, traffic is light, and you will probably want your bicycle to get around.

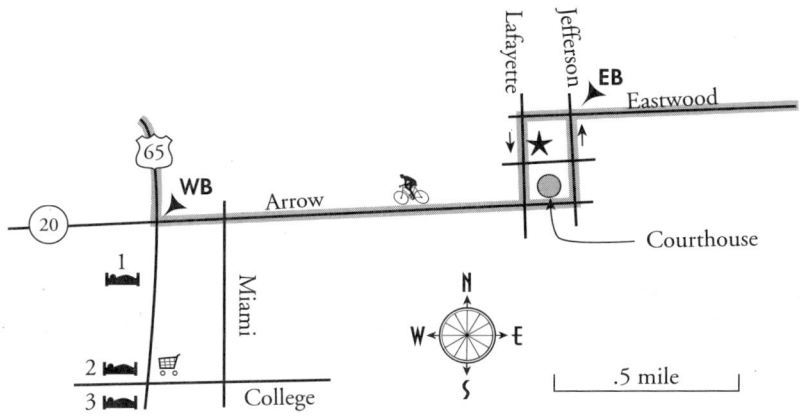

Marshall, MO — Zip: 65340

★   **Marshall Chamber of Commerce:** 241 N Lafayette, 816-886-3324

1) Marshall Lodge ($$),
   660-831-0022

2) Super 8 Motel ($$), 660-886-3359

3) Comfort Inn ($$), 660-886-8080

*Saline County Courthouse,
Marshall, MO*

Lexington, MO

Population: 5,000

Back on the Missouri River, Lexington is another regional center with all services except camping. There are two B&Bs near downtown, one motel, good food shopping, and a variety of restaurants.

The primary attraction in Lexington is the Battle of Lexington State Historic Site and Visitor's Center. As an Easterner, I always think of the Battle of Lexington (Massachusetts) in the Revolutionary War; but Missouri was the site of many vindictive and bloody Civil War battles. This site commemorates and interprets the three-day battle fought here.

Once an important river port, Lexington was later superceded by Independence and then Kansas City, as steamboats were able to navigate farther and farther upriver. Lexington has a number of attractive historic homes and the Wentworth Military Academy.

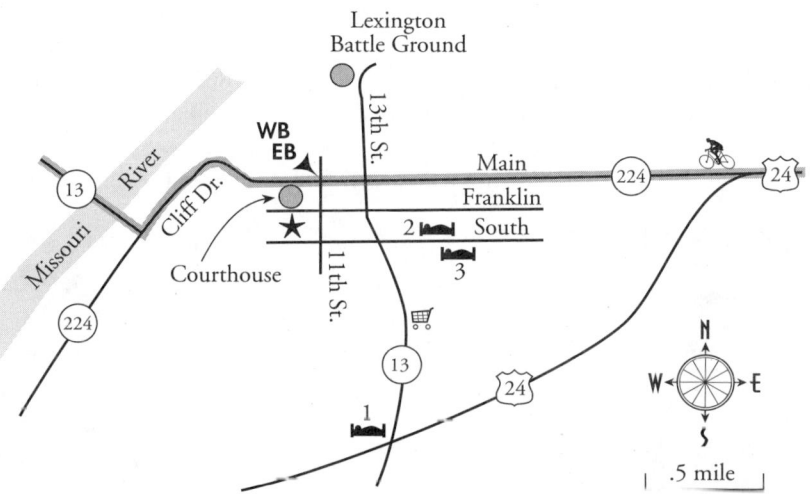

Lexington, MO — Zip: 64067

★ **Lexington Tourism Bureau:** 1029 Franklin Ave., 660-259-3082, www.historiclexington.com

🛏 1) Lexington Inn Motel ($$), Routes 24 and 13 (13th St.), 800-259-4641

   2) Victorianne B&B ($$), 1522 South, 660-259-2868

   3) Parsonage B&B ($$), 1601 South, 660-259-2344

Liberty, MO

Population: 25,000

Liberty is the county seat of Clay County on the north side of the Missouri River about twelve miles from Independence. It is a good resting place, with B&Bs and motels. Although there are several good restaurants and good food shopping, there is no camping in the area. The Fork and Spoon Café on Kansas, a block west of the courthouse, is worth a special mention. There are wonderful murals by Jeff Parson on the walls outside, and their breakfast is especially good. We also enjoyed an excellent dinner at the Hardware Café, another long time institution on Liberty Square across from the courthouse.

Although Liberty is inland from the river and was never visited by Lewis and Clark, our bicycle route passes through here for several reasons. First, it offers pleasant cycling and avoids the heavy traffic and dangerous Missouri River bridges near Kansas City. Second, for anyone wishing to begin or end their tour here, our route passes right by Kansas City International Airport between here and Platte City. Finally, it offers some unique and interesting historic points of interest.

The first daylight bank robbery in peacetime (notice all the qualifications!) occurred at the Clay City Savings Bank on February 13, 1866, resulting in the accidental shooting death of an innocent spectator. There is speculation that the robbers were Jesse James and his brothers, whom we'll meet again in St. Joseph. Nearby is the former Clay County Jail, where the Mormon leader Joseph Smith was held

One of two murals by Jeff Parson at the Fork & Spoon Café, Liberty, MO

awaiting trial in 1838. He was later murdered by a mob, and the jail is now a shrine run by the Church of Jesus Christ of Latter Day Saints.

Liberty is also a good staging point for those wishing to visit Independence and/or Kansas City. See the next section for this option.

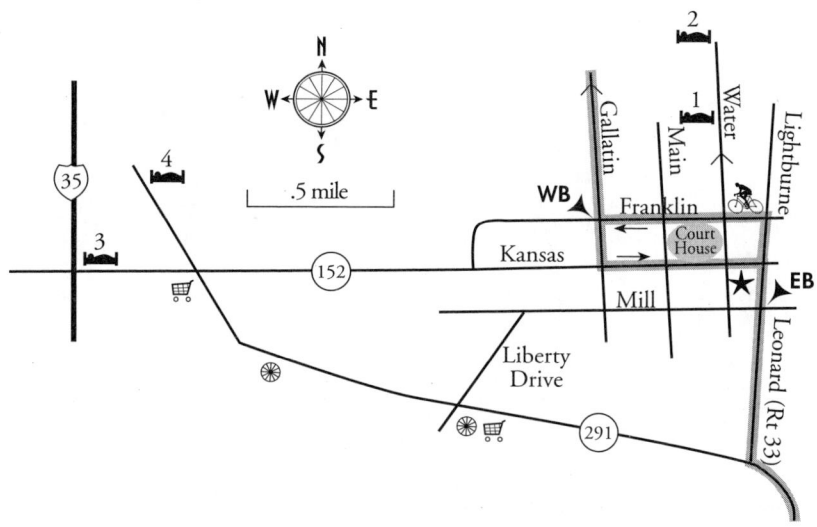

Liberty, MO — Zip: 64068

★ **Liberty Chamber of Commerce:** 9 S Leonard, 816-781-5200, www.ci.liberty.mo.us

🛏 1) Dougherty House B&B ($$), 302 N Water, 816-792-4888, www. doughertyhouse.com, historic home, porches, gardens, gazebo, private baths, jetted tubs, TV-VCR, full breakfast; historic photos, documents; direct link to Major John Dougherty and Lewis and Clark.

2) James Inn B&B ($$), 342 N Water, 816-781-3677

3) Super 8 Motel ($$), Route 152 at I-35, 816-781-9400

4) Best Western Hallmark Inn ($$), 209 N Route 291, 816-781-8770

✸ Biscari Brothers, 884 S Route 291, 816-792-8877

Sunshine Bicycles, 352 S Route 291, 816-792-1331

SIDE TRIP TO INDEPENDENCE AND KANSAS CITY

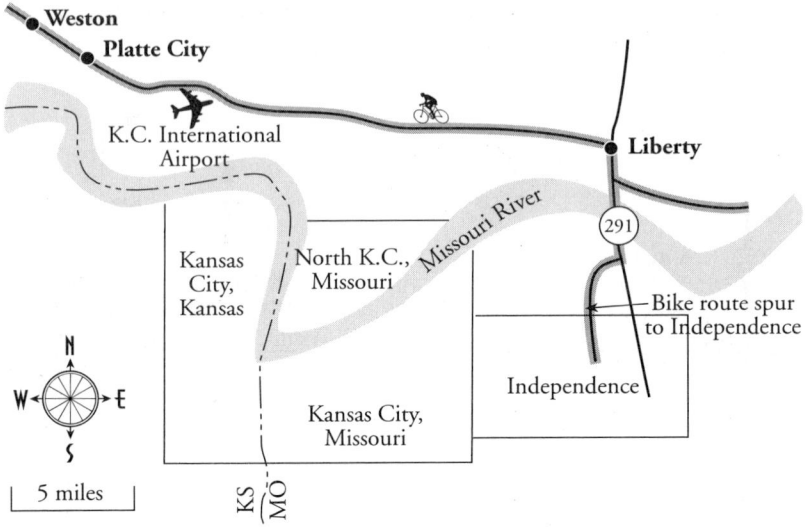

Both these cities have lots of attractions and are great to visit—but not necessarily by bicycle. If you are determined to visit one or both of these cities, there are three options. First, you can ride a thirteen-mile spur route from Liberty to Independence (see Chapter 5 for detailed Cue Sheet), and it is possible to take a bus from Independence to downtown Kansas City. Second, there is express bus service between Liberty and downtown Kansas City (The Metro, 816-221-0660). Third, you can take a bus between downtown Kansas City and the airport, which our route passes in the next section.

Visiting the attractions in Independence is quite possible by bicycle if you are willing to invest the time and indulge in some urban riding. Although Route 291 between Liberty and Independence is a large four-lane divided highway, traffic is not too bad outside of commuting hours, the Missouri River bridge is wide, and the bicycle spur route takes back roads just south of the river. However, riding from Independence into downtown Kansas City is strongly discouraged, and the Kansas City bridges across the Missouri River to get back on our bicycle route are very dangerous and/or closed to bicycles.

Independence—Queen City of the Trails—was originally a thriving river port before Kansas City even existed. As the population pushed westward across Missouri in the early 1800s, the overland starting point for the Santa Fe Trail moved up the Missouri River from New Franklin to Independence, and later to Westport, now on the western edge of Kansas City. For several years this was also the starting point for the Oregon and California Trails.

In 1831 Joseph Smith and the Mormons attempted to build their city of Zion here, but they were quickly pushed farther westward. Ironically, today there is a significant Mormon population, and the Mormon Center with its distinctive spiral architecture is open to the public.

Although Independence today is still technically a separate city of 100,000, it appears more like an eastern appendage of Kansas City. It is perhaps most famous as the home of Harry Truman. The Truman Library and Museum offers excellent displays and interpretations of his life and times, and it is also possible to visit the Truman home a few blocks away. Nearby, the National Frontier Trails Center offers displays, mementos, and interpretations of the Santa Fe, Oregon, and California Trails.

If you have special interests in these cities, contact the Visitor Centers listed below:

★ **Independence Tourism Department**
800-748-7323, www.ci.independence.mo.us

Kansas City Convention and Visitors Bureau
1100 Main, Suite 2550, Kansas City, MO 64105
800-767-7700, www.kansascity.com, info@visitkc.com

Special Attractions

Truman Library and Museum, Hwy. 24 at Delaware,
800-833-1225, www.trumanlibrary.org

National Frontier Trails Center, 318 W Pacific, 816-325-7575

Truman House, Independence, MO

C. TURNING NORTH

LIBERTY, MO TO COUNCIL BLUFFS, IA

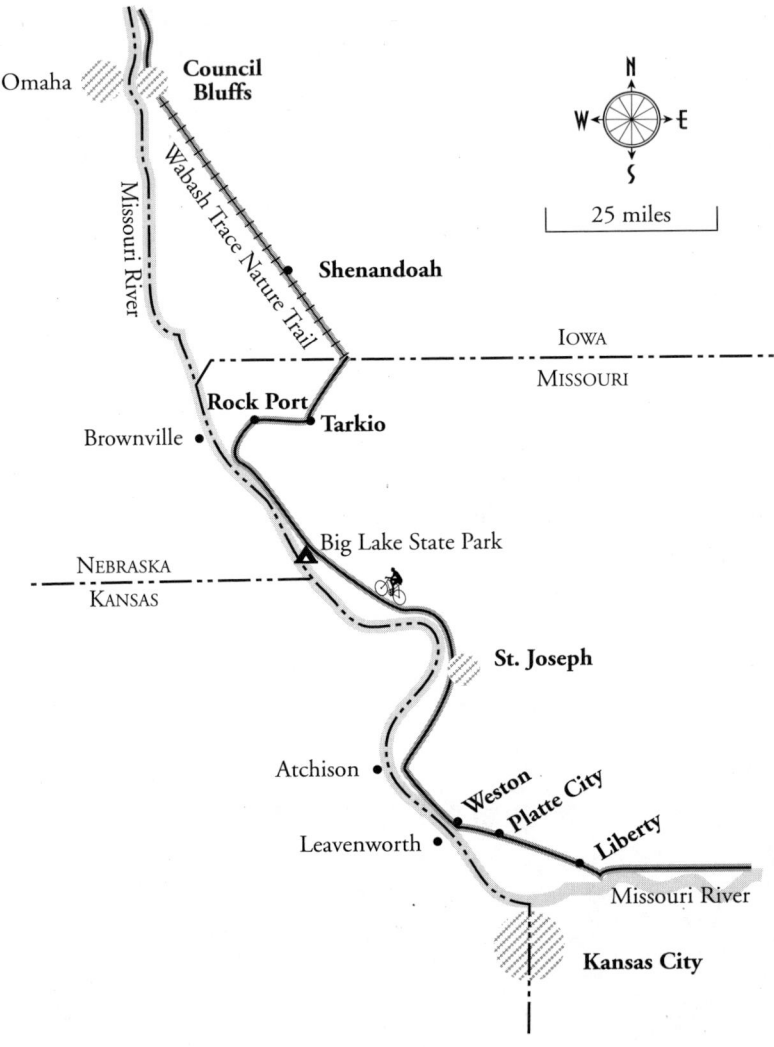

mile 262

On the border of Missouri and Kansas, there are actually two cities: Kansas City, Missouri, and Kansas City, Kansas. Our bicycle route avoids this large urban and industrial area by staying north through pleasant rural suburbs and the much more manageable towns of Liberty and Platte City. However, the route also passes conveniently by Kansas City International Airport for those wishing to join or leave the route here.

Although Kansas City is a major geographical milestone in our route today, where the river changes direction from westerly to northerly and the large Kansas River joins the Missouri River, it was not a significant milestone for Lewis and Clark. On June 26 *"we Killed a large rattle Snake, Sunning himself in the bank passed a bad Sand bar, where our tow rope broke twice, & with great exertions we rowed round it and Came to & Camped in the Point above the Kansas River. I observed a great number of Parrot queets this evening, our Party Killed Several 7 Deer today."* Clark anticipated the future of this strategic location where *"the high lands Coms to the river Kanses on the upper Side at about a mile, full in view, and a butifull place for a fort, good landing place, the waters of the Kansas is verry disigreeably tasted to me."*

Our bicycle route continues north along the eastern side of the Missouri River. The terrain alternates between gently rolling farmland and flat rich river bottom farmland up to St. Joseph—a bicycle-friendly, medium-size city with some hills and many services. This was the starting point for the Pony Express, and I recommend a visit to the excellent Pony Express Museum.

If you have a special interest in military history and modern military bases, it is possible to detour seven miles across the river from Weston and visit Fort Leavenworth in Leavenworth, Kansas. Today it is a large army complex with a museum of western U.S. military history. From here you can either return to the Missouri side or ride 24 miles north on the hillier Kansas side to Atchison, a very pleasant town with a rich railroading history and many beautiful historic homes—including the home of Amelia Earhart, the aviation pioneer. From Atchison it is four flat miles east across the river to rejoin the main route south of St. Joseph.

Leaving St. Joseph there are a few hills and then 72 miles of rich bottomland to Rock Port. The route heads northeast and inland here for 27 miles of hilly farm country to the tiny town of Blanchard on the Missouri-Iowa state line. Here our route picks up the Wabash Trace Nature Trail for 65 relatively flat and very scenic miles through beautiful hilly farmland into Council Bluffs.

This last stretch of hills is part of Iowa's Loess (pronounced "luss") Hills that run north and south along the western side of the state. This range of 200-foot hills was created by very fine soil similar to that found in parts of China and farther along our route in the Palouse of eastern Washington. This dirt was ground as fine as flour by the last glaciers 18,000 years ago, and then was blown by the wind into rounded hills.

Platte City, MO

Population: 3,000

Platte City is a possible place to find a motel and restaurant, or to shop for food before continuing on to camp at Weston Bend State Park five miles farther west.

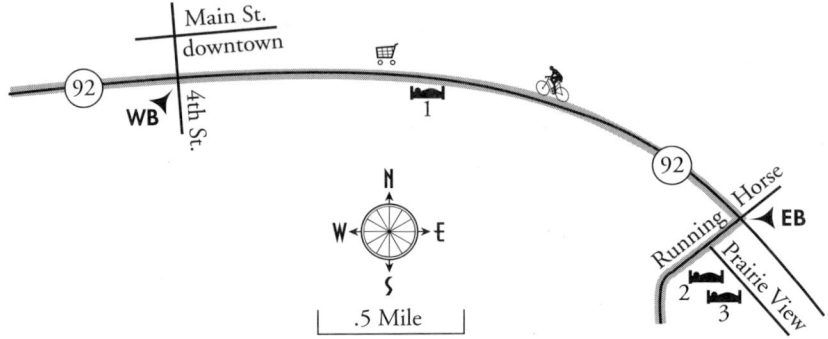

Platte City, MO — Zip: 64079

1) Comfort Inn ($$), 1200 Route 92, 800-228-5150

2) Super 8 Motel ($$), Prairie View Rd., 800-800-8000

3) AmericInn ($$), Prairie View Rd., 816-858-0200

Weston, MO

Population: 1,600

Weston was originally founded as a shipping port for the tobacco and hemp grown in the area. At one time Weston was the largest hemp port in the world, and it served many pioneers on the Oregon and California Trails. After Fort Leavenworth was built across the river, the town took advantage of its strategic location to sell both tobacco and liquor to the soldiers. The town died in the late 19th century after the Missouri River shifted its course westward, and then two large fires destroyed many buildings. In the last 30 years many people have worked successfully to bring Weston very much back to life.

It is now a very pleasant small town that is part "real" and part restored for tourists. The blend works well. There are several good restaurants, B&Bs, and interesting shops in restored historic buildings; but the town is not at all overrun with tourists. The Weston Café serves a great breakfast to both visitors and local working people. Just east of town is the McCormick Distillery, which claims to be the oldest distillery in the country (disputed by Jack Daniels!). If you want to taste their bourbon, you can buy some at their downtown store.

When Lewis and Clark camped near Weston on the night of June 30, 1804, *"one of the Sentinals challenged either a man or Beast, which run off, all prepared for action."* Keep in mind that this was a military expedition venturing into unknown Indian territory. On a lighter note, *"Turkeys are plenty on the Shore, G. Drewyer inform that he Saw PueCanns (pecan) Trees great quantities of raspburies and grapes."*

Main Street, Weston, MO

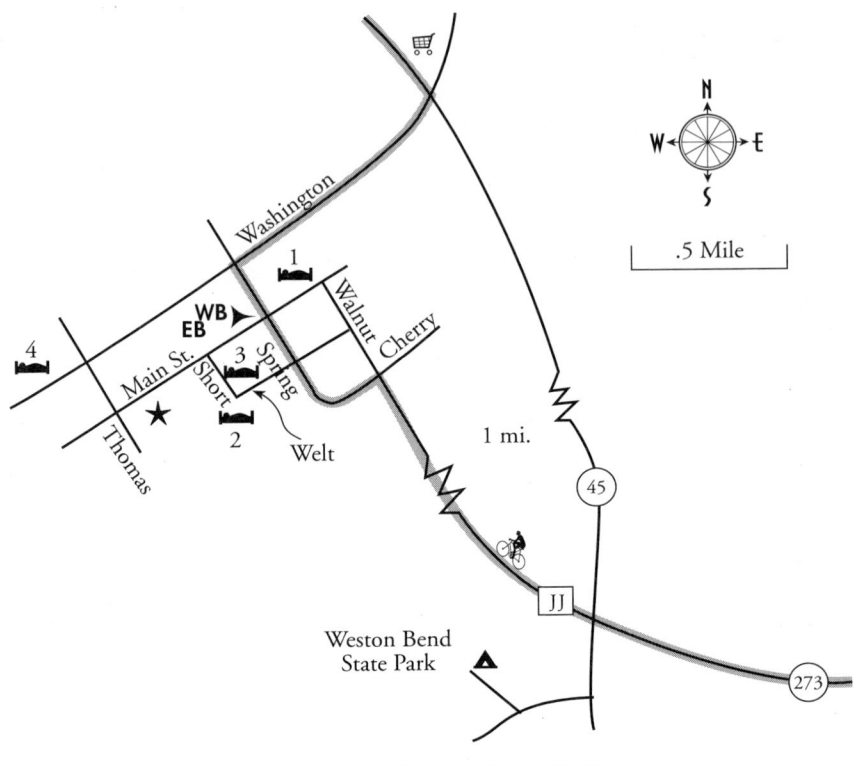

Weston, MO — Zip: 64098

★   **Weston Development Company:** 502 Main, 816-640-2909, www.ci.weston.mo.us

Missouri Department of Natural Resources (State Parks), Box 176, Jefferson City, MO 65102, 800-334-6946

🛏 1) Benner House ($$–$$$), 645 Main, 816-640-2616; http://ci.weston.mo.us; restored 1898 gothic home; quiet downtown location; pool and hot tub; queen beds and private baths; full breakfast; reduced weekday rates; reservations recommended.

   2) Inn at Weston Landing ($$), Short and Welt, 816-640-5788

   3) Hatchery B&B ($$), 618 Short, 816-640-5700

   4) Lemon Tree B&B ($$), 407 Washington, 816-386-5367

▲ 1) Weston Bend State Park, on Route 45 one mi. south of Route JJ and 273, about 3.5 hilly mi. east of town, good grass/shade/privacy, clean restroom with showers and laundry

   2) Lewis and Clark State Park, 13 mi. north on Route 45 on Sugar Lake (old oxbow from Missouri River), flat, good grass and shade, less privacy, covered

picnic pavilion, swimming and boating, clean restroom with showers and laundry

Lewis and Clark passed the site of this state park on Independence Day, July 4, 1804. They *"ussered in the day by a discharge of one shot from our Bow piece, proceeded on, passed the mouth of a Bayeau lading from a large Lake on the Starboard Side."*

St. Joseph, MO

Population: 72,000

St. Joseph was founded as an Indian trading post on the bluffs above the Missouri River by Joseph Robidoux 20 years after the Lewis and Clark expedition. Although it is best known as the starting point for the Pony Express, it was a also a very large and prosperous trading port, manufacturing center, and staging point for many westward pioneers. It was considered as the possible eastern terminus for the first transcontinental railroad, but questions about slavery and stability led Lincoln to choose Council Bluffs instead. Unlike Weston, St. Joseph has changed and adapted over the years and continued to grow as a regional business center.

Since the city is mostly a "low-rise" city, traffic is not bad for bicycles, except for the downtown area and the modern mall area on the Belt Highway. However, this also means the city is pretty spread out, and you will need your bicycle to get around. Our bicycle route through town meanders a bit to try to avoid traffic and unnecessary hills.

I consider the Pony Express Museum a "must see" attraction. The displays and interpretations of this short-lived—but exciting and romantic—venture are very well done. A visitor center is around the corner from the Pony Express Museum, and it's easy to stop in here to figure out what other attractions you might like to visit.

The Jesse James home, where the famous bank robber was shot and killed by one of his gang members, and several other museums are nearby. The Stetson hat factory and outlet store are located a couple of miles east of downtown if you are interested in western style and protection from the elements.

Historic mansions on Hall Street, St. Joseph, MO

If you still crave more riding, St. Joseph's Parkway offers 26 miles of very pleasant hilly riding through a series of inter-connecting parks and greenways in a semicircle around the city.

St. Joseph offers several B&Bs in historic mansions and a wide variety of restaurants spread around the city. Most of the motels are either downtown or clustered along with franchise restaurants near the intersection of I-29 and Frederick Blvd. two miles east of downtown. Camping is available at two private campgrounds six miles north of Frederick Blvd., and you should do your food shopping before you head out there.

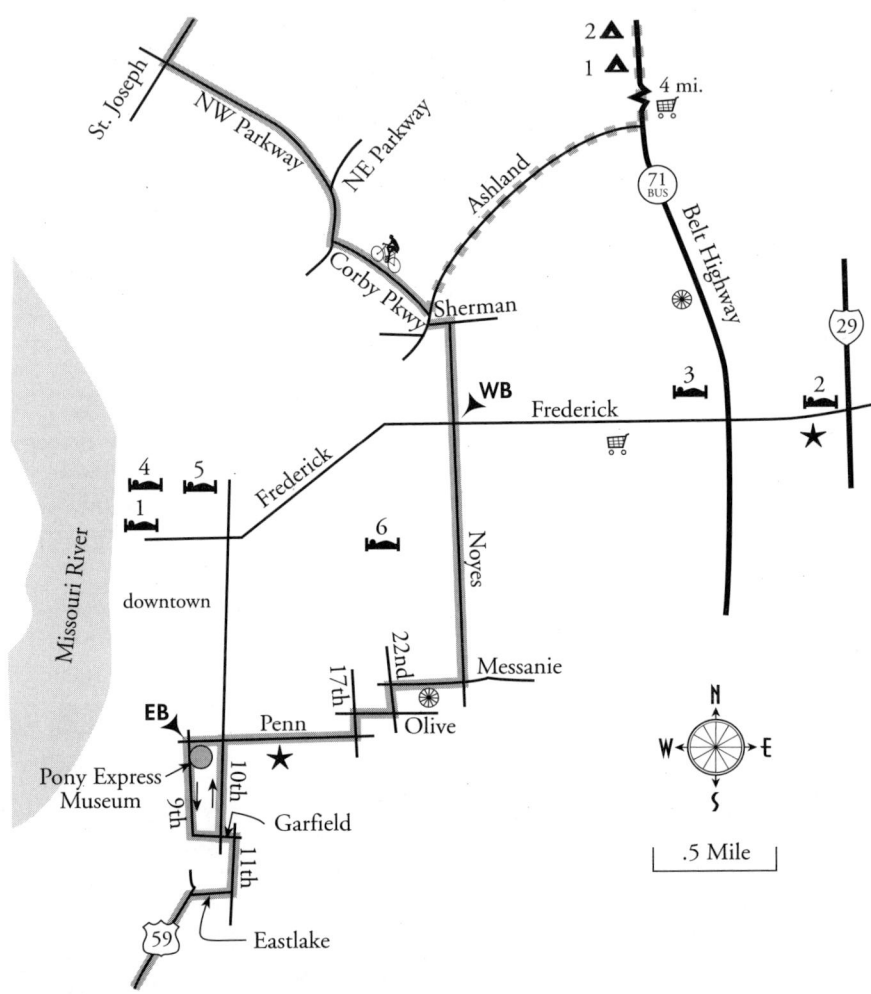

St. Joseph, MO — Zip: 64502

★ **St. Joseph Convention and Visitors Bureau:** 109 S 4th, seasonal offices on Penn and near I-29 interchange, 800-785-0360, www.stjomo.com, cvb@stjomo.com

🛏 1) Holiday Inn ($$), 102 S 3rd, 800-824-7402

2) Motel 6 ($), 4021 Frederick, 816-232-2311

3) Budget Motor Inn ($), 1328 Belt Hwy., 816-233-3146

4) Schuster Mansion B&B ($$), 703 Hall, 816-233-6017

5) Shakespeare Chateau B&B ($$), 809 Hall, 816-232-2667

6) Harding House B&B ($$), 219 N 20th, 816-232-7020

▲ 1) Walnut Grove Campground (816-233-1974) is located 0.2 mi. down a gravel road off the Belt Highway near I-29. Sites are somewhat hilly, but there is some grass, shade, and privacy. Restrooms are old but clean.

2) AOK Campground (816-324-4263) is located 0.4 mi. down a gravel road off the Belt Highway. The tenting area next to a pond is level, grassy, and open with some shade and some covered picnic tables. Restrooms are satisfactory, and there is a small pool.

⊛ 1) Bicycles by Savarino, 2402 Messanie, 816-364-1488

2) Ride Bicycles, 2320 N Belt Highway, 816-233-1718

ROUTE NORTH (WESTBOUND) FROM ST. JOSEPH

You should be aware that the recommended route north (westbound) has four miles of moderate dirt road with eight little nuisance hills of about 50 vertical feet each. I had no trouble riding this road on my touring bike with 35c tires. There is no food shopping for 40 miles, so you should stock up on whatever you need before leaving St. Joseph. The good news is that there is NO traffic, only a few hills near St. Joseph, and beautiful quiet riding along the flat bottomland near the river.

One of eight "little nuisance hills" on scenic dirt road north of St. Joseph, MO

If you really hate dirt roads, or if you are camping north of town and don't want to double back, the alternative is to ride north on Business 71 through Savannah and west on Route 59 through Oregon to rejoin the main route in Forest City. This alternate route includes 20 miles of four-lane divided highway, with traffic varying from heavy near St. Joseph to light in Oregon, and 2.6 miles on Interstate 29 with big dirty shoulders and very fast (but light) traffic. The advantages of this alternate route are paved roads and good food shopping in Savannah. Also, if you're camping, you're already six miles into this route and only have 39 miles to Big Lake State Park.

Big Lake State Park, Big Lake Village, MO 64437, 660-442-5432, (800-334-6946 for state reservation system)

This large flat park has grass and shady trees next to a lake which used to be an oxbow in the Missouri River. Camping, boating, and fishing are very popular, and there is a separate swimming pool. The unusual thing about this park is that it also offers motel rooms, suites, and cabins at reasonable prices. There is a camp store that sells some groceries and a dining lodge that offers buffet meals. The catch is that this park is very popular for family weekends and reunions, and reservations are required—well in advance if you want a room or cabin.

It was near here on July 12, 1804, that Captains Lewis and Clark held a court martial for Alexander Willard, who was accused of lying down and falling asleep while on guard duty the night before. This may seem like a natural thing to do and a minor crime, but the military considered this very significant—punishable by death. After all, the lives of the whole party depend on the sentinel. Willard got off lucky with 25 lashes each evening for four days, and once again all the men were reminded of the seriousness of their mission and the need for discipline.

Rock Port, MO

Population: 1,500

Rock Port is a possible place to find a motel and restaurant, and to shop for food before continuing on to camp along the Wabash Trace or at the KOA just west of the I-29 interchange. There are restaurants both downtown and on Route 136 near I-29.

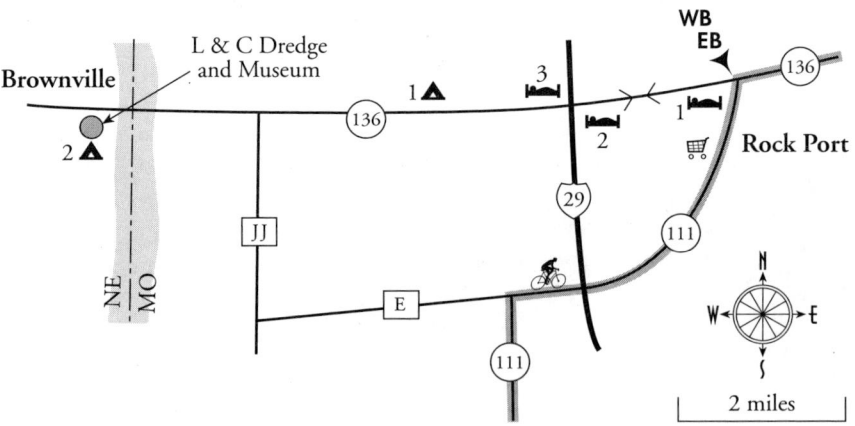

Rock Port, MO — Zip: 64482

🛏 1) White Rock Motel ($), 660-744-5363

    2) Rock Port Inn ($$), 660-744-6282

    3) Oak Grove Inn ($$), 660-744-5357

▲ 1) KOA, 660-744-5485

Brownville, NE

Population: 150

mile 400

Although it requires an additional 14 miles (45 vs. 31) between Big Lake and Rock Port, and probably an extra day to enjoy the attractions, a visit to this delightful town will be worth it for many people. In 1956 a group of local residents set out to preserve this historic small river town, and they have done an admirable job. It now includes a historical museum which is open afternoons, the Brownville Village Theatre (402-825-4121) that offers weekend summer performances, the Belle of Brownville river cruise boat (402-825-6441), and the Captain Meriwether Lewis—a 269-foot river dredge boat that operated on the river from 1932 to 1969 and is now a museum of early life on the river.

The town was originally founded in 1854, 40 years after Lewis and Clark came up the river. It was a major steamboat landing and river crossing, with as many as ten steamboats stopping each day. The bridge across the Missouri River was completed in 1939 and was quite advanced for its time. In 1857 the Brownville Medical College was established here, and the main building can still be seen as the Methodist church. Today there are several other historic buildings to enjoy.

If you are thinking of staying overnight, there are two restaurants in town and a primitive campground near the bridge. See Rock Port for more camping, lodging, and restaurants five to eight miles east—and on our route. More information about the town can be obtained from the Brownville Historical Society, Box 1, (402-825-6001), and the Brownville fine Arts Association, Box 4, (402-825-3331).

Zip: 68321

▲ 2) Brownville State Recreation Area, primitive camping near Route 136 bridge in Brownville, rough grass, shade, pit toilet, no water

Captain Meriwether Lewis Museum of Missouri River History, located in a restored 269-foot Corps of Engineers side-wheeler dredge, Brownville, NE

Tarkio, MO

Population: 2,200

Tarkio is a possible overnight stop in the middle of hilly farming country, with a motel, medium supermarket, and small restaurants.

Zip: 64491

🛏 Big T Motel ($), 816-736-4174

Shenandoah, IA

Population: 6,000

Shenandoah is a regional farm center and a good stopping place on the Wabash Trace Nature Trail. It has three motels and several restaurants in a flat town almost small enough to walk around. There are also two places to camp and good food shopping, and there may be more accommodations as the town gradually builds up its tourist business for the Wabash Trace. Shenandoah also claims some national fame as the home of the Everly Brothers.

The Wabash Trace is a 63-mile rail trail running from Blanchard on the Missouri state line northwest to Council Bluffs. It is surfaced with hard packed crushed limestone and is good riding for all but thin racing tires. If the southern section is muddy after a lot of rain, it's easy to ride to Shenandoah on nearby county roads that are laid out in a square grid. The quality of the Trail improves as it ages and you pedal closer to the population centers near Council Bluffs.

This trail was originally used as a pioneer and military road. In 1878 tracks were laid by the Council Bluffs and St. Louis Railway, which was later acquired by the Wabash Railroad. It is amazing how they found an almost level route through the Loess Hills of western Iowa. The trail provides wonderful quiet views of rich rolling farmland and small towns.

Depot Restaurant and Wabash Trace Nature Trail Headquarters, Shenandoah, IA

Wabash Trace headquarters is located in the Depot Restaurant in the middle of downtown. This local institution is owned and operated by Bill Hillman, the force behind the Wabash Trace; and you can get good meals in this historic restoration from early morning until late at night.

mile 444

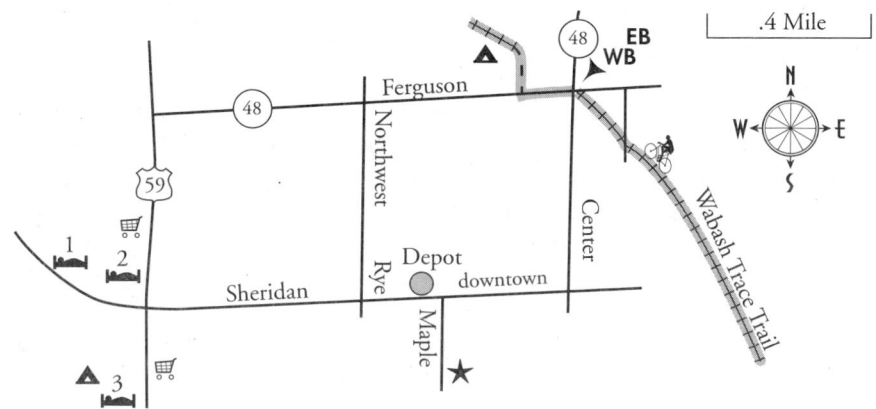

Shenandoah, IA — Zip: 51601

★ **Shenandoah Chamber and Industry Association:** 301 Maple, 712-246-3455

🛏 1) Country Inn ($$), Sheridan and Route 59, 712-246-1550

2) Days Inn ($$), Route 59 and Sheridan, 712-246-5733

3) Fifty Niner Motel ($), Route 59 and Nishna, 712-246-2925

▲ 1) Fifty Niner CG, Route 59 and Nishna, 712-246-2925

2) City Park, Ferguson and Wabash Trace, 712-246-3409

Cycling on the Wabash Trace Nature Trail, Iowa

Council Bluffs, IA

Population: 55,000

Although Council Bluffs sometimes feels like a poor relation of Omaha across the river, it has everything a bicycle tourer needs and a number of things to recommend it. Lake Manawa offers pleasant lakeside camping just south of town. There is a wide selection of motels, mostly located near exits of the two major interstate highways. There are many restaurants, which tend to be spread out around the downtown area or clustered near the motels around the interstate exits. The city is too spread out for walking; you need your bicycle to get around. Traffic can be heavy in some areas, so the recommended bicycle route appears somewhat indirect on the city map. Sixth Street (Route 192) may look appealing as a direct north-south route, however it is very busy; and the elevated section north of I-29 is very fast, narrow, dirty, and dangerous for bicycles.

Although Lewis and Clark camped at present day Long's Landing (south of Lake Manawa) for five days looking for Indians, they actually had their first "council" with the Otos and Missouris several days later about 20 miles upriver on the "bluffs" near present day Fort Calhoun. Today's city of Council Bluffs was settled as Kanesville in 1846 by Mormons travelling west to escape religious persecution. The name was changed to Council Bluffs in 1853, and the town was thriving before Omaha was settled.

I consider the new Western Historic Trails Center a "must see" in the southwest edge of the city along the Missouri River. It features very good displays and interpretations of the Lewis and Clark, Mormon, Oregon, and California Trails. The Lewis and Clark Monument and Scenic Overlook just north of town provides a great view of the river and Omaha, but it's up a steep hill. Railroad fans might like the Railswest Museum, HO Model Display, and Railroad Transportation Museum. The General Dodge House is a beautiful restoration of the home of Grenville Dodge—Civil War General, friend of Lincoln, and surveyor for the first transcontinental railroad.

Council Bluffs, IA — Zip: 51502

★ **Council Bluffs Convention and Visitor's Center:** 7 N 6th St., 800-228-6878, www.councilbluffsiowa.com

🛏 The Visitor's Center lists 19 motels and 2 B&Bs.
  A small sample of convenient locations is listed here:

  1) Motel 6 ($$), 6th St. south of I-80, 800-466-8356

  2) Econo Lodge ($$), 6th St. south of I-80, 800-229-5150

  3) Settle Inn ($$), 500 S 30th Ave., 888-980-5555

▲ Lake Manawa State Park, South Shore Drive, (south on 6th St.), 712-366-0220

⊛ Endless Trail, 506 S Main, 712-322-9760

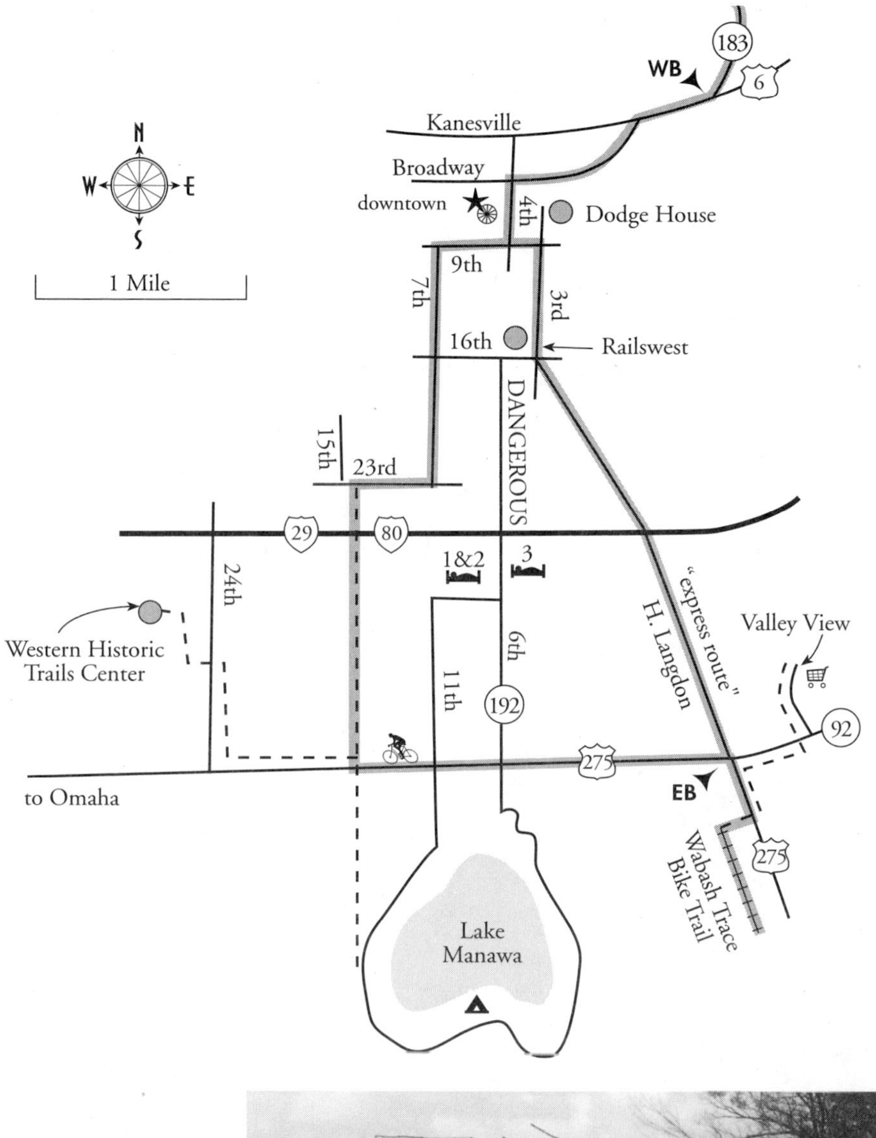

mile 490

183
6
WB
Kanesville
Broadway
downtown
4th
9th
Dodge House
7th
3rd
16th
Railswest
N
W · E
S
DANGEROUS
1 Mile
15th
23rd
24th
29 80
1&2
3
Western Historic
Trails Center
"express route"
Valley View
H. Langdon
11th
6th
192
92
to Omaha
275
EB
Wabash Trace
Bike Trail
275
Lake
Manawa

Modern and historic obstacles on the Missouri River, behind the Western Historic Trails Center, Council Bluffs, IA

D. BOTTOMLAND

COUNCIL BLUFFS, IA TO YANKTON, SD

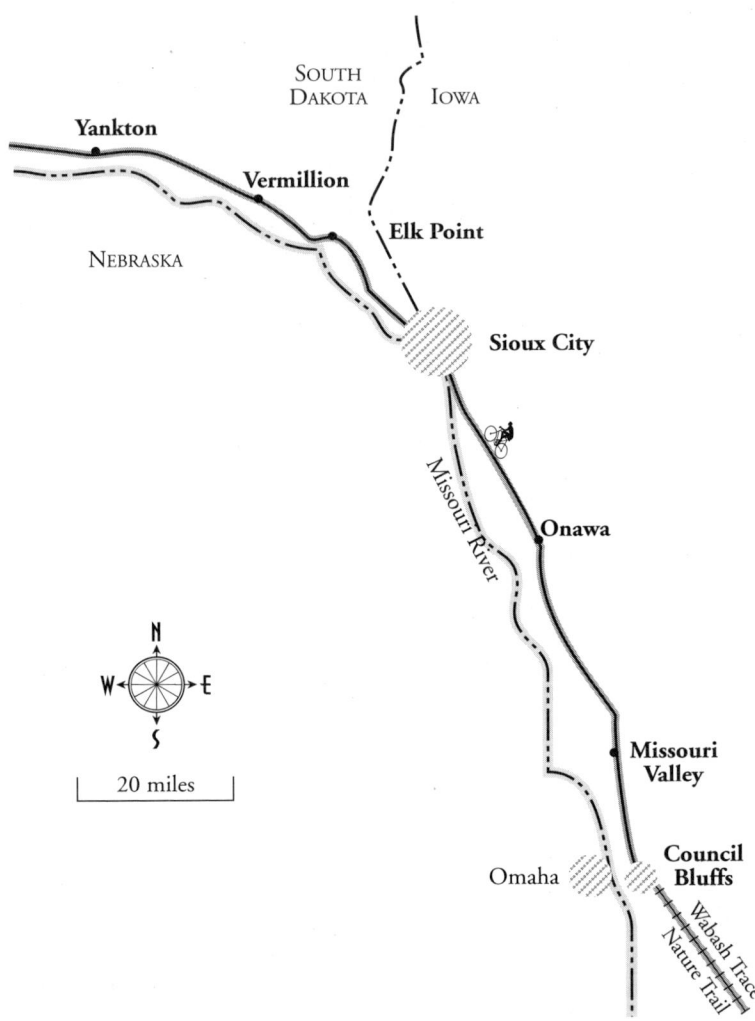

Although we've already seen flat bottomland along the river in Missouri, north of Council Bluffs there is an even wider and more extensive flood plain— mostly on the Iowa side. This provides relatively flat riding for 170 miles to Yankton. Savor the flat riding here and hope that the wind is blowing your way on these wide open spaces.

IOWA VS NEBRASKA

The 110 miles between Council Bluffs and Sioux City can be ridden on either side of the river, but I prefer the Iowa side for several reasons. First, it is about ten miles shorter and flatter. There are some hills just north of Council Bluffs, but most of the route is along river bottomland. Second, camping is better in Iowa with two excellent state parks near Missouri Valley and Onawa. Third, motels are a little better in Iowa, with options evenly spaced in Missouri Valley and Onawa. Finally, traffic is a little lighter in Council Bluffs than Omaha, and you can avoid riding the bridge across the Missouri River between the two cities.

The Iowa side offers the DeSoto National Wildlife Refuge and its natural and cultural history. In spring and fall migrations, half a million snow geese fill the air and feed here. There is also a permanent display of an 1860 sternwheeler and its artifacts found here in 1968. Near Onawa, Lewis and Clark State Park offers good camping on a lake that used to be an oxbow of the river. It also offers replicas of the keelboat and pirogues used by the Corps of Discovery.

However, there are some valid reasons for visiting Omaha and riding up the Nebraska side. The Omaha Airport is reasonably convenient for cyclists wanting to start or end a segment here. Omaha has a number of interesting attractions which are easily accessible to cyclists, like the Old Market, Union Station, Mormon Winter Quarters, and the Joslyn Art Museum. Boys Town and the Strategic Air Command Museum are interesting, but not easily accessible by bicycle.

Nebraska also offers Fort Atkinson State Park (in the town of Fort Calhoun) and its history. This is the spot where Lewis and Clark had their first big council with Indian chiefs, although the state park is mostly devoted to displaying and interpreting the fort built here in 1820 on the recommendation of Lewis and Clark. It was the first U.S. fort west of the Missouri, and was important in the early years of fur trade, river traffic, and Indian relations.

Up a 300-foot hill just above Decatur, Nebraska, is a memorial to Chief Blackbird, who died of smallpox along with 400 of his tribe four years before Lewis and Clark arrived. Although Blackbird was friendly to white traders, even though they brought the smallpox, he had a reputation of ruthlessly poisoning his personal enemies. On August 11 Lewis and Clark stopped to climb Blackbird Hill to pay their respects and enjoy the view.

It is also possible to cross the river back and forth to see things that are important to you. To visit Omaha (Nebraska) from Council Bluffs (Iowa) is about a 15-mile round trip of highway riding with a busy hilly bridge. To cross between Blair (Nebraska) and Missouri Valley (Iowa) is 10 flat miles with light traffic, and between Decatur (Nebraska) and Onawa (Iowa) is 8 flat miles with light traffic.

Although our bicycle route goes up the Iowa side, it's not hard to get a Nebraska map and follow Route 75 in Nebraska. The town description for Omaha includes a route to the airport and sources for more information about both Omaha and Nebraska.

mile 490

The final 70 miles from Sioux City to Yankton is more flat bottomland with a nice break in the middle in Vermillion, home of the University of South Dakota, sitting on a treed bluff oasis above the bottomland.

A different kind of cycling at Old Market, Omaha, NE

Omaha, NE

Population: 355,000

Omaha is a *big* city on the west bank of the Missouri River opposite Council Bluffs. It has grown from a major river port and regional farm center to also become the financial, insurance, and telemarketing center for much of the Midwest.

The spur route to the airport passes directly by the Western Heritage Museum in the refurbished Union Pacific train station and the Old Market—several blocks of restaurants and shops in old warehouses. North of downtown is Eppley Airfield (Omaha's airport). Just a few blocks off the route is the Joslyn Art Museum—which houses an excellent collection of Western United States art by Bodmer and others, as well as a broad sampling of classical art in an art deco building. North of the airport is the Mormon Winter Quarters Museum and Cemetery, which commemorates their winter encampment here before they moved on to Salt Lake City. No matter what your religious convictions, you have to be impressed by their determination, as illustrated by the statue of the family travelling on to Utah pulling all their belongings in a handcart.

If you want to explore Omaha west of the river, be prepared for hills. Although there are several pleasant paved bike trails that follow river beds, they generally don't go where you want to go. If you have access to transportation, Boys Town is 12 miles west of downtown on Route 6, and the new SAC (Strategic Air Command) Museum is now 28 miles southwest on I-80.

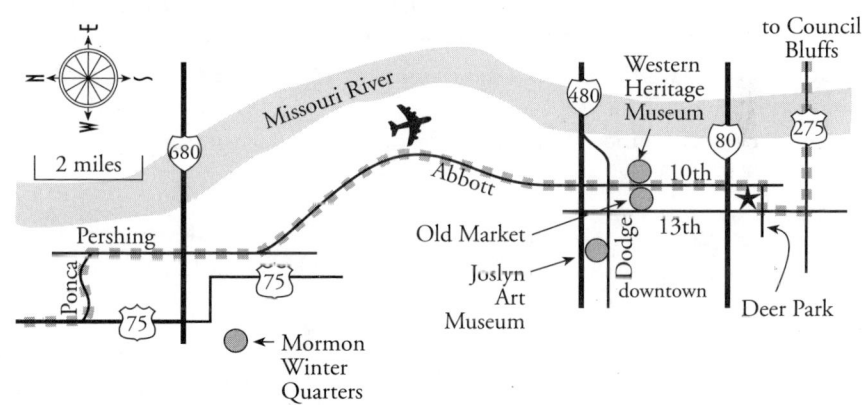

Omaha, NE — Zip: 68106

★ **Greater Omaha Convention and Visitors Bureau:** 6800 Mercy Rd., (10th St., just south of I-80), Omaha, NE 68106-2627, 800-332-1819; www.visitomaha.com

Nebraska Office of Tourism, 700 S 16th St., Lincoln, NE 68509, 800-228-4307; www.visitnebraska.org

Missouri Valley, IA

Population: 3,000

Missouri Valley grew as an agricultural center after the Union Pacific Railroad came through in 1871. In the early 1900s the Lincoln Highway was established as the first transcontinental highway, and today Route 30 marks this historic route

through town. The town is also on the crossroads of I-29 and Route 183, part of today's Loess Hills Scenic Byway.

You can find motels and restaurants out by the I-29 interchange, as well as a B&B and several restaurants within walking distance in the downtown area. The map below shows a pleasant detour through the DeSoto National Wildlife Refuge and Wilson Island

Varied architecture on Main Street, Missouri Valley, IA

State Park. Although it's seven miles off the route, Wilson Island offers very pleasant camping, and it's all flat. The refuge is most famous for the spring and fall migrations of ducks and geese, as well as a museum of relics recovered from the steamboat Bertrand. To summarize distances, camping at Wilson Island adds 15 miles, and completing the loop through DeSoto Refuge adds an extra 5 miles.

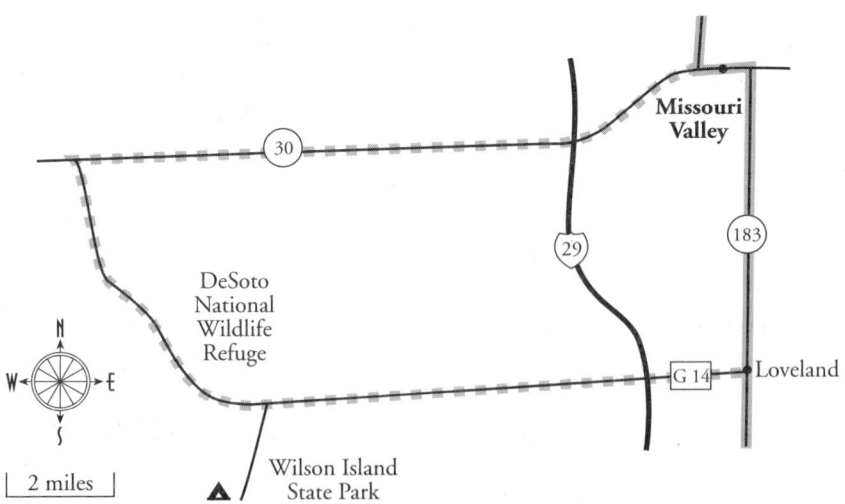

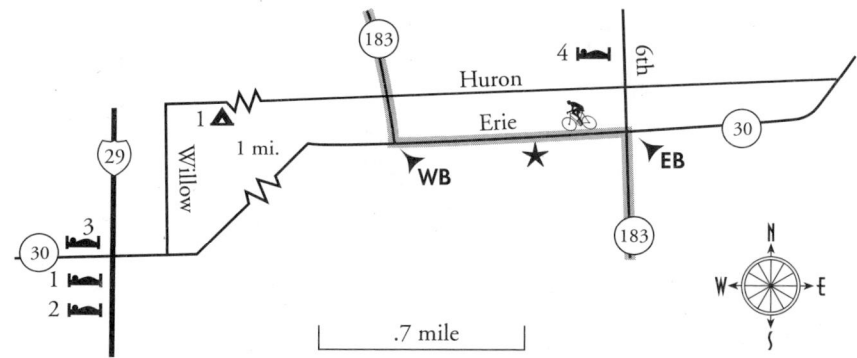

Missouri Valley, IA — Zip: 51555

★ **Missouri Valley Chamber of Commerce:** 400 E Erie, 712-642-2553, www.missourivalley.com, chambermv@aol.com

🛏 1) Super 8 Motel ($$), 800-800-8000

2) Rath Travelers Inn ($$), 712-642-2723

3) Days Inn ($$), 712-642-4003

4) White House B&B ($$), 217 N 5th, 888-204-6873

▲ 1) Missouri Valley City Park, restrooms, no showers

2) Wilson Island Recreation Area, 7 flat mi. west of Route 183 just above Loveland, near river, grass, shade, showers, 712-642-2069

Special Events

Gospel Sing, 4th weekend in June
Harrison County Fair, 4th weekend in July

Special Attractions: DeSoto National Wildlife Refuge, Box 114, Missouri Valley, IA, 51555, 712-642-4121

Onawa, IA

Population: 3,000

Originally an agricultural center in the middle of a corn and soybean area, Onawa is now the county seat of Monona County, and many people are employed in government and services. "Onawa" means "wide awake," and "monona" means "beautiful valley" in the local Omaha Indian dialect.

In this century Onawa has gained some fame as the home of the Eskimo Pie. It is also proud of having the widest main street in the United States, which is used to host car shows and promote a welcoming environment. There are several restaurants, good food shopping, a motel out by the I-29 interchange, and two campgrounds on Blue Lake—a former oxbow in the Missouri River.

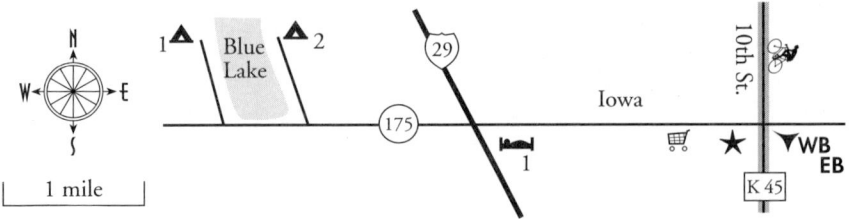

Onawa, IA — Zip: 51040

★ **Onawa Chamber of Commerce**
1009 Iowa Ave., 712-423-1801, www.onawa.com, chamber@onawa.com

⊨ Super 8 Motel ($$), Route 175 and I-29, 712-423-2101

▲ 1) Lewis and Clark State Park, 4 flat mi. west on Route 175, replica keelboat
and pirogues, swimming, showers, 712-423-2829

2) Onawa Blue Lake KOA, 4 flat mi. west on Route 175, pool, showers,
laundry, convenience store, 800-562-4182

Special Events

Lewis and Clark Festival, 2nd weekend in June (keelboat display, muzzle-
loader shoot, quilt show, etc.)

Graffiti Night, 3rd Saturday in June (music, car show)

Car Show, 3rd Saturday in August

Monona County Fair, July

Widest Main Street in America, Onawa, IA

Sioux City, IA, So. Sioux City, NE, N. Sioux City, SD

Populations: 85,000 — 9,700 — 2,000

Sioux City is located in Iowa, on the north bank of the Missouri River, sandwiched between the Sioux and Floyd rivers. It is also the intersection of three states; and all these rivers, bridges, railroads, and boundaries make bicycle travel somewhat complicated. It is also potentially confusing, because there are actually three cities in three states—Sioux City, Iowa; South Sioux City, Nebraska; and North Sioux City, South Dakota (actually located west of Sioux City). This is a relatively large metropolitan area with lots of traffic and lots of services spread out over a wide geographic area. However, by using the map below with a little thought and planning, it can be a very pleasant place with easy riding.

This is an ideal resting point for bicycle tourers, and most will want to stop either in South Sioux City, Nebraska—one mile from downtown on the south side of the Missouri River—or North Sioux City, South Dakota—about six miles north and west of downtown Sioux City. It is possible to breeze through the edge of downtown Sioux City on a pleasant bike path along the Missouri River. Fortunately, the excellent Sergeant Floyd Visitor Center and Riverboat Museum are located right on this bike path.

South Sioux City, Nebraska, is both a self-contained town of 9,700 and an appendage of Sioux City, Iowa. There is good camping right on the river, good food shopping, several motels, and many restaurants. Although it's possible to get around town by walking, traffic is light and you

Our bike route along the Big Sioux River, Sioux City, IA

will probably want to use your bicycle. An easy half-mile ride across a sidewalk on the Veteran's Bridge on Dakota Ave. takes you to a bike path along the north side of the river.

The bike path runs east along the river through Gateway Park, with a connector into downtown Sioux City, Iowa. Our route follows the bike path west through Larsen Park to the Sergeant Floyd Visitor Center and Riverboat Museum. It continues four miles farther west—running between I-29 and the river to provide scenic riding and a pleasant relief from traffic. After a stretch along the Big Sioux River, ride through Riverside Park and return to the highway.

The other good option for spending the night is in North Sioux City, South Dakota, about six miles west of Sioux City. Near I-29 is a KOA campground, several motels listed below, and several restaurants. There is food shopping between Riverside Park and this area.

The free Sergeant Floyd Visitor Center and Riverboat Museum is housed in an old landlocked riverboat, and is definitely worth a visit. It has a number of exhibits on the Lewis and Clark expedition, as well as life on the river. Blair Chicoine, who

recently died from leukemia, had a shop on board where he made wonderful boat models. His model of the Lewis and Clark keelboat helped me understand this boat much better than all the descriptions, sketches, and replicas I have seen. Having grown up

Sergeant Floyd Museum and Welcome Center

on a farm in the Missouri River bottomland nearby, he knew a lot about back roads, the shifting course of the river over the last 200 years, and the Lewis and Clark expedition's campsites in this area.

Sioux City is also known as the place where Sergeant Floyd died—the only man to die on the expedition. Death was probably caused by a burst appendix, which probably would have resulted in death even in a major city with good medical facilities and doctors. On August 20 Clark wrote, *"I am Dull & heavy been up the greater Part of last night with Serjt. Floyd, who . . . expired with a great deel of composure, having Said to me before his death that he was going away and wished me to write a letter— we Buried him to the top of a high round hill over looking the river & Countrey for a great distance Situated just below a Small river without a name to which we name & call Floyds river, the Bluffs Sergts. Floyds Bluff."*

Although the grave had to be moved twice as the river changed course and ate away at the bluff, today there is a tall obelisk on a nearby bluff on the east bank of

the river just south of the city. The roads to the monument are quite dangerous for cyclists, because they have curbs, no shoulders, and carry lots of traffic. It's best to honor Floyd and enjoy this visible memorial from a distance.

Lewis & Clark Keelboat

Red Pirogue

Models by Blair Chicoine, Sergeant Floyd Museum, Sioux City, IA

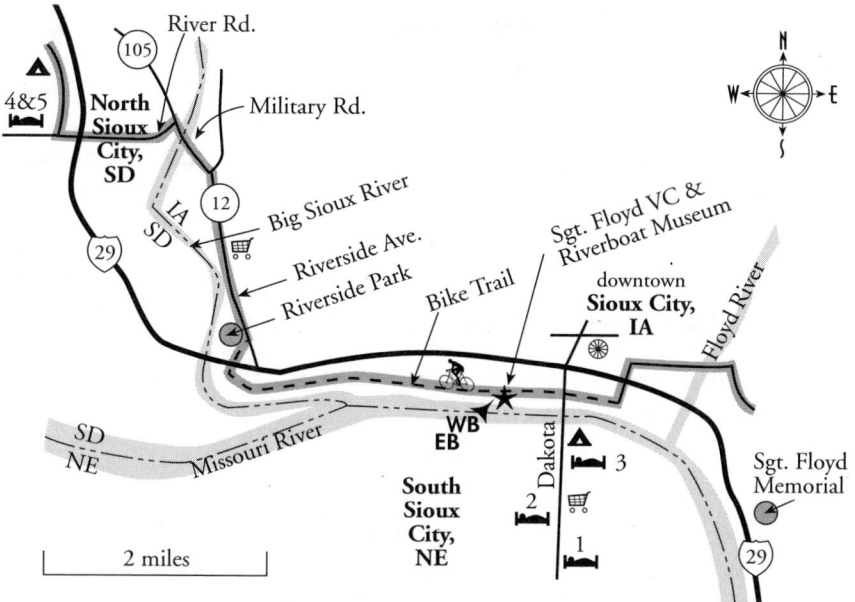

Sioux City, IA — Zip: 51102, **South Sioux City, NE** — Zip: 68776
North Sioux City — Zip: 57049

★   **Sioux City Convention and Visitors Bureau:** 801 4th St.,
800-593-2228; www.sioux-city.org

     Sergeant Floyd Welcome Center and Riverboat Museum, Larsen Park, on
north side of Missouri River bike path just west of Veteran's Bridge

   The Visitors Bureau lists 27 hotels and motels in the tri-city area. Below are
five that are convenient to the Trail:

     South Sioux City

1) Econo Lodge, 4402 Dakota, 402-494-4114

2) Ramada, 2829 Dakota, 800-962-2545

3) Travel Lodge, 400 Dakota, 402-494-3046

     North Sioux City

4) Comfort Inn, Streeter Dr., 605-232-3366

5) Super 8, Streeter Dr., 605-232-4716

▲   **South Sioux City**
Scenic Park CG, 6th and E St.: pleasant and convenient camping on the
river across from downtown Sioux City; good grass, shade, little privacy, and
satisfactory restrooms and showers

     North Sioux City: KOA, 601 Streeter Dr., 605-232-4519

⊛   Albrecht Cycle Shop, 200 5th St., Sioux City, IA, 712-258-6050

Elk Point, SD

Population: 1,400

Elk Point is a small town with a motel, town park with camping, several restaurants, and a grocery store. Near here the Corps of Discovery elected Patrick Gass as a sergeant to replace Sergeant Floyd. It was four days later when Lewis first used the term "corps of volunteers for North Western Discovery" in his orders.

Zip: 57025

🛏   Home Towne Inn ($), I-29 interchange, 605-356-2667

⛺   Town Park, near high school south of Main, grass, shade, satisfactory restrooms with showers

Vermillion, SD

Population: 10,000

Located on a relatively lush, tree-covered bluff above the small Vermillion River (Wase Wakpala, or "red stream" in the Sioux language), Vermillion is a very pleasant oasis in the middle of the flat Missouri River bottomland farm country. It is also the home of the University of South Dakota.

Six miles north of town is Spirit Mound—which the Indians told Lewis and Clark was inhabited by fierce people eighteen inches tall with large heads. The explorers could not resist visiting this site, but found only great views of the prairie. Today it is on private property and difficult to visit.

Vermillion can be a very pleasant stopping point for bicycle tourers, although it's tough competing with both Sioux City and Yankton in either direction. A basic Lion's Club campground is located across the street from a huge food supermarket. There are also several motels in town, which sometimes fill up for special events at the university. Finally, there is the typical wide variety of restaurants you would expect in a college town. You'll want your bicycle to get around in this flat, spread out, low-traffic town.

In addition to the university, Vermillion has some interesting attractions. The Shrine to Music contains a collection of 6,000 rare and antique musical instruments from all over the world. The Austin-Whittemore House is a modest Italian Villa style home filled with Victorian furniture appropriate to the late 19th century.

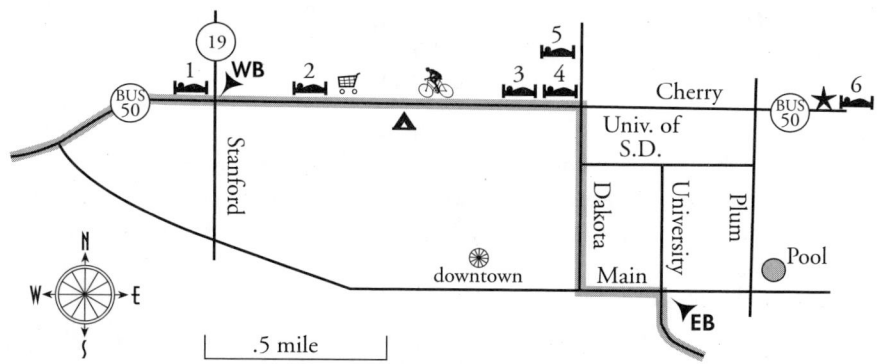

mile 633

Vermillion, SD — Zip: 57069

★ **Vermillion Area Chamber of Commerce:** 906 E Cherry, 800-809-2071, www.vermillionsouthdakota.com

🛏 1) Budget Host Tomahawk ($), 1313 W Cherry, 800-283-4678

2) Comfort Inn ($$), 701 W Cherry, 800-228-5150

3) Lamplighter ($), 112 E Cherry, 605-624-4451

4) Coyote ($), 702 N Dakota, 605-624-2616

5) Travelodge ($$), 912 N Dakota, 605-624-2824

6) Super 8 ($$), 1208 E Cherry, 605-624-8005

▲ Lion's Club Campground, Cherry at Princeton, good grass, shade, little privacy, satisfactory restroom, showers available at town pool a few blocks away (see map)

✺ Bike Plus, 28 Center, 605-624-6200

Yankton, SD

Population: 14,000

Yankton was the capital of the original Dakota Territory before it was split into two states. Today it is the seat of Yankton County and a regional center with many services. There are still many attractive Victorian buildings around the downtown area. During the warm months it is a gateway to the recreational areas of nearby Lewis and Clark Lake, and it can be crowded with fishermen and other vacationers on weekends and holidays.

There is a wide variety of lodging, restaurants, and stores, as well as excellent camping at Lewis and Clark Lake five miles west of town. The best camping areas are Midway Unit and Gavins Point Unit, located directly on the lake just west of the dam, marina, and restaurant. However, availability may be better at the unit below the dam, which is still a very pleasant campground without the view. A bike trail starts just east of the dam, climbs the dam, winds several miles along the lake through the various campgrounds, and ends directly on our route west towards Springfield.

There is a visitor center with wonderful views located on a hill overlooking the south side of the Gavins Point Dam. It has displays of both the history of the area and the modern building of the dam and power plant. This is the first of many dams and lakes created by the Army Corps of Engineers to "tame" the Missouri River for flood control, electricity, and recreation.

The visitor center is near Calumet Bluff, where the Corps of Discovery camped for four days on August 28–31, 1804, and had a friendly meeting with the Yankton Sioux. One reason this encounter went so well was the expedition's new translator, Pierre Dorion, whom they had picked up farther down river as he was returning from a trading trip. Dorion had a Sioux wife and lots of experience with the local people, who had caused problems with earlier groups of white traders.

Beach and camping on Lewis & Clark Lake, Yankton, SD

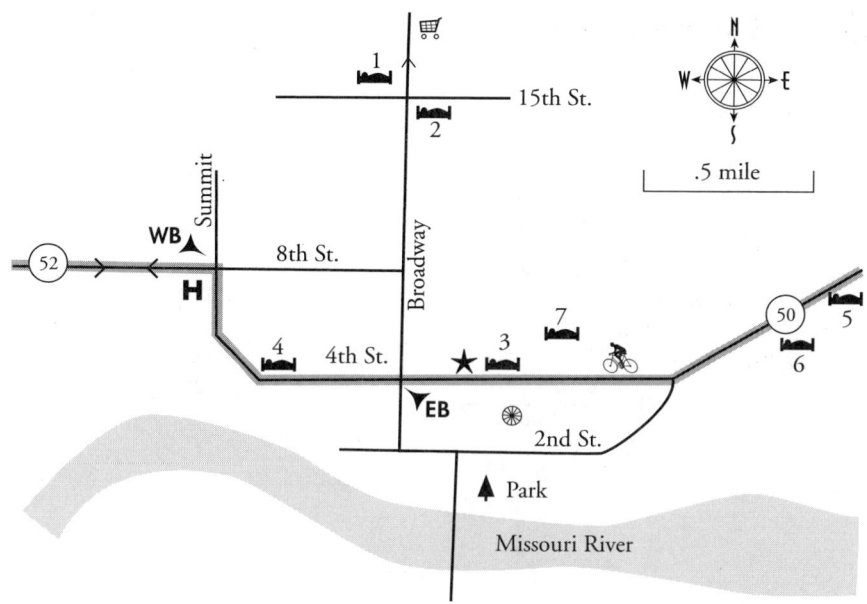

Yankton, SD — Zip: 57078

★ **Chamber of Commerce:** 218 W 4th St., 605-665-3636
www.yanktonsd.com

1) Colonial Inn ($), 1509 Broadway, 605-665-3647

2) Broadway Inn ($), 1210 Broadway, 800-665-7805

3) Star-Brite Inn ($), 412 E 4th St., 605-665-7856

4) Star-Lite Inn ($), 500 Park St., 605-665-7828

5) Best Western Kelly Inn ($$), 1609 E Hwy. 50, 800-635-3559

6) Super 8 Motel ($$), 1705 E Hwy. 50, 800-800-8000

7) Mulberry Inn B&B ($$), 512 Mulberry, 605-665-7116

▲ Lewis and Clark Lake, 5 mi. west on Hwy. 52, several beautiful units on lake above dam and below dam, showers, 402-667-7873

✺ Ace Hardware and Bike Shop, 3rd and Douglas, 605-665-2813

🚲 E. LAKES AND DAMS

YANKTON, SD TO BISMARCK, ND

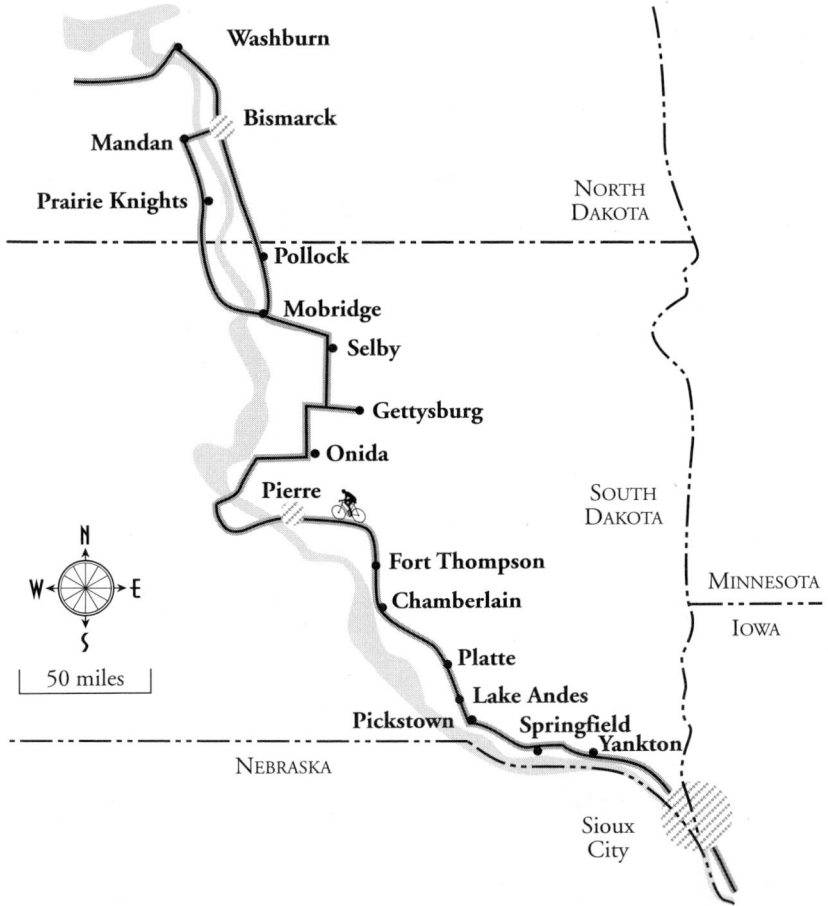

There seems to be a subtle, but significant, east-west dividing line right around Yankton. Farmers and local people will tell you it's the James River, flowing south to join the Missouri just east of Yankton. Scientists will tell you it's the 98th meridian just west of Yankton. Whichever line you choose, west of here there is less rain, the grass is shorter, the hills are lower, and the wind is stronger.

Upriver from Yankton a series of six large dams changes the nature of the Missouri River from a free flowing river into a collection of huge lakes. Lewis and Clark might not recognize this part of the river today. These dams were built in the mid-1900s by the Corps of Engineers for flood control, irrigation, and power generation. Together these lakes have a shoreline equal in length to the Atlantic, Pacific, and Gulf of Mexico shorelines all put together.

Although the Corps of Engineers is sometimes criticized for spending vast amounts of money to change—and sometimes challenge—nature, one thing they do well is public relations. All their projects include very good campgrounds, picnic areas, boat launching ramps, and recreational facilities to please fishermen and local residents. The campgrounds, picnic areas, and beaches on Lake Lewis and Clark just west of Yankton provide a beautiful stopping point.

It was in the Dakotas that Lewis and Clark first encountered the "Dakota" Indians. *"This Great Nation who the French has given the nickname of Sciouex, Call them selves Dar co tar." (Moulton, Vol 3, p. 32)* Unfortunately, but not surprisingly, white people first heard them called "Sioux" (meaning "cutthroat" or "little snake" in Ojibwa and "enemy" in Chippewa) by the French trappers, and that is the name that stuck.

Missouri River emerging from the power plant and surge tanks below Oahe Dam, Pierre, SD

Roads in this area traverse a mixture of flat bottomland, gently rolling hills, and occasional long 400-foot hills. The road is generally located away from the river, although it returns to the river—or lake—at many places for good overnight stops.

There is very little traffic. I once rode for two hours west of Springfield without seeing another vehicle on the road. However, I felt comforted by occasional farms with tractors working in the fields, and I always felt that help would be freely given if needed. Although I carried four bottles of drinks in areas like this, it was often interesting and rewarding to stop and ask for water.

One rainy morning in Lake Andes I was hoping to find a restaurant for breakfast. The small town looked mostly closed up, but a person on the street directed me to the Wolf's Den. It looked more like a nightclub—built of cinder blocks covered with graffiti, no windows, and one solid door. But the dozen pickup trucks parked outside were a good sign. It was dark inside; but as my eyes adjusted, I saw several men at one long table and a few other people at nearby tables. As I walked up to the counter in my purple tights and bright yellow rain jacket, all conversation stopped. However, after the initial shock, they started asking me about my trip, and they were very friendly and helpful. As the men's table broke up, one of them came over, introduced himself, and we talked for another half hour about my trip and the area.

Farther north near Onida, SD, I first noticed something I would see over and over again—abandoned farmhouses with brand new farm equipment parked nearby. These are farms that are still very productive, but are no longer supporting a family. We've all heard and read about this; family farms are being consolidated. You can look at this negatively or positively, but it seems inevitable.

One day in South Dakota I loaded my bike aboard a bus, because I needed to make serious time to get home for the 4th of July. There were only seven people on the bus, and I sat in the front row with my state highway map on my lap. One of several signs in the front of the bus said, "Talking with the driver while underway is strictly forbidden." Less than a minute after pulling out of the gas station bus stop the driver started chatting.

I figured it was his problem, not mine, and we had a fascinating talk for a couple of hours. He was one of six children raised on a family farm of one "section" of one square mile, the basic unit of land in the settlement of the midwest. Today one of his brothers farms this land, but only part time with several other sections. His brother's primary job is manager of a fertilizer store. Even though he owns and leases several sections, he contracts out with other specialists to do the plowing, seeding, fertilizing, harvesting, etc. The equipment today is so expensive and efficient that a farmer needs a huge amount of land to justify it.

I wondered if the driver was sad about these developments, but he volunteered that most people are better off today. He recognizes the reality that there's no way a family could survive farming a single section, and he feels he's better off driving a bus. He went on to list all the things his brothers and sisters are doing today—teacher, lawyer, nurse, etc. It struck me that this is probably a healthy view of reality.

Modern farm equipment and abandoned home.
Although this farm is still "productive," it no longer supports a family.

Springfield, SD

Population: 900

Springfield has several restaurants, a small food market, and a motel in the downtown area. A mile east of town, on Lewis and Clark Lake, is a small state campground with a couple of basic cabins. Reservations are definitely needed for the cabins during fishing season (i.e. most of the year!), but are not accepted for camping. A new bypass allows you to skip this town, but most cyclists will welcome the break for at least a quick stop and diversion from the long lonely roads.

mile 694

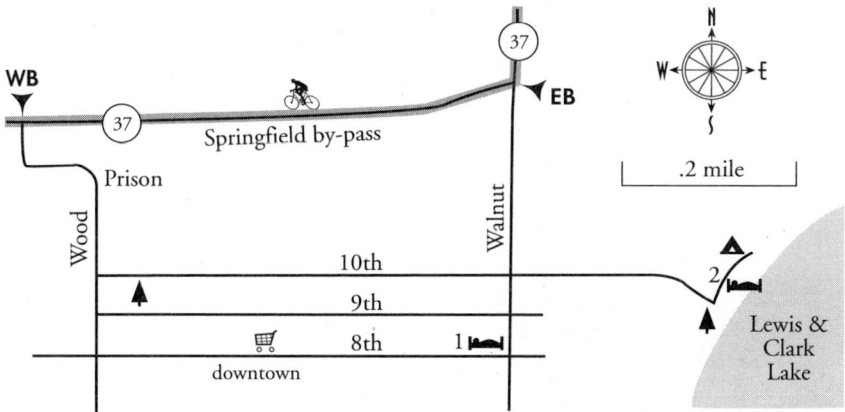

Springfield, SD — Zip: 57062

1) Wagon Wheel Inn ($), 811 Walnut, 605-369-2431

2) Lewis and Clark Lake ($), east on 10th, bare cabins, 800-710-2267

▲   Lewis and Clark Lake, east on 10th, restrooms with showers, 605-668-2985

Pickstown, SD

Population: 100

Although the population is listed at only 100, Pickstown is well situated for an overnight stop on our route. The town's defining feature is the Fort Randall Dam, and there is an interesting small visitor center on the near (eastern) side of the dam, as well as several recreation areas for boating, picnicking, and camping.

Food shopping is a problem, since the last real supermarket is in Yankton, and the last small market is in Springfield. However, I was able to buy a frozen hamburger at the café and convenience store in town to go with rice I was carrying. There are also a couple of small motels with a restaurant in town. Reservations would be a good idea during fishing season. Three miles east, up a long hill on Route 46, is the Fort Randall Casino. This has a restaurant and hotel rooms to go along with the casino and evening entertainment. Although I have mixed feelings about the efficacy of Indian gambling casinos, I learned from a teacher at the nearby Marty Indian School that the Yankton Sioux, who own and operate this casino, are using a lot of their profits to educate their young people.

Camping on Lake Francis Case in Pickstown, SD

An oasis visible for miles: Marty Indian School, Marty, SD

Martin Marty, Apostle of the Sioux Indians, First Abbot of the Benedictines, Vicar Apostolic of Dakota Territory, First Bishop of Sioux Falls. Marty, SD

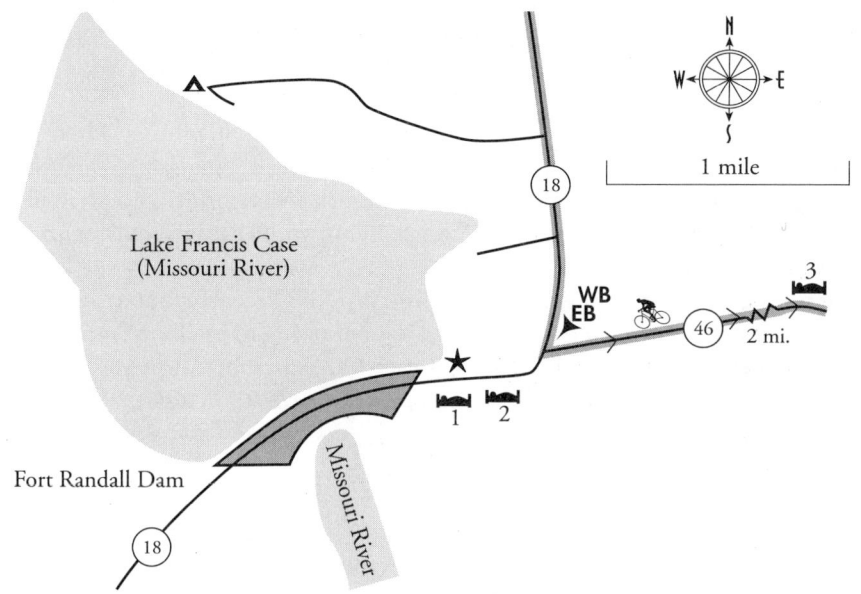

Pickstown, SD — Zip: 57367

★ **Visitor Information Center:** The Corps of Engineers maintains a Visitor Center near the east end of the dam. It displays information about the dam, the river, and the history of the area.

🛏 1) Dakota Inn ($$), 605-487-7404

2) Fort Randall Inn ($$), 605-487-7801

3) Fort Randall Casino Hotel ($$), 605-487-7891

▲ **North Point Recreation Area:** 1 mi. north of Pickstown (intersection of Routes 46 and 18), then 2 mi. west on paved access road. Look for the sign to North Point Recreation Area. Do NOT take the first road at 0.6 mi. to North Point Beach Area. On lake, rough ground, good shade, picnic tables, good restroom with shower, 605-487-7046

Lake Andes, SD

Population: 850

Lake Andes has two "sportsman's" motels that cater primarily to hunters and fishermen, so reservations are a good idea. There is also a restaurant, bar, convenience store, and small food market in this small town.

Zip: 57356

🛏 1) Circle H Motel ($), 605-487-7652

2) River Hills Motel ($), 605-487-7680

Platte, SD

Population: 1,300

If you don't want to ride the whole distance to Chamberlain in one day, Platte provides a choice of motels and a B&B, as well as several small restaurants. The nearest camping is Snake Creek, 14 miles west of town on the Missouri River and 5 miles off our route. Besides being a regional farm center town, Platte is popular with hunters and fishermen.

It was just upriver from Platte where the Corps of Discovery found George Shannon, one of their hunters, after sixteen days of trying to catch up with the group—not realizing he was ahead of the boats. On September 11 he was *"nearly Starved to Death, he had been 12 days without any thing to eate but Grapes & one Rabit, which he Killed by shooting a piece of hard Stick in place of a ball."*

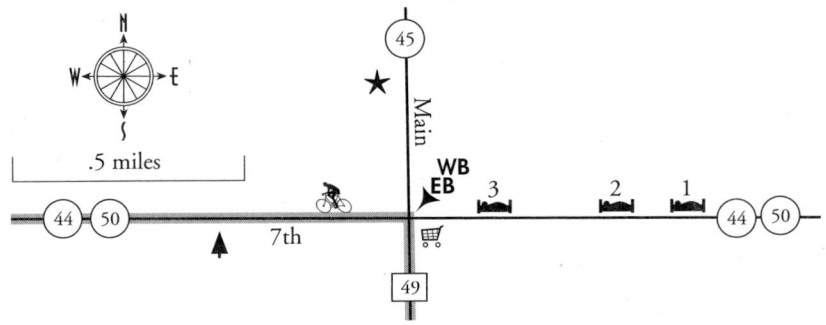

Platte, SD — Zip: 57396

★   **Platte Chamber of Commerce:** 500 S Main, 800-510-3272

1) Dakota Country Inn ($$), 800-336-2607

2) Grandma's House B&B ($$), 605-337-3589

3) King's Inn ($), 800-337-7756

▲   Snake Creek Campground: on Missouri River 14 mi. west of Platte (5 mi. off route). 605-337-3484

Chamberlain, SD

Population: 2,500

Chamberlain is located where I-90 and the railroad cross the Missouri River. Because of its strategic location and distance from other towns, it's almost impossible not to stop here for the night. There are several motels and restaurants located within walking distance in the downtown area. There is also good camping right on the river just a few blocks north of downtown. 3.5 miles north of town (and up a big hill) is Riverview Ridge B&B with long views over the Missouri River.

Besides being a significant crossroads town on I-90 and the river, Chamberlain is a center for boating and fishing enthusiasts. Just north of town is St. Joseph's Indian School, including an interesting chapel with a tapestry of "the Indian Christ" behind the altar, and the Akta Lakota Museum with displays of Native American life. It's well worth at least a quick visit here.

mile 829

Missouri River at Chamberlain, SD

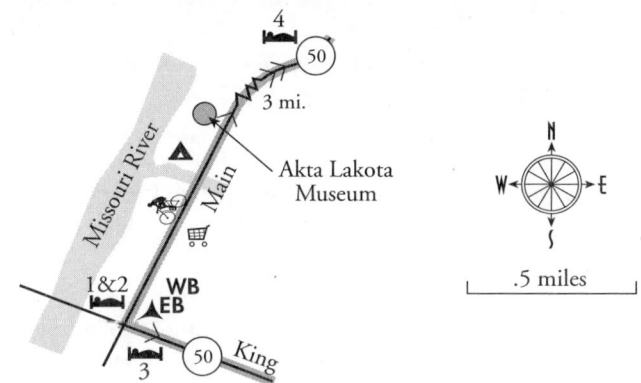

Chamberlain, SD — Zip: 57325

★ **Chamber of Commerce:** 115 W Lawler, 605-734-6541
www.chamberlainsd.org

🛏 1) Alewel's Lake Shore Motel ($), 115 N River, 605-734-5566

2) Best Western Lee's Motor Inn ($$), 220 W King, 605-734-5575

3) Bel Aire Motel ($), 312 E King, 605-734-5595

4) Riverview Ridge B&B ($$), 3.5 mi. north on Route 50, 605-734-6084

▲ American Creek Campground: grassy shaded level tent area with tables right on river; covered pavilion with tables; good restrooms with shower; convenient to downtown, food shopping, and restaurants. 605-734-6772

Fort Thompson, SD

Population: 1,100

Fort Thompson is near Big Bend Dam, the third of six major dams on the river. Just below the dam is the historic site of Fort Randall with the ruins of the chapel and a walking tour of the old sites.

Today Fort Thompson is the headquarters of the Crow Creek Reservation. If you don't want to pedal the whole 80 miles between Chamberlain and Pierre, there is a new casino, with a hotel and restaurant to go along with opportunities to gamble.

Just northwest of here is the Big Bend of the Missouri River. In the days of steamboats, passengers would often get off the boat and walk 1.5 miles across the sandbar while the boat travelled more than 30 miles around the huge oxbow in the river. Unfortunately the road is far from the river here, and it's not possible to see the oxbow.

Zip: 57339

▟ Lode Star Motel ($$), 888-268-1360

Pierre, SD

Population: 13,000

Pierre (pronounced Peer) is the smallest state capital in the United States and the only one without an interstate highway. It was founded by Pierre Chouteau, Jr., nephew of the fur trader who knew Lewis and Clark personally and had already established a string of trading posts along the Missouri.

The people of Pierre are friendly and proud of their down-to-earth small city. The wide variety of services in a relatively small geographical downtown area makes it an excellent stopping point for bicycle tourers. Most of the services, including motels, restaurants, bike shop, and food shopping, are located along the flat stretch near the river. There is also a large mall about two miles up a big hill on Harrison St. A bike trail runs along the river in town and extends four miles east to Farm Island Recreation Area.

The State Capitol has been beautifully restored, and it is quick and easy to take a self-guided tour through the building. The governor's secretary was very friendly when I accidentally wandered into his office in my cycling clothes. The Cultural Heritage Center a half mile up the hill tells the story of South Dakota from the Lakota culture to the pioneering families and the railroads.

Just north of Pierre is Oahe Dam, the fourth in the series of six major dams. Dedicated in 1962 by President Kennedy, this dam creates the huge Lake Oahe, running for 200 miles, almost as far as Bismarck, ND. There is a small visitor center on the east side of the dam with displays and restrooms.

Lewis and Clark first arrived in Pierre on September 24, 1804, passing Good Humored Island—now La Framboise, a public park which can be reached by a causeway. At the mouth of the Teton River (now called the Bad River) they held their famous meeting with the Teton Sioux, the first time they were seriously threatened by Indians. They had been warned about this tribe, who had refused river passage to many earlier traders, and who, in fact, influenced later pioneers to avoid this area and follow the Platte River through Nebraska.

At the height of this confrontation, with the Indians refusing to let go of Clark's boat near shore, Clark drew his sword. Clark's men had their guns primed and aimed, Lewis and the men on the keelboat had guns ready, and many Indians at point blank range on the shore reached for arrows for their already strung bows.

It was a tense moment, and it could have been the end of the expedition. Although the guns would have done serious damage, the Corps of Discovery was overwhelmingly outnumbered. Fortunately, both parties realized that discretion was the better part of valor, regained their composure, and defused the situation with talk. After the confrontation, the Corps of Discovery spent an uncomfortable night anchored off an island they named Bad Humored Island.

State Capitol, Pierre, SD

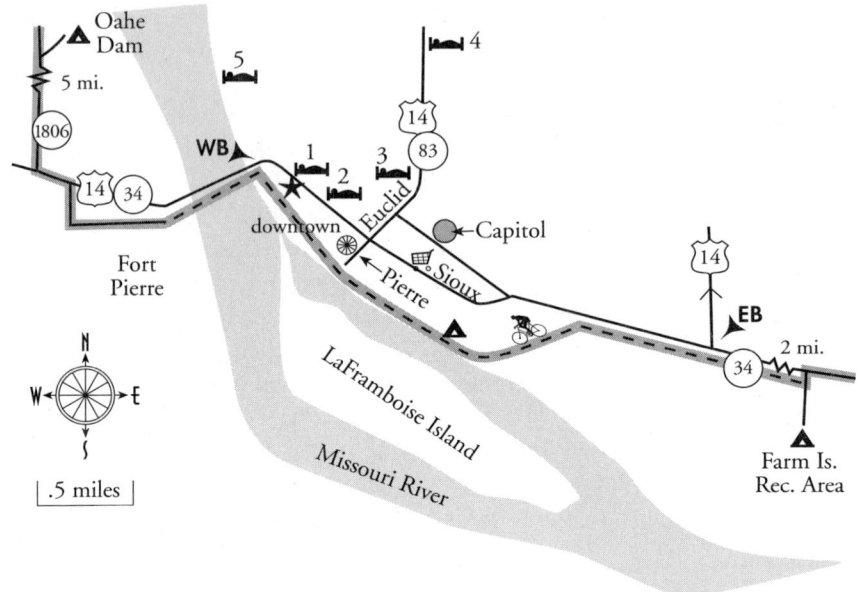

Pierre, SD — Zip: 57501

★   **Pierre Chamber of Commerce:** 800 W Dakota, 800-962-2034, www.pierre.org

🛏 1) Day's Inn ($$), 520 W Sioux, 800-329-7466

   2) Comfort Inn ($$), 410 W Sioux, 605-224-0377

   3) Terrace Motel ($), 231 N Euclid, 605-224-7797

   4) Budget Host Motel ($), 640 N Euclid, 605-224-5896

   5) River Place Inn B&B ($$), 109 River Place, 605-224-8589

▲ 1) Griffin Park: on river downtown, free, grass, shade, satisfactory restrooms, no showers

   2) Farm Island Recreation Area: 4 mi. east on Route 34 on river; big, grass, shade, no privacy, showers, 800-710-2267

   3) Oahe Dam: 6 mi. north on Route 1806 just below Oahe Dam, grass, shade, showers, 605-223-9805

✺   Pedal & Paddle, 411 S Pierre, 605-224-8955

Special Event: Walleye fishing tournament, mid-June

Onida, SD

Population: 760

Onida is the county seat of Sully County. There is a convenience store on our route at the intersection of Route 83 and Onida Road. The center of town is a mile east, with an attractive courthouse, a motel, a couple of cafés, and a small food market.

Zip: 57564

Wheatland Inn, 200 S Main, 605-258-2341

mile 956

Sully County Courthouse, Onida, SD

Gettysburg, SD

Population: 1,500

Although Gettysburg is five miles off the main route, it is a flat five miles; and this small town offers a strategic and pleasant stopping point. There is good free camping at the town park just a few blocks south of town. There are also motels, several restaurants, and a food market.

The Dakota Sunset Museum offers a wonderful glimpse into the history of a small town in South Dakota. Among the many displays are Charles Person's collection of 3,000 ball point pens, the dentist chair used by Dr. Budde, and eighteen trophy animals shot by Coe Frankhauser and stuffed for display.

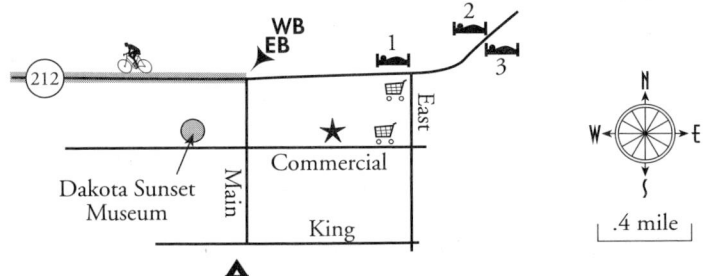

Gettysburg, SD — Zip: 57442

★   **Gettysburg Development Corp:** 109 E Commercial, 605-765-2731

🛏 1) Trail Motel ($), 211 E Garfield, 605-765-2482

2) Super 8 Motel ($$),719 E Hwy. 212, 605-765-2373

3) Sage Motel ($$), 804 E Hwy. 212, 605-765-2471

▲   The town park offers good grass and shade, a covered picnic pavilion, and a satisfactory restroom with a shower. The park also has a lighted baseball field that is surprisingly active with well organized games for a town this size. Next door is the town pool.

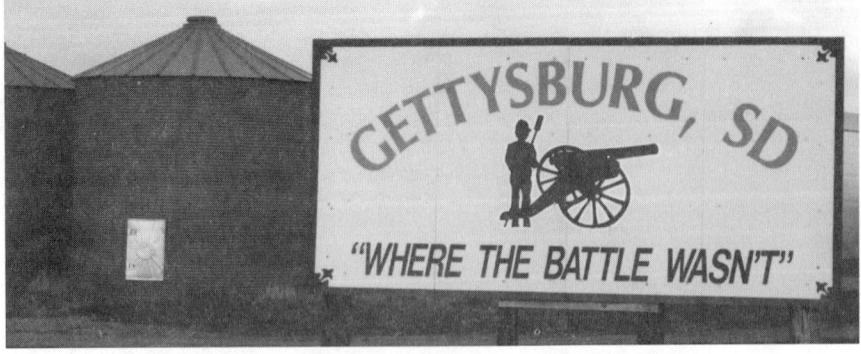

Selby, SD

Population: 700

Selby is the county seat for Walworth County and a very pleasant working town. There are two motels directly on Route 12 and a food market and older family hotel with a restaurant and bar on Main St., a half mile east of the highway. I stayed there one afternoon and night to avoid a tornado, and the owners just happened to be celebrating their twentieth year with the hotel. The entire town was invited for a free dinner that evening, and I received a huge dose of friendly hospitality from many people.

Zip: 57472

1) Berens Hotel ($), Main St., 605-649-7621

2) Super 8 Motel ($$), Hwy. 12, 605-649-7979

3) Hilltop Motel ($), Hwy. 12, 605-649-7622

▲   Hilltop Motel, Hwy. 12, tenting in yard behind motel, 605-649-7622

Berens Hotel, Café, and Lounge, Selby, SD

mile 1023

Mobridge, SD

Population: 3,800

A succession of Native Americans has occupied this area for centuries. First mound dwellers, then woodland Indians, then Arikaras and Mandans. On October 8, 1804, Lewis and Clark found three Arikara villages at the mouth of the Grand River in Mobridge. Here they encountered Joseph Gravelines, a trader who had lived with the Arikara tribe for thirteen years, who helped them translate smoothly. This was also their first encounter with bullboats—bowl shaped boats made from buffalo hide stretched over a frame of willow branches. The men were amazed at how well the Indians—often women—could navigate in these boats, even in very rough water.

White settlers did not move into this area until the late 1800s. In 1885 General Olson realized this would be a good location for the Milwaukee Railroad to cross the Missouri River. He formed the Grand Crossing and Improvement Company to convince the railroad to cross the river here and to market the land to new settlers. The town was named when an early railroad telegrapher signed his transmissions with the abbreviation "MO Bridge."

Lake Oahe was formed by Oahe Dam in 1962, and recreation has since become a key industry in the area. Reading the sports section of the *Mobridge Tribune* one morning at breakfast, I found stories on fishing, hunting, rodeo, and baseball—in that order. That says something about the priorities here.

Today Mobridge is a good overnight stop for bicycle tourers. It is quite spread out, but mostly flat. There is a wide variety of motels, camping, restaurants, food shopping, and other services.

Across the river from Mobridge, about four miles south of Highway 12, are two noteworthy monuments. One is a monument to Sacagawea, who died in 1812 a short distance north of here. The other marks the final grave of Sitting Bull, the great Sioux chief—shot and killed by Indian police who claimed he was resisting arrest. Although it's a beautiful spot high above the river, you'll have to decide for yourself whether it's worth the long hilly detour.

Two other special attractions merit mention. The Klein Museum has many displays of both Indian and pioneer cultures. The City Auditorium, next to the Chamber of Commerce, displays ten murals of Sioux culture by the Indian artist, Oscar Howe.

*Sitting Bull Memorial,
Mobridge, SD*

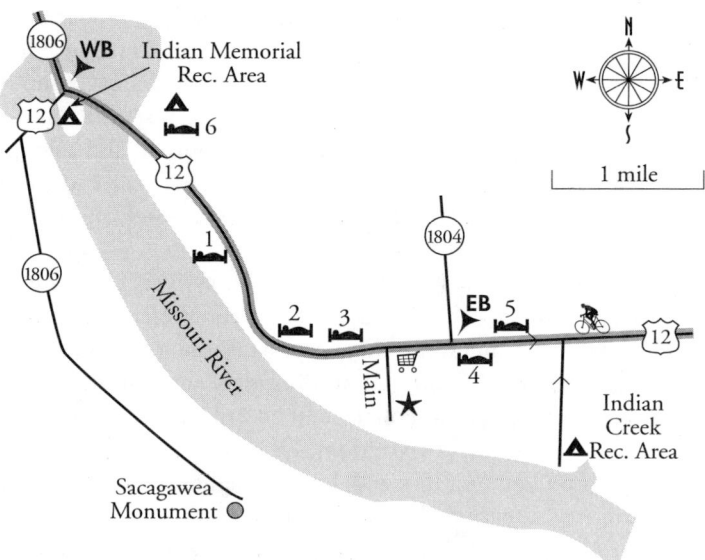

Mobridge, SD — Zip: 57601

★ **Chamber of Commerce:** 212 Main, 605-845-2387, www.mobridge.org

1) Super 8 Motel ($$), Hwy. 12, 605-845-7215

2) Wrangler Motor Inn ($$), Hwy. 12, 800-341-8000

3) MoRest Motel ($), 706 Hwy. 12, 605-845-3668

4) Mark VI Motel ($), 317 Hwy. 12, 605-845-3681

5) East Side Motel ($), 510 E 7th Ave., 605-845-7867

6) Kountry Cabins ($), 800-648-2267

▲ 1) Indian Creek Recreation Area, full service Corp of Engineers campground, 140 feet of climbing to/from downtown, 605-845-2252

2) Kountry Kamping, full services, 800-648-2267

3) Indian Memorial Recreation Area, full service Corp of Engineers campground, 605-845-2252

MOBRIDGE TO BISMARCK

There are two possible routes between Mobridge and Bismarck. I recommend Route 1806 on the west side of the Missouri River for three reasons: First, it is 11 miles shorter (112 vs. 123 miles). It can actually be 25 miles shorter (98 vs. 123) if you camp at Indian Memorial in Mobridge and Fort Abraham Lincoln below Mandan. Second, it is less hilly (3,300 feet of climbing vs. 5,100 feet). Third, there is slightly less traffic (very low on both sides) and slightly more views of the river.

If you choose Route 1806, you basically have two choices: One is to ride the whole 112 miles (or 98 miles from Indian Memorial to Fort Abraham Lincoln) in a single day. The other choice is to stay overnight at Prairie Knights Casino in the middle (61 miles from Mobridge and 51 miles from Bismarck). The casino has hotel rooms, an inexpensive buffet (all you can eat!) restaurant, and a gourmet restaurant, as well as gambling. There is no campground between Indian Memorial and Fort Abraham Lincoln, only a couple of convenience stores, and most of the land is part of the Standing Rock Nation.

The alternative is Route 1804 on the east side of the river. There are two related reasons why you might choose this route. First, if you prefer shorter days, it allows you to break the 123 miles into three days by camping or staying in a motel or fishing camp near Pollock (36 miles from Mobridge) and camping at Beaver Creek Campground (33 miles from Pollock and 54 miles from Bismarck). Second, if you prefer camping, it provides two options. Of course, this side could also be ridden in two days of 69 and 54 miles with a single night camping at Beaver Creek.

If you take this east side route, be aware that there are only small cafés and a small grocery store in Pollock; so you might want to stock up on food in Mobridge. This alternate route is not described in Chapter 5, but it's easy to follow Route 1804 all the way between Mobridge and Bismarck.

ALTERNATE ROUTE 1804

Pollock, SD

Population: 350

This whole town was moved by the Corps of Engineers in 1962, just before the Oahe Dam near Pierre raised the water level to create Lake Oahe. Since Pollock is remote and popular with fishermen, reservations are a good idea.

Zip: 57648

🛏 Lakeview Motel ($) (no view of lake!), Box 208, Pollock, SD, 800-521-6951

🛏 & ▲ Jensen's Resort ($), Box 14, Pollock, SD 57648, 605-889-2448, near lake, hard dirt, no trees, showers, restaurant

▲ 1) Lake Pocasse, half mile north of Pollock, primitive campground on lake, pit toilets, no water

   2) Beaver Creek Recreation Area, 33 mi. north of Pollock and 54 mi. south of Bismarck, Corps of Engineers campground, on lake, some grass and trees

Bismarck, ND, Mandan, ND

Populations: 55,000 — 15,000

Bismarck and Mandan are unbalanced twin cities that face each other across the Missouri River. It is very possible to find everything you need in smaller Mandan and bypass the larger Bismarck altogether. There are motels, restaurants, camping, and excellent food shopping all within a square mile that makes up the heart of Mandan. The Five Nations Depot in the old railroad station on Main Street is

worth a visit. Craft and artwork of over 200 North Dakota Native Americans are on display for purchase here. There is good camping right on the river five miles south at Fort Abraham Lincoln. There is also camping available behind the Colonial Motel for those who value convenience to town more than pleasant scenery.

For those who want

This brick silo and farmhouse were built to last. Mandan, ND

more variety of motels and B&Bs, more choice of restaurants, shopping malls, and generally more of everything, Bismarck offers all this spread over a wider area with more traffic. Main Avenue is the older part of town—offering more established restaurants and older and less expensive motels. The Bismarck Expressway, near the southern edge of town, offers newer motels, big malls, and franchise restaurants. Four flat miles south of here, on a bike path and road with very light traffic, is General Sibley County Campground near the river.

There are three bridges connecting these cities across the Missouri River. Cyclists can use either the older Memorial Bridge (middle) on a narrow bikeway or the newer Expressway Bridge (south) on a wider bikeway. Both connect to a good 17-mile system of bike trails that run along the river on the east side with several spurs heading east towards the business areas of Bismarck. There are maps posted on periodic signs along the trail. Bicyclists cannot cross the I-94 Bridge (north).

Fort Abraham Lincoln State Park (five miles south of Mandan) is a gem of a state park, and there is no admission charge for bicyclists! Note the instructions on the detailed directions in Chapter 5, because bicyclists can use the "old road" on the north side and avoid a hill and some light traffic. There is a good visitor center that offers displays and interpretations of the three different areas in the park—earth homes in On-A-Slant Village where the Mandan Indians lived before Lewis and Clark arrived, an infantry post high on a hill overlooking the river and Bismarck, and the lower fort grounds which housed General Custer and the 7th Cavalry just before they rode off to the fatal Battle of the Little Bighorn.

It was near this site that Private Cruzatte first encountered a grizzly bear—which they called a "white bear."

Bismarck exists because of the Northern Pacific Railroad. When Jay Cooke was trying to build this line, he had plenty of land from the government, but no money. His strategy was to attract German farmers from middle America, so he named it Bismarck, after the famous 19th century German emperor. Although the railroad was delayed financially for another ten years, enough Germans came to give the area a real German flavor. Notice the number of Lutheran churches. Today Bismarck is primarily a government town—an urban island in the middle of rural wheat country.

The 19-story State Capitol of North Dakota (sometimes called "the skyscraper on the prairie") offers free tours hourly. Although somewhat bland and not looking like a typical state capitol should look on the outside, it is much more attractive and interesting on the inside. The tours finish on the top floor for a great view of the surrounding area. Nearby is the North Dakota Heritage Museum and the historic Governor's Mansion. The Visitor Center offers many other attractions in these two small cities.

Mandan earthlodge at Fort Abraham Lincoln State Park, Mandan, ND

Cruising the Missouri River, Bismarck, ND

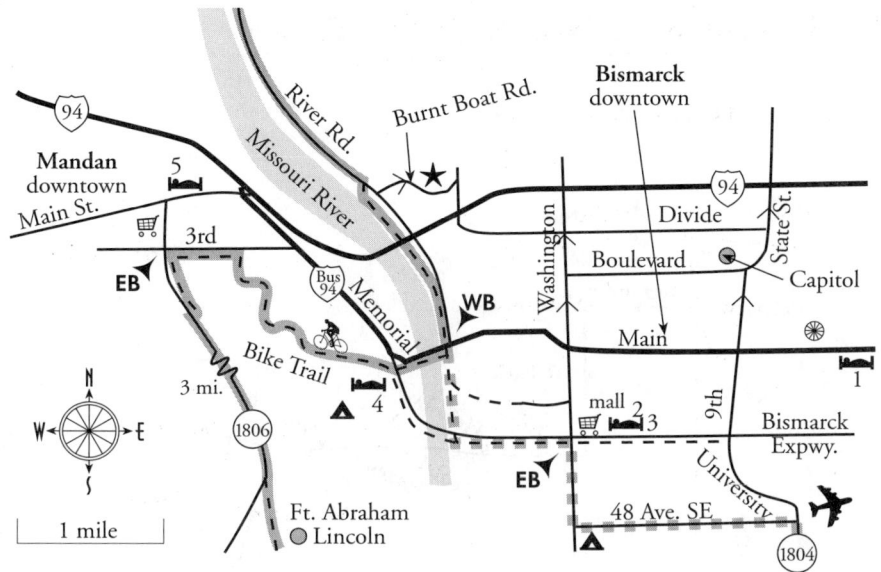

mile 1146

Bismarck, ND — Zip: 58501, **Mandan, ND** — Zip: 58554

★ **Bismarck-Mandan Convention and Visitors Bureau:**
1600 Burnt Boat Rd., Bismarck, ND 58501, 800-767-3555,
www.bismarck-mandancvb.org, visitnd@bismarck-mandancvb.org

Bismarck

1) Bismarck Motor Hotel ($), 2301 E Main, 701-223-2474

2) Expressway Inn ($$), 200 Bismarck Expwy., 800-456-6388

3) Fairfield Inn South ($$), 135 Ivy Ave., 800-228-2800

▲ **Bismarck**

1) General Sibley County Campground, 4 mi. south of Bismarck Expwy. on
Washington, 701-222-1844; good grass, shade, satisfactory restrooms with
showers

⊕ **Bismarck:** Dakota Cyclery, 1606 E Main, 701-222-1218

Mandan

4) Colonial Motel ($), 4631 Memorial Hwy., 701-663-9824

5) North Country Inn Motel ($$), 1200 E Main, 800-464-0158

▲ **Mandan**

2) Colonial Motel, 4631 Memorial Hwy., 701-663-9824

3) Fort Abraham Lincoln State Park, 5 mi. south of Mandan on Route 1806,
701-663-9571

F. ACROSS THE NORTH DAKOTA PRAIRIE

BISMARCK, ND TO FAIRVIEW, MT

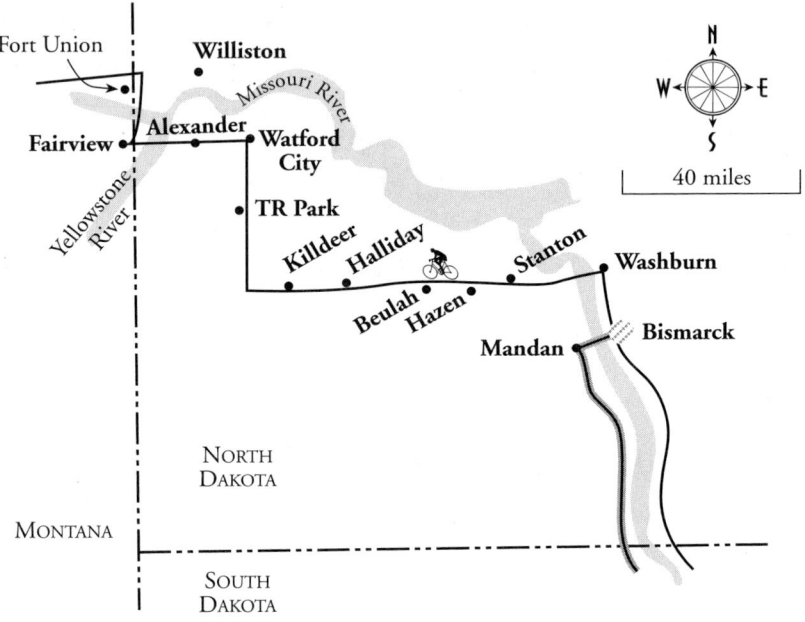

From Bismarck the Lewis & Clark Trail runs 40 miles north along the Missouri River to Washburn. Gentle hills provide beautiful vistas of the river and prairie. Although Bismarck, with its airport and broad array of services, is the logical transition point in today's journey, Washburn was a much truer geographical and historical transition point for Lewis and Clark. Washburn is near the actual site of the Mandan villages—the farthest point reached by white men in 1804 and the place where the Corps of Discovery stopped and hunkered down for the winter of 1804–1805. It is also the place where the Missouri River turns west, and our bicycle route leaves the river to head west across the North Dakota prairie.

On the eve of their departure from Fort Mandan, Lewis was in one of his thoughtful moods as he pondered the journey ahead. *"Our vessels consisted of six small canoes, and two large perogues. This little fleet altho' not quite so rispectable as those of Columbus or Capt. Cook were still viewed by us with as much pleasure as those deservedly famed adventureres ever beheld theirs; and I dare say with quite as much anxiety for their safety and preservation. we were now about to penetrate a country at least two thousand miles in width, on which the foot of civillized man had never trodden; the good or evil it had in store for us was for experiment yet to determine, and these little vessells contained every article by which we were to expect to subsist or defend ourselves.*

however as this the state of mind in which we are, generally gives the colouring to events, when the immagination is suffered to wander into futurity, the picture which now presented itself to me was a most pleasing one. entertaining as I do, the most confident hope of succeading in a voyage which had formed a darling project of mine for the last ten years, I could but esteem this moment of my departure as among the most happy of my life. The party are in excellent health and sperits, zealously attatched to the enterprise, and anxious to proceed; not a whisper of murmur or discontent to be heard among them, but all act in unison, and with the most perfect harmony."

Early settlers came to this region because farmland was cheap, and today agriculture is still the leading industry in the state. Although the land is drier and colder as you head farther north and west, it's still good for both grazing animals and growing wheat. Only 2% of the land is covered with forest.

The dams on the Missouri River have provided additional power and water for irrigation to make this such a rich agricultural area. North Dakota ranks first in the country in production of barley, durum spring wheat, dry edible beans, oats, and sunflowers,

Friendly hay bales along the North Dakota highway

and it ranks among the top four states in production of all wheat, navy beans, potatoes, sugar beets, and honey.

During the 20th century modern pioneers have come for energy, and this area of western North Dakota has produced a lot of soft coal and oil shale. Even though soft coal produces significant pollution and strip mining has been unpopular with environmentalists, mining has flourished here in an area of low population density and low per capita income. Deep wells also tap vast resources of oil and natural gas.

Much of North Dakota's character has been formed by its challenging climate and relative isolation. Far from the modulating forces of either ocean, temperatures vary from extremely hot in the summer to extremely cold in the winter. Long distances from population centers has made it a poor location for manufacturing. All this has produced hardy and hard-working people. Although per capita income is low, the divorce rate is also very low, and the percentage of families with two parents is very high.

Heading west across North Dakota on Route 200, rolling hills become more pronounced as you approach the Killdeer Mountains. It can be a long way between services here, but people are correspondingly more friendly and helpful; and traffic is light. Heading north on Route 85 you'll ride through more wide open and hilly prairie, which is stunningly interrupted by the Little Missouri River and the beautiful open gashes it has created known as the Badlands. What was "bad" for early settlers who wanted to graze animals and build farms is "good" for modern tourists who want fantastic scenery. The North Unit of Theodore Roosevelt National Park offers lots of this scenery for those able to camp and carry food supplies to this remote area. (See page 119 on Killdeer for more information about the park.)

After climbing out of the valley created by the Little Missouri, the last 60 miles from the park to the Montana border cross more rolling prairie. Just before the state border you cross the Yellowstone River, which was the return route for Clark.

Washburn, ND

Population: 1,500

In 1804 this area was home to Mandan and Hidatsa Indians living in several compact and crowded villages of round earth homes. Sometimes described today as "the Mall of the West," the Mandan Villages made up a large regional trading center, where each summer tribes from the west brought beaver pelts to barter with French, English, and American traders from both Canada and St. Louis. In 1804 this was the farthest west that white men had ever travelled in the Louisiana Territory.

Although Lewis had originally planned to spend the winter at the Knife River Indian Villages with the Hidatsas, the captains felt that a site on the north side of

the river, opposite a Mandan village and about seven miles below the Knife River, provided a better location for timber and game. The original site has long since been washed away by the changing river.

Today Washburn is the county seat for McLean County. North of town is an electric generating plant, powered by coal from a large surface mine nearby. There is one motel on Highway 83 with a restaurant and grocery store nearby, a couple of restaurants a mile down the hill in the center of town, and a primitive campground down by the river. Because it is so close to Bismarck, Washburn is not a regional center and does not have the variety of services you might expect in a town with this population.

Keeping warm in a buffalo robe.
Lewis & Clark Interpretive Center,
Washburn, ND

mile 1186

The excellent Lewis and Clark Interpretive Center at the intersection of Highways 83 and 200A deserves a visit. Along with general displays and artwork that you might expect in such a center, there are several innovative displays to help the visitor better understand and appreciate the expedition of Lewis and Clark. One is a 36-foot dugout canoe made by several local people. The story of their difficulties in building this modern dugout provides many insights into the challenges the Corps of Discovery must have faced when they built six similar canoes in 22 days in the spring of 1805. You can also try on a buffalo robe to feel both how warm and how heavy and awkward it feels.

Fort Mandan, Washburn, ND

2.7 miles down the hill to the west is a reproduction of Fort Mandan—about ten miles downriver from the actual location where the Corps of Discovery spent their first winter. Although it's only a small stockade fort, it is impressive to stand there and ponder what it must have been like to build it in just 52 days and then spend a North Dakota winter inside it.

It was during this winter camp that Lewis and Clark met Toussaint Charbonneau, a French trader with two young Shoshoni wives, whom he had either purchased or won in a card game. Both these women had been captured near Three Forks, Montana, four years earlier by a Hidatsa hunting party. When Charbonneau offered to join Lewis and Clark for their trip west, a contract was eventually negotiated; but they only allowed him to take one wife. Although Charbonneau himself was of questionable value in many respects, the captains really wanted one of his wives to translate when they reached Shoshoni territory at the end of the Missouri River and would need to acquire horses to cross the Rocky Mountains.

Charbonneau chose the pregnant Sacagawea to accompany him, and she delivered her baby in February, two months before their departure. At the Interpretive Center you can try on a packboard loaded with the weight of a baby to get a better feel for Sacagawea's trip from here to Oregon and back.

Although some later books have exaggerated Sacagawea's role as a guide for the expedition, she often proved to be very helpful in daily life on the trip. She gathered roots to improve their diet, and she was probably a civilizing influence among the men of the expedition. One day she helped save both people and equipment when a canoe capsized and her husband panicked. When the Corps of Discovery finally started meeting Indians in Montana, Oregon, and Washington, she was an unintended symbol of the peaceful intentions of the expedition. War parties don't usually travel with a woman and young child. Her most incredible contribution to the success of the expedition—perhaps making the critical difference between the success and failure of the entire project—occurred several months later at Camp Fortunate. If you can't wait to find out what happened, look up Clark Canyon Reservoir and Dam (page 157).

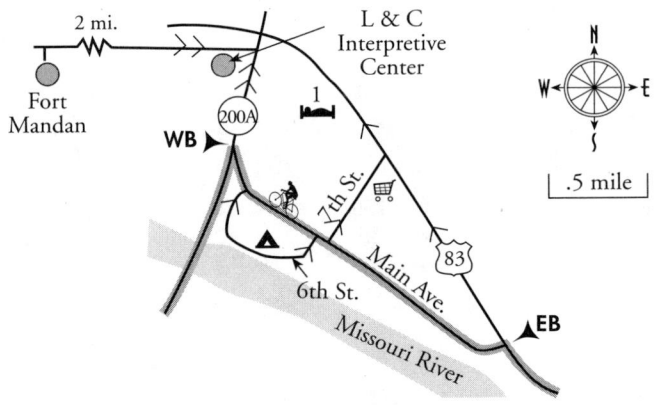

Washburn, ND — Zip: 58577

★ **Lewis and Clark Interpretive Center:** Box 607, 877-462-8535, www.fortmandan.com, info@fortmandan.org

🛏 ScottWood Motel ($), Route 83, 701-462-8191

▲ Riverside Park: primitive, on river, grass, shade, bathroom

mile 1206

Stanton, ND

Population: 500

This small town is located two miles north of our route on Route 31. A mile farther north is Knife River Indian Villages National Historic Site with a good visitor center and an excellent guided tour of a furnished Hidatsa earth home. If you're interested in learning about plains Indian life in the early 1800s, this detour is definitely worthwhile. If you're not sure, write or call for their excellent brochure. (PO Box 9, Stanton, ND, 58571, 701-745-3309, www.nps.gov/knri)

Back in downtown Stanton are several small restaurants, bars, and a grocery store. A few blocks east is Sakakawea Town Park (701-745-3202) on the Knife River. Although there is water and covered picnic tables, the poorly maintained restroom has neither roof nor shower.

Hazen, ND

Population: 2,800

Hazen is located on flat land very close to our route, making it a convenient possibility for an overnight stop. Two campgrounds, a motel, and a restaurant are all visible from the highway. About a half mile south is the downtown area with a variety of restaurants, food shopping, and other services.

Zip: 58545

★   **Hazen Chamber of Commerce:** Box 717, 701-748-6848

🛏   Roughrider Motor Inn ($), Hwy. 200, 701-748-2209

▲   1) John Moses Memorial Town Park, 701-748-6948, grass, shade, water, and poorly maintained outhouses, no showers

2) Lewis and Clark Campground, Main St. at west end of town, new restrooms with showers

Strip mining is BIG in North Dakota.

Beulah, ND

Population: 3,400

Beulah calls itself the Energy Capital of the Midwest, because of the billions of tons of lignite coal in the area. The town is two miles down a big hill. Halfway down the Route 49 hill to town are several motels and restaurants. For more restaurant selection, food shopping, and camping, you will have to go all the way down the hill.

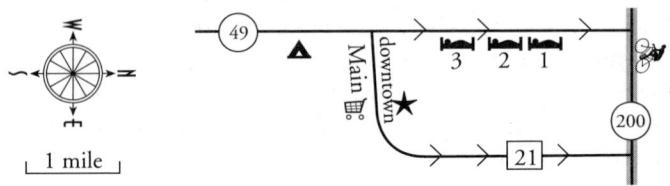

Beulah, ND — Zip: 58523

★   **Chamber of Commerce:** 120 Central Ave., 800-441-2649, www.tradecorridor.com/beulah, chamber@westriv.com

1) AmericInn ($$), Hwy. 49, 800-634-3444

2) Dakota Farms Inn ($$), Hwy. 49, 701-873-2242

3) Super 8 Motel ($), 1008 Hwy. 49, 701-873-2850

▲   Riverside Recreation Area, 0.7 mi. south of Main on Hwy. 49, 701-873-5852, pleasant grass, shade, showers

Zap, ND

Population: 300

Zap is one mile off our route with 100 feet of climbing. There is a bar, small grocery store, and town campground with water, pit toilets, and no showers.

Golden Valley, ND

Population: 250

Golden is one mile off our route with 100 feet of climbing. There are two bars and a small grocery store.

Halliday, ND

Population: 300

This small town is a mile north of the Trail down a 100-foot hill. Partway down the hill is a motel. Downtown are several small restaurants, bars, grocery store, and a town park.

Zip: 58636

🛏 Halliday Motel ($), 680 7th St., 701-938-4777

⛺ Town Park, grass, shade, poorly maintained outhouse, and water that may be locked. Camping is allowed, although you may have to hunt around to find someone to unlock the water.

Killdeer, ND

Population: 725

Since your next overnight stop from Killdeer is either camping at Theodore Roosevelt National Park in 38 miles, or motels and camping in Watford City in 52 miles, this is almost a required overnight stop. The town is two flat miles north of Route 200 on Route 22.

Downtown you will find a motel, several restaurants, and a supermarket. If you are planning to camp at Roosevelt National Park, do food shopping here before you leave. The next food shopping is in Watford City in 52 miles (14 miles beyond Roosevelt Park).

Killdeer Mountain Battlefield State Historic Site is ten miles north of Killdeer on Route 22. In 1864 2,000 Army troops under General Alfred Sully battled 6,000 Sioux Indians there.

Zip: 58640

🛏 Mountain View Motel ($), Route 22, 701-764-5843

⛺ Killdeer RV Park, 701-764-5295, Route 22 halfway into town, pleasant grass, no shade or privacy, clean restrooms with showers

mile 1252

Theodore Roosevelt National Park

As you descend into the Little Missouri River Canyon on Route 85, you will experience an excellent view of the North Dakota Badlands and the national park off to the west. If this looks appealing, there is much more of this gorgeous scenery on a fourteen-mile hilly park road to Oxbow Overlook—and another fourteen miles back. Be careful around the buffalo; they are faster and more agile than they look. The road climbs up and down some side canyons on the north side of the canyon for spectacular views. There is also a variety of hikes for those who would like to spend some time out of the saddle. If you're still in doubt about whether or how long to stay, you can talk with Rangers at the Visitor Center just inside the Entrance Station or contact them in advance.

The campground is five miles from the entrance. It is a pleasant and typical national park campground with separate sites among Cottonwood trees near the river. There are good clean restrooms, but no showers. There is also camping at the National Grasslands just north of the Little Missouri River. It's cheaper and the views are great, but there is only rough ground, water, pit toilets, and a rough 1.1-mile dirt road to get in there.

▲   Theodore Roosevelt National Park, Box 7, Medora, ND 58645,
        701-623-4466, www.nps.gov/thro

*Badlands in
Theodore Roosevelt
National Park, ND*

mile 1326

Little Missouri River in Theodore Roosevelt National Park, ND

Watford City, ND

Population: 1,800

This regional center with a relatively flat and compact downtown area makes a good overnight stop. It offers a pleasant municipal campground, three motels, several restaurants, food shopping, and a Pioneer Museum.

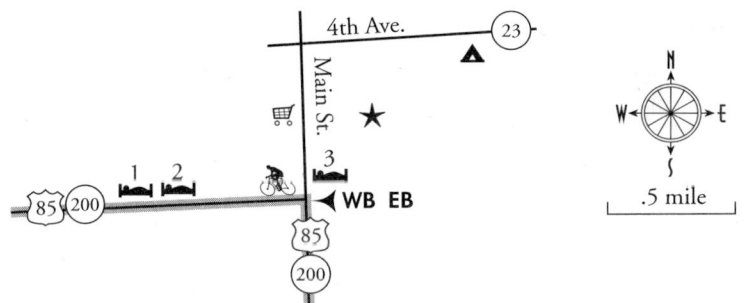

Watford City, ND — Zip: 58854

★ **Chamber of Commerce:** Box 458, 701-842-2526

🛏 1) Roosevelt Inn ($), Hwy. 85 W, 888-206-0400

   2) McKenzie Inn ($), Hwy. 85 W, 800-842-3989

   3) Four Eyes Motel ($), 122 S Main, 701-842-4126

▲   Tourist Park, 0.7 mi. east of town on Route 23, quiet, grass, shade, covered picnic tables, clean restrooms with showers

Alexander, ND

Population: 220

If you are willing to live with less variety of services, this small town offers a motel, a small restaurant next door, grocery store, and town park for camping. For some people, the real advantage of staying overnight in Alexander or Fairview is the way it splits up daily riding mileage. It also offers flexibility if you want to spend more or less time at Roosevelt National Park, Fort Union, and/or Fort Buford.

Zip: 58831

🛏 Ragged Butte Inn Motel and Café ($), 701-828-3164

⛺ Town Park, grass, shade, covered picnic tables, clean restrooms, no shower

Fairview, MT

Population: 900

This is another small town just one flat mile west of our route on Route 200, where it is possible to spend the night. There is a grocery store, several small restaurants, a basic motel, and a pleasant town park for camping with showers at the pool next door.

Zip: 59221

🛏 Korner Motel ($), 800-656-7637

⛺ Town Park, grass, shade, covered picnic tables, satisfactory restroom, showers next door at town pool

G. Eastern Montana Big Sky Country

Fairview, MT to Great Falls, MT

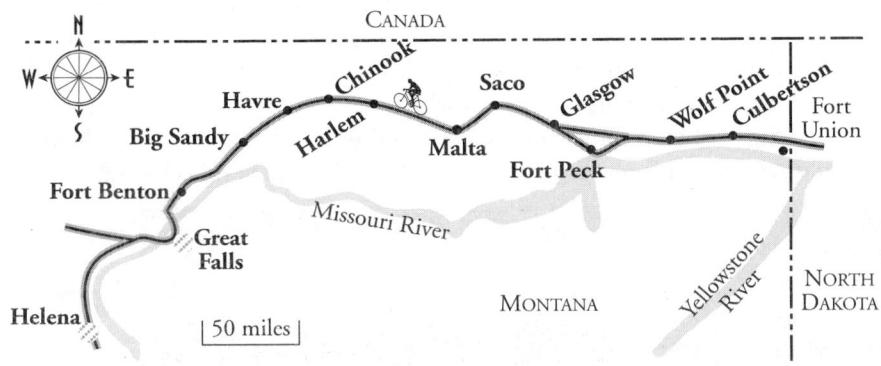

If you've ever wondered why Montana is called "Big Sky Country," a few days riding here will answer that question beyond any doubt. Especially in eastern Montana, there are gently rolling plains, few trees, little shade, and long vistas from horizon to horizon. This state is just plain big. It is 535 miles across, which is big enough, but our route will require from 800 to 1060 miles (depending on which route you choose over the Bitterroots). Lewis and Clark travelled more than one quarter of their journey in this state.

But don't let this bigness scare you. It's only 400 miles of gorgeous grand prairie to Great Falls, towns with good services are well spaced along the route, and traffic is light. It's lucky the traffic is light, because it's also fast. At least Montana now has a daytime speed limit of 70 mph instead of the previous "reasonable and prudent."

The directions for this section are simple: follow Route 2 west for 285 miles to Havre, and then take Route 87 southwest for 115 miles to Great Falls. Route 2 is also known as the Hi-Line, because it generally follows the route of the Great Northern Railroad—the northernmost railroad across the western states.

The directions are actually slightly more complicated. There are three opportunities to get off the main highway if you're tired of traffic. The first alternate (between Brockton and Poplar) is recommended and is built into the cue sheets in Chapter 5. The other two are not recommended—one because of added distance, and the other because of poor pavement—but both are noted in the cue sheets and described in the town descriptions of Wolf Point and Saco.

Although trappers, gold miners, and other adventurers prowled Montana in the 1800s, this part of the West was not really settled until after the Great Northern Railroad was built across Montana in 1877—seventy years after Lewis and Clark. Most early pioneers and settlers avoided the Missouri River route above Omaha because of the hostile Sioux Indians in the Dakota Territory. This made the Platte River route through Nebraska much more attractive, leading to the 1824 discovery of the relatively easy South Pass over the Continental Divide in Wyoming—which became the main route for the Oregon, California, and Mormon Trails.

The eastern two-thirds of Montana is rolling prairie similar to North Dakota. Geologically, both are part of the Missouri Plateau. As in neighboring North Dakota, agriculture is the primary industry in Montana, especially in the eastern part. This means primarily cattle grazing and wheat, because the land is dry.

Montana is also a big grain growing state, and you may see bulldozers towing wide gangs of farm implements across large dry fields. Everything here is big; they even use huge bulldozers instead of tractors.

Speaking of "big," dinosaurs once roamed this area. There are good exhibits in the Phillips County Museum, just east of Malta and at the Fort Peck Dam Visitor

*Along the
Milk River
in Montana*

Center. The Fort Peck Dam is the largest earth dam in the world, blocking the Missouri River to form Fort Peck Lake and creating 1,500 miles of shoreline.

Although the railroads first opened Montana to settlement in the 1880s, it was mining that really attracted people. First it was gold in Helena, but later it was the cheap electricity generated by Great Falls that made copper production much bigger and more sustainable. After 1915, oil and natural gas were discovered, and the state now produces and exports coal, oil, natural gas, and energy. As copper demand and prices have fallen in the late 20th century, the growth of energy production has helped Billings eclipse Great Falls as the largest city.

As a New Englander, I never really understood the large size and low population density of Montana until someone explained it to me like this: Take the six New England states plus most of New York and Pennsylvania and move all the people out except for those living in Hartford, Connecticut. Then tell the people of Hartford to spread out. That's Montana.

The stretch of river between Fort Peck and Fort Benton is called the Missouri Breaks, because the river cut into the land here to create a rugged and stunning landscape of limestone cliffs and side canyons. When the Great Northern Railroad was built across Montana, it was much easier to follow the Milk River than the Missouri River in this area. Road builders had the same thoughts. No roads follow the Missouri River from Fort Peck to Fort Benton, and only a few north-south roads cross the river.

It's unfortunate that you can't see the river for 250 miles until Fort Benton. The good news is that the river runs through beautiful wilderness that looks much as it did when Lewis and Clark first saw it, and you can have a similar experience on a half-day to multi-day river trip out of Fort Benton. You deserve this kind of break, as the name "Missouri Breaks" takes on a new meaning!

NORTH DAKOTA / MONTANA BORDER AREA

It's worth doing some planning about how much time you want to spend at the two historic forts near the confluence of the Yellowstone and Missouri Rivers at the border between North Dakota and Montana. You may then want to consider an overnight stop in one of the towns nearby in order to split up daily riding mileage better. See the map and descriptions below.

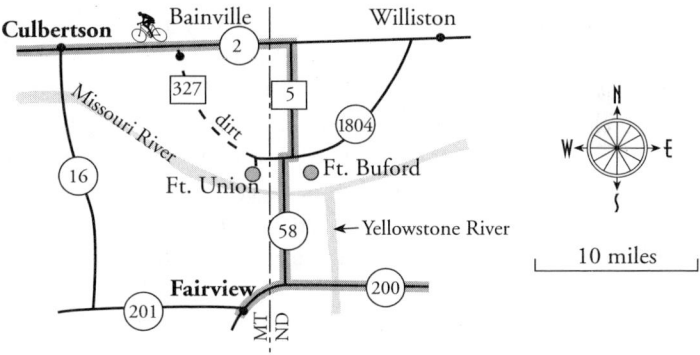

FORT UNION

Lewis and Clark were the first to recognize the strategic importance of both the relatively flat land and the strong riverbank where the Yellowstone River joins the Missouri. They recommended this site for a key government outpost. Although called a fort and built like a stockade, Fort Union was really a trading post constructed for John Jacob Astor's American Fur Company. It became a very successful commercial center, where Indians brought in buffalo and beaver skins to trade for manufactured goods from the east. As the railroads superceded river transportation, this fort became obsolete and was dismantled.

Fort Union, MT

The National Park Service has built a full scale reproduction of much of the original stockade trading post. It's an impressive structure with good exhibits and a knowledgeable and enthusiastic staff. Although the river has moved, you can still see where boats used to tie up at the levee near the main entrance.

The fort is two flat miles off our route, and admission is free. I recommend at least an hour to walk around, enjoy the setting, see the exhibits, and ponder what life was like here during the 1800s. People who are interested in American history, trade, and relations with the Indians may want to spend more time. For more information, contact Fort Union Trading Post National Historic Site, Williston, ND (701-572-9083). The Fort Union Rendevouz is held during the 2nd week in June.

FORT BUFORD

After the Civil War, the U.S. Army built Fort Buford two miles downstream from Fort Union and closer to the Yellowstone River. This was a real fort, with soldiers stationed here to protect railroad workers and settlers. It was useful for about 30 years before it too was abandoned. The fort is most famous for some of the prisoners held here—including Chief Joseph of the Nez Perce and Sitting Bull of the Sioux.

Today the fort is long gone, and there's not much to see at this historic site. If you are interested in the military history of this time period, the state manages a small museum and cemetery here. For more information, contact State Historical Society of North Dakota, North Dakota Heritage Center, Bismarck, ND 58505 (701-224-2666).

DIRT SHORTCUT (option)

Although it's possible to save 4 miles and avoid some significant hills by taking Route 327 west from Fort Union to Bainville, MT, it includes 14 miles of fairly rough and dry dirt road. The scenery is beautiful, and there are very few cars; but the riding is rough (even on a mountain bike), and the few cars and trucks generate a lot of dust. The main route heads due north on paved 153rd Ave. (County Road 5) from Fort Buford to Route 2.

PAVED SHORTCUT (option)

If you want to skip Fort Union, or you decide to return to Fairview for the night after visiting Fort Union, it's possible to save 10 miles (36 vs. 46) by heading west from Fairview on Route 201 for 12 miles and then north on Route 16 for 24 miles to Culbertson, MT. This shortcut has a little more climbing (1500 feet vs. 1100 feet) and about the same light traffic.

WILLISTON, ND (option)

If you need a big town, Williston, North Dakota, is 23 miles northeast of Fort Buford; the last 7 miles is a busy four-lane highway with poor shoulders. Williston has a population of 12,000 and Amtrak service between Chicago and Portland or Seattle.

Culbertson, MT

Population: 1,000

Culbertson is a flat town that is small enough to get around easily on your bicycle.There are two motels, camping, several restaurants, and a small supermarket. Across from a highway rest area on Route 2, just east of town, the Visitor Center is located in an interesting free local museum. It is divided into rooms that display an old general store, school classroom, kitchen, doctor's office, barber shop, and beauty shop.

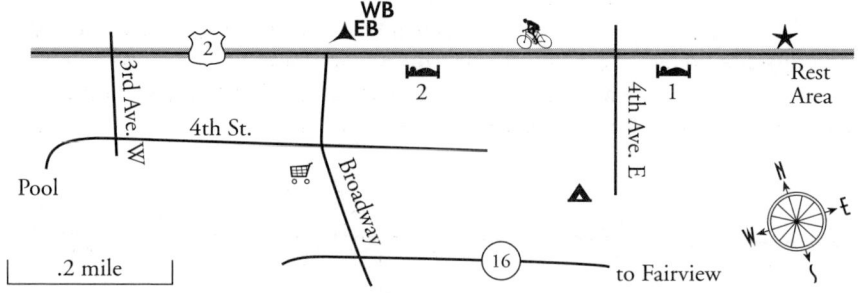

Culbertson, MT — Zip: 59218

★   **Culbertson Museum and Visitor Information Center**
     1 mi. east of town on Route 2, 406-787-5821

🛏 1) King's Inn Motel ($), 406-787-6277

   2) Diamond Willow Inn ($), 406-787-6218

▲   Bruegger Centennial Park, 4th Ave. E, free, open grass area, bathroom, showers available at town pool (small fee) at western end of 4th St.,

Poplar, MT

Population: 900

Located on the Fort Peck Indian Reservation, Poplar is home to two museums. The Fort Peck Assinniboine and Sioux Culture Center and Museum contains exhibits of Native American arts and crafts. The City Museum chronicles the growth of an Indian camp into a frontier town, focusing on the fur trade in the mid-19th century and the homesteading in the early 20th century. Poplar also has a motel, several small restaurants, convenience store, and grocery store.

Zip: 59255

🛏   Lee Anns Motel ($), 406-768-5442

Wolf Point, MT

Population: 2,900

Wolf Point is an open flat town with a variety of restaurants and many services. A historical kiosk near Albertson's explains, "A party of trappers poisoned several hundred wolves one winter, hauled the frozen carcasses in and stacked them until spring for skinning. It taught the varmints a lesson. No wolf has darkened the door of a house in this town since."

The Historical Society and Museum in the town library features displays of early settlers and Indians. If you're interested in old John Deere tractors, you can call the Toavs (406-392-5294) and make an appointment to view more than 500 old tractors at a private museum on his farm. At the east end of town Bell Enterprises Indian Market has a variety of items to view and buy. On the second weekend in June the Wild Horse Stampede includes a rodeo.

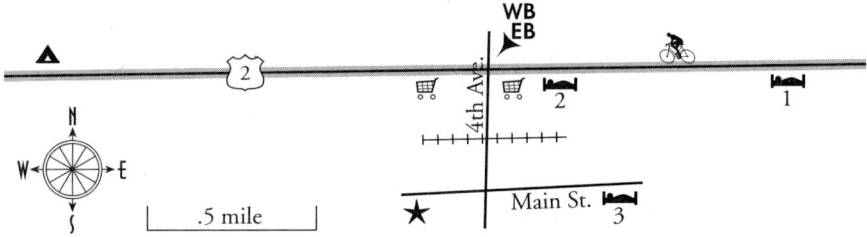

Wolf Point, MT — Zip: 59201

★ **Chamber of Commerce:** 218 3rd Ave. S, 406-653-2012

1) Big Sky Motel ($), 406-653-2300

2) Homestead Inn ($), 406-653-1300

3) Sherman Motor Inn ($$), 406-653-1100

▲ El Rancho Campground, 1.4 mi. west of town on Route 2; some shade, some tables, some grass, satisfactory restrooms and showers

ALTERNATE ROUTE

It is possible to avoid 25 miles on Route 2 by taking the old road, which runs parallel to the south. It is good pavement, but it adds 5.4 miles to this stretch. Westbound, turn left 2.2 miles west of Wolf Point and follow the pavement west for 30.8 miles to reconnect with Route 2 6.8 miles east of Nashua.

Glasgow, MT

Population: 3,600

Glasgow bills itself as the "whist capital of the world" with major tournaments in November and January. Are you wondering what winters are like here? The town was originally built along with the railroad in the 1880s, and is now a thriving regional center in an area of wheat farming and cattle grazing. The flat downtown area is located just south of Route 2. There are several motels and chain restaurants along Route 2, and more restaurants are located downtown. The Governor's Cup Walleye Tournament is held the second weekend in July.

mile 1516

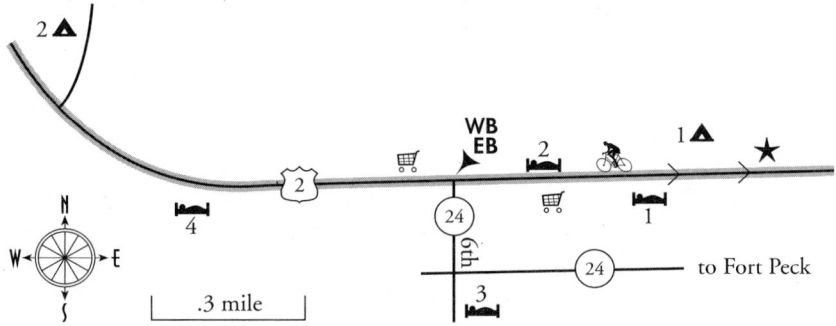

Glasgow, MT — Zip: 59230

★ **Glasgow Area Chamber of Commerce and Agriculture:** Route 2 at east end of town, Box 832, 406-228-2222

▬ 1) Cottonwood Inn ($), 800-321-8213

  2) La Casa Motel ($), 406-228-9311

  3) Campbell Lodge ($), 406-228-9328

  4) Star Lodge ($), 406-228-2494

▲ 1) Shady Rest RV and Campground, 406-228-2769; small and pleasant, grass sites, clean restroom and shower

  2) Trails West Camp and RV Park, 406-228-2778; 0.4 mi. off Route 2, dry and open; restrooms and showers

Fort Peck, MT

Population: 325

The town of Fort Peck was built in the 1930s to house the 30,000 workers and families involved in building the Fort Peck Dam—the largest earth dam in the world. The town was literally owned by the U.S. Army Corps of Engineers until 1986, when it became a self-governing town serving the needs of today's power plant workers and the many people fishing and camping at Fort Peck Lake. If you want to get away from Route 2 for 14 miles and don't mind adding another 16 easy miles between Wolf Point and Glasgow, you can easily detour down to Fort Peck from either Nashua (11 miles on Route 117) or Glasgow (19 miles on Route 24). Either way, be sure to check out Bergie's home-made ice cream in Nashua.

There are four main attractions in Fort Peck. One is the huge Fort Peck Lake—135 miles long with 1,500 miles of shoreline. Another is the huge Fort Peck Dam—4 miles across and two-thirds of a mile thick at the base. At the base of the dam is a power plant and a visitor center that displays many of the dinosaur parts and fossils found in this area. In the early 1900s an 18-foot high 47-foot long skeleton of a Tyranosaurus Rex was discovered here; it now resides in the American Museum of Natural History in New York.

The third attraction is the Fort Peck Theatre. Built in 1934 as a magnificent log chalet, it showed movies 24 hours a day to workers who were building the dam in shifts around the clock. Today the theatre has been beautifully restored and is used for all kinds of summer productions. The fourth attraction is the Fort Peck Hotel, a vintage 1930s hotel with a restaurant and bar. During the summer reservations are essential.

Fort Peck Theatre, Fort Peck, MT

Zip: 59223

🛏 Fort Peck Hotel ($), 800-560-4931

⛺ Downstream Campground, below Fort Peck Dam, grass, shade, showers

Saco, MT

Population: 225

If you like small towns, you will like Saco (pronounced Say-co). It would be easy to miss in a car, if you blinked; but you will definitely see it on your bicycle. There is a motel, B&B, café, grocery store, and a couple of bars.

Zip: 59261

1) Saco Motel ($), 800-752-3051

2) Big Dome Hotel B&B ($$), 406-527-3498

ALTERNATE ROUTE

It is possible to avoid 21 miles on Route 2 on the old Route 2, which bears south 5 miles west of Saco and 1.6 miles east of Malta. The pavement is very rough on this stretch; mileage is the same.

Sleeping Buffalo Hot Springs, MT

56 miles west of Glasgow, 10 miles west of Saco, and 18 miles east of Malta, this aging, but still pleasant and reasonably priced family resort lies 1.5 miles north of Route 2 on a gentle hill with sweeping views of the plains. Developed around three hot mineral pools, it includes a golf course, campground with good restrooms and showers, laundromat, older motel rooms, a café, and a restaurant. Soaking in the hot mineral pools can be very soothing after a hard day of cycling!

& ▲ Sleeping Buffalo Resort ($), 406-527-3370

mile 1558

Malta, MT

Population: 2,400

Malta is a flat town located on the Milk River, named by Lewis and Clark. *"The water of this river possesses a peculiar whiteness, being about the colour of a cup of tea with the admixture of a tablespoonfull of milk. from the colour of it's water we called it Milk river. we think it possible that this may be the river called by the Minitares the river which scoalds all others."* (*May 8, 1805, Lewis*)

Today Malta has a variety of motels and restaurants, food shopping, and camping. The free Phillips County Museum is located on Route 2 one mile east of Route 191. Along with artifacts, beadwork, and articles from early Native Americans and pioneers, it also has a large dinosaur exhibit—including a life-size model of an Albertosaurus, and a Tyrannosaurus Rex skull. Northeastern Montana is a rich area for fossil hunting.

The Milk River Wagon Train on the first weekend in September includes a parade, rides, and festivities.

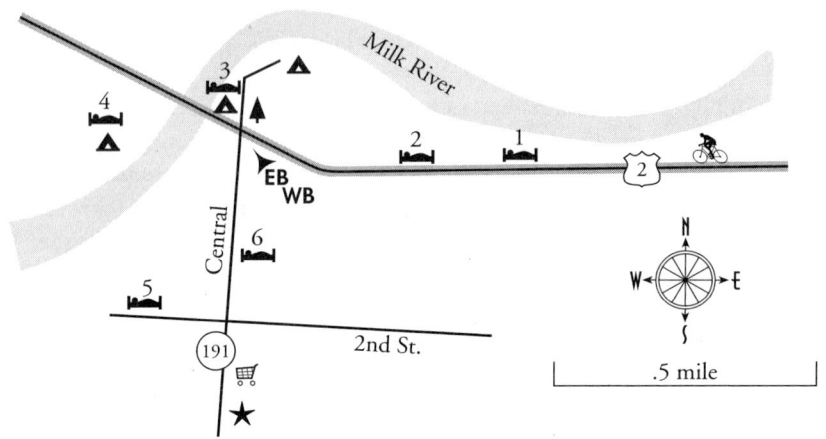

Malta, MT — Zip: 59538

★   **Chamber of Commerce:** Box 1420, 800-704-1776

🛏 1) Sportsman Motel ($) 406-654-2300

2) Royal Inn ($) 406-654-1150

3) Riverside Motel and Campground ($) 406-654-2310

4) Edgewater Inn and Campground ($$) 800-821-7475

5) Maltana Motel ($$) 406-654-2610

6) Great Northern Hotel ($$) 406-654-2100

▲ 1) Town Park, Central Ave. north of Route 2

2) Riverside Motel and Campground (3 above)

3) Edgewater Inn and Campground (4 above)

Harlem, MT

Population: 900

Harlem has a motel on the highway, with food shopping and a couple of restaurants located in the downtown area about a mile north of the highway.

🛏 McGuires' Motel ($), 406-353-2433

Chinook, MT

Population: 1,600

Chinook is an Indian word meaning "warm thawing winds of late winter." It's an appropriate name for a town that is friendly to cyclists. There are two motels, an inexpensive hotel, two parks for camping, several restaurants, and good food shopping. Although located on both the Milk River and the railroad, passenger trains no longer stop here. Chinook is the county seat for Blaine County.

The Blaine County Museum houses a collection of early fossils, Indian and pioneer artifacts, and an introduction to the Bear's Paw Battlefield 16 miles south of Chinook. This is the place where the U.S. Cavalry finally caught up with Chief Joseph and his band of Nez Perce Indians struggling to escape to Canada. Just 40 miles short of freedom, Chief Joseph surrendered with these famous words, "From where the sun now stands, I will fight no more forever."

Captain Lewis was probably looking at the Bear's Paw Mountains when he wrote in his journal, *"on arriving to the summit one of the highest points in the neighbourhood I thought myself well repaid for any labour; as from this point I beheld the Rocky Mountains for the first time, I could only discover a few of the most elivated points above the horizon . . . these points of the Rocky Mountains were covered with snow and the sun shone on it in such manner as to give me the most plain and satisfactory view, while I viewed these mountains I felt a secret pleasure in finding myself so near the head of the heretofore conceived boundless missouri; but when I reflected on the difficulties which this snowy barrier would most probably throw in my way to the Pacific, and the sufferings and hardships of myself and party in them, it in some measure counterbalanced the joy I had felt in the first moments in which I gazed on them; but as I have always held it a crime to anticipate evils I will believe it a good comfortable road untill I am compelled to beleive differently." (May 26, 1805)*

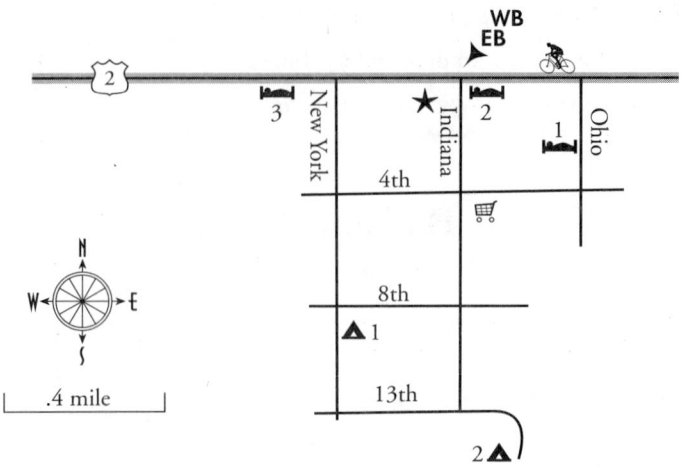

Chinook, MT — Zip: 59523

★   **Chamber of Commerce:** Box 744

🛏   1) Chinook Hotel ($), 406-357-2231

    2) Chinook Motor Inn ($$), 406-357-2248

    3) Bear Paw Court ($), 406-357-2221

▲   1) Town Park, grass, shade, restrooms with no showers

    2) Griffin Park, grass, shade, showers

Havre, MT

Population: 11,000

mile 1673

Havre (pronounced Have-er) is the largest town on the Hi-Line, a major railroad junction, and a regional farming and commercial center. Although the surrounding land was originally used for grazing cattle and sheep, in the 20th century it has been primarily used for growing both winter and spring wheat.

The downtown area is compact, flat, and easy to get around. There is a variety of restaurants, entertainment, and other services. Fort Assinniboine, built in 1879 six miles southwest of town, was once home for 500 soldiers protecting the Montana frontier. Summer tours are offered at 5 pm. "Havre Beneath the Streets" on 3rd Ave. offers tours of a rebuilt historic underground mall, including the Sporting Eagle Saloon, a bordello, and an opium den.

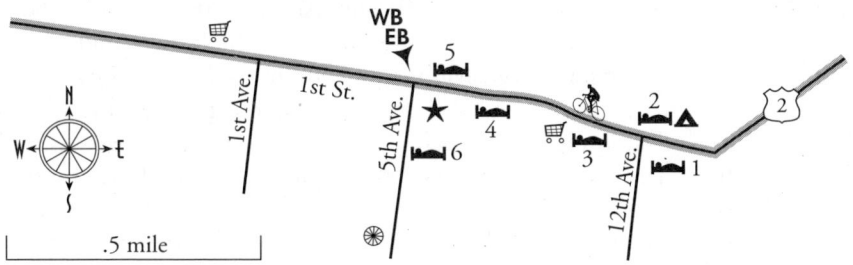

Havre, MT — Zip: 59501

★ **Chamber of Commerce:** 518 1st St., 406-265-4383

🛏 1) Duck Inn ($), 406-265-9615

2) Best Western Great Northern ($$), 888-530-4100

3) Budget Inn ($), 888-868-8625

4) Siesta Motel ($), 406-265-5863

5) El Toro Motel ($), 406-265-5414

6) Rails Inn ($), 406-265-1438

▲ Havre RV Park, very convenient open campground on main street with beautiful soft grass, little shade, pool, hot tub, and clean restrooms with showers. 406-265-8861

✳ Havre Bicycle, 425 5th, 406-265-3654

Special Event: Havre Festival Days, mid-Sept., (parade, arts & crafts, concerts)

Big Sandy, MT

Population: 750

Big Sandy has a town park that allows camping, combined with a highway rest area with restrooms, but no showers. Within walking distance are a couple of restaurants and a food supermarket.

Loma, MT

Population: 80

In the small town of Loma, 11 miles north of Fort Benton, the Marias River joins the Missouri River. The Corps of Discovery stopped at this critical point for nine days trying to decide which river was the Missouri. Although the Indians in the Mandan villages had told them about "the great falls," the Milk River, and many other features to look out for, no one had mentioned this confluence of two rivers. Both appeared to be "the main river," and there were good arguments for each. After several days of exploring each branch, both Lewis and Clark were convinced the southern branch was correct; all the men were equally convinced the northern branch was correct.

Since everyone in the party understood this was a military expedition, they obeyed their commanders and proceeded on the southern branch. Two days later Lewis, hiking out ahead of the boats, heard and then saw the first of "the great falls," and they knew they had made the right choice.

Today there is a dirt road just south of the bridge that goes 0.7 miles out to Decision Point. From a small hill you can look down on the confluence of the Marias and the Missouri. Today it's obvious which is the main river, because so much water from the Marias has been used for irrigation.

For twelve years before Fort Benton was established farther upriver, Loma was the head of navigation on the Missouri River. In 1831 James Kipp built Fort Piegan here to trade with the dreaded Blackfeet Indians. Kipp succeeded where earlier traders and trappers had failed, because he had a translator who convinced the Indians of the benefits of trade. However, the peace did not last, and this important river junction was the scene of much bloodshed over the ensuing years. Today there is a café and convenience store here.

Fort Benton, MT

Population: 1,700

mile 1747

In 1846 the American Fur Company decided to replace Fort Mackenzie (in today's Loma) with Fort Lewis on this site twelve miles farther upriver. The name was later changed to Fort Benton to honor the company's best friend in Congress—Thomas Hart Benton. Originally a fur trading post, it became a gold trading town with the gold rush in the 1860s. As many as 50 steamboats arrived each summer—bringing settlers, adventurers, and manufactured goods. In one year over 10,000 miners disembarked here, and there would have been 1,000 oxen pulling wagons on the streets. From here wagon trains took over and spread out to carry people and goods farther north and west. It remained the head of navigation on the Missouri River until the railroad replaced steamboat travel in the late 1880s.

The town is working on several restorations that will make it even more interesting. The original fort is being rebuilt, and is the site of ongoing archeological study. The Grand Union Hotel has been restored to its original glory next to the river. The town is also home to the Museum of the Upper Missouri (describing life in the area) and the Museum of the Northern Great Plains (describing the history of farming and agricultural machinery in the area).

Fort Benton marks the upper end of the 150-mile stretch of river designated and protected as the Wild and Scenic Missouri River. It's only "wild" in the sense that it looks very much like it did when Lewis and Clark first travelled on it 200 years ago. This is an ideal place to rent a canoe for a day trip or sign on with an outfitter for a multi-day trip down the river. Contact the Chamber of Commerce for information about rentals and

Grand Union Hotel, Fort Benton, MT

Can you find the canoe? Missouri River near Fort Benton, MT

trips. Canoes can often be rented at the last minute, but reservations are strongly recommended for longer guided and catered trips.

Although lodging is scarce, there is very pleasant free camping at the town park along the river at the north end of town. The town is flat and compact enough to walk around easily. There are several restaurants, a small supermarket, and many shops along Front Street. It's both fun and educational to walk along the levee side of Front Street and read the history of the area on a series of signs. Besides the wonderful statue of Lewis, Clark, and Sacagawea, and a keelboat, there is also the statue and touching story of the faithful dog, Shep, who waited every day at the train station for his dead master—whom he had last seen at the station.

Notice the carefully researched details on this statue by Robert M. Scriver in Fort Benton, MT.

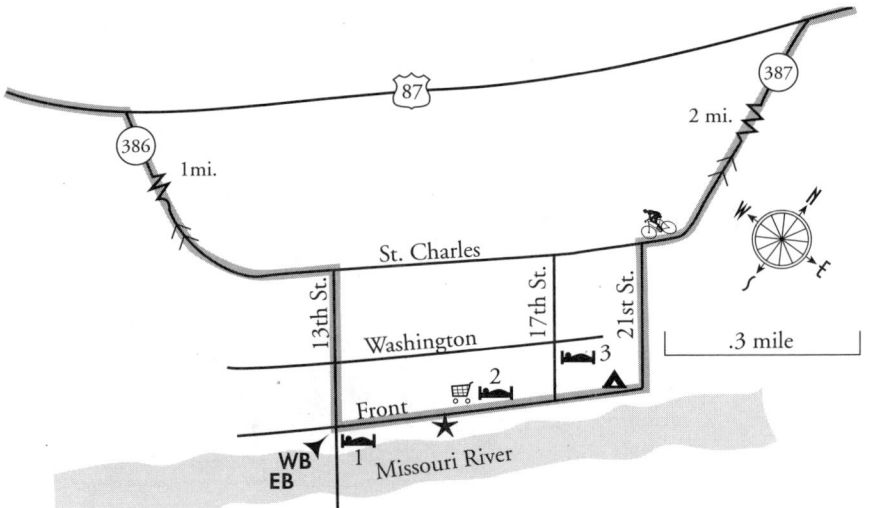

Fort Benton, MT — Zip: 59442

★   **Chamber of Commerce:** along the Steamboat Levee, PO Box 879, 406-622-3864

🛏 1) Grand Union Hotel ($$), Front, 888-838-1882

   2) Pioneer Lodge Motel ($$), Front, 406-622-5441

   3) Long's Landing B&B ($$), 17th and Washington, 406-622-3461

▲   Town Park at north end of Front St., pleasant grass and shade, water, satisfactory restrooms with no shower (possible shower at town pool or swim in river across street), easy walk to restaurants and shopping

Great Falls, MT

Population: 60,000

Great Falls emerged as a planned city in the 1880s, and it grew rapidly as five dams were built to take advantage of the hydroelectric power available by the drop in the river. The copper industry was booming, and huge amounts of electricity were required to refine copper from ore. The Anaconda Copper Company once employed 60% of the workers in Montana, and Great Falls was the largest city in the state. In fact, many people would tell you that Anaconda "owned" Montana—including many of its politicians. As copper declined and oil and gas boomed in the late 20th century, Great Falls was surpassed by Billings as the largest city.

Great Falls today is about 4 miles by 1.5 miles in size with moderate hills and traffic, so you need your bicycle to get around and see things. I recommend heading to the very helpful visitor center overlooking the river as soon as you arrive to get oriented, get a detailed city map, and figure out what you want to see and do.

It's helpful to understand that two areas have evolved in Great Falls. The old downtown area is in the ten blocks east of the river around Central Ave., while the entire three-mile stretch of 10th Ave. South near the south edge of the city provides many newer motels, shopping malls, chain restaurants, and other stores.

The Corps of Discovery learned about the great falls from the Indians at Fort Mandan, but the information turned out to be unduly optimistic. They were told about *"a most tremendous cataract . . . the noise it makes can be heard at a great distance . . . a precipice of solid and even rock, many feet high . . . there is a fine open plain on th X. side of the falls, through which, canoes and baggage may be readily transported. this portage they assert is not greater than half a mile." (Moulton, Vol 4, p. 367)*

Only one of the "Great Falls," now tamed by dams, Great Falls, MT

What Lewis discovered when he arrived on June 13 was much worse. There were actually a series of five large falls in a ten-mile stretch of river, and steep rocky banks on both sides. After scouting both sides of the river, they decided to use an eighteen-mile portage route on the south side. It required a very difficult month to get by these falls, and it must have dealt a discouraging blow to the idea of a commercial Northwest Passage.

The new Lewis and Clark Interpretive Center (4201 Giant Springs Rd., 406-727-8733) is a "must see" for anyone, especially people following the Lewis & Clark Trail. On the south side of the river at the north edge of the city, it can be reached by a pleasant ride along the River's Edge Bike Trail. This trail also provides a glimpse of the falls, rapids, and steep side walls that provided such a huge barrier to Lewis and Clark—even though today's dams make the river somewhat different.

The C.M. Russell Museum Complex (400 13th St. N, 406-727-8787) is well worth a visit for anyone who enjoys western art. Charlie Russell (the son of a prominent St. Louis family) left home in 1880 at age 16 to pursue his dream of becoming a cowboy. Instead, he gained fame as a self-taught artist. The museum complex includes a museum of western art, featuring works of Russell and others, his home, and the restored cabin and studio where he worked.

Although it's a little hard to get to, the 3-D International Restaurant across the river in Black Eagle offers an excellent all-you-can-eat Mongolian Grill buffet at a reasonable price. You can see their sign atop the restaurant from the Great Falls side of the river.

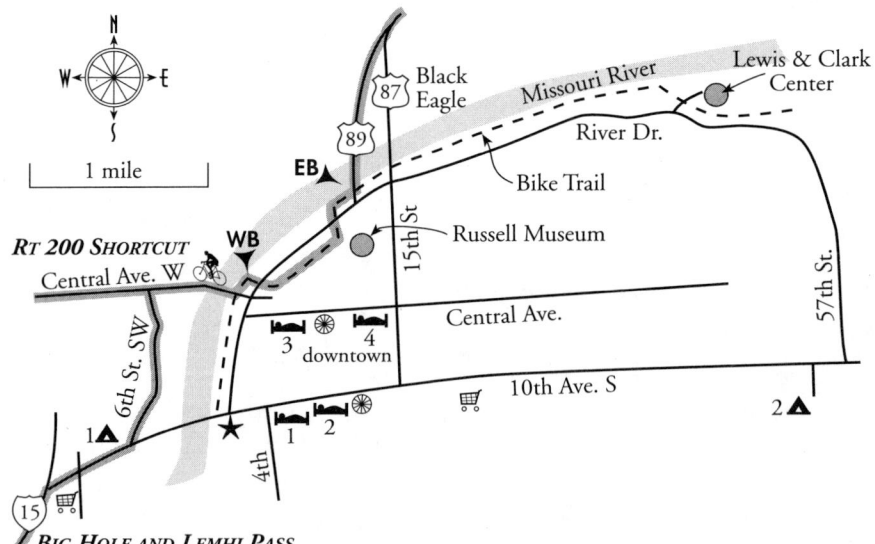

Great Falls, MT — Zip: 59403

★ **Visitor Center:** 10th Ave. S at the river, PO Box 2127, 800-735-8535, www.greatfallscvb.visitmt.com

▬ The Visitor Center lists 33 motels. Several older and newer ones are grouped in the downtown area, around Central Ave. in the 10 blocks east of the river. Another grouping can be found scattered along 10th Ave. S along with many franchise restaurants and several shopping malls. A sample from both locations:

1) Holiday Inn ($$), 400 10th Ave. S, 800-257-1998

2) Village Motor Inn ($), 726 10th Ave. S, 406-727-7666

3) Best Western Ponderosa ($$), 220 Central, 406-761-3410

4) Royal Motel ($), 1300 Central, 406-452-9548

▲ 1) Dick's RV Park, at intersection of 6th St. SW and 10th Ave. S just west of the river, a few tent sites distant from clean restrooms with showers, rough grass, no shade, near noisy roads, about 2 mi. from downtown, expensive. 406-452-0333

2) KOA, 1500 51st St. S just south of 10th Ave. S at east end of city, quiet area, some shade and grass, tent sites near excellent restrooms with showers, pool, hot tub, about 4 mi. from downtown, more expensive. 406-727-3191

✺ 1) Scheels, Holiday Village Mall, 10th Ave. S at 9th St., 406-453-7666

2) Bighorn Wilderness Equipment, 600 Central, 406-453-2841

Special Events

Lewis and Clark Encampment, weekend late June or early July (living interpretation of portage around falls),

State Fair and Rodeo, late July

International Dixieland Jazz Festival, Labor Day weekend

mile 1786

H. THREE ROUTES OVER THE DIVIDE

GREAT FALLS, MT TO MISSOULA, MT

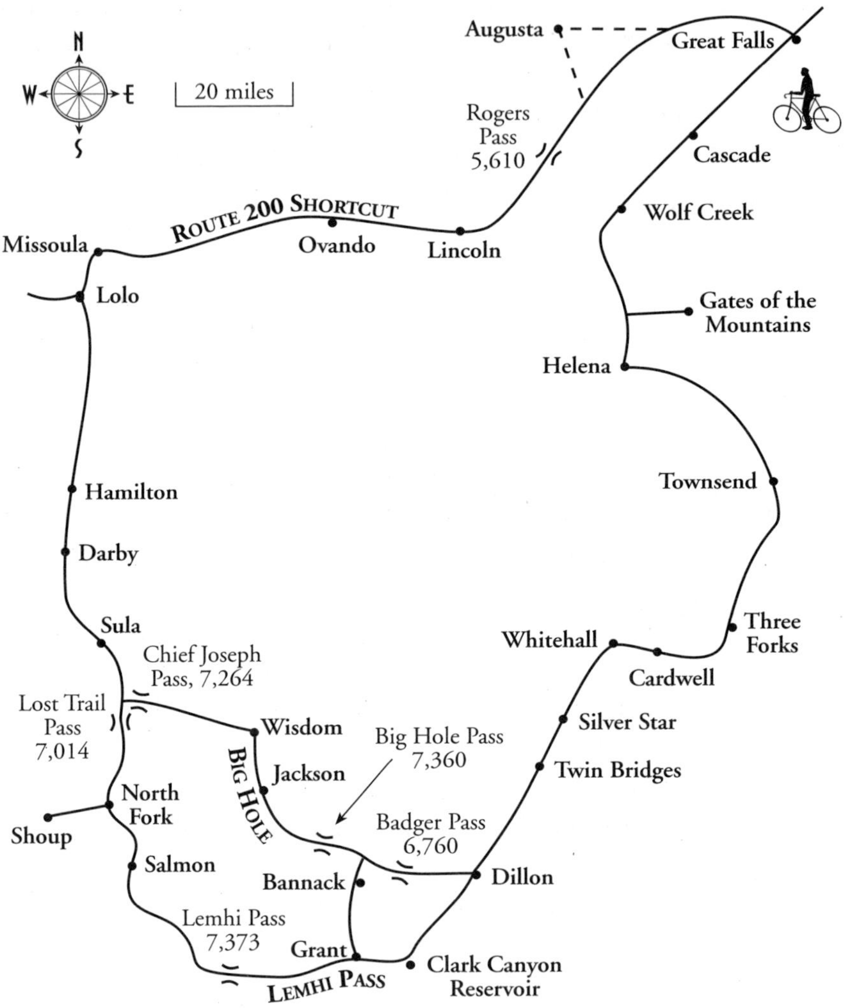

Augusta

Great Falls

Rogers
Pass
5,610

Cascade

Wolf Creek

ROUTE 200 SHORTCUT

Missoula

Ovando   Lincoln

Lolo

Gates of the
Mountains

Helena

Hamilton

Townsend

Darby

Sula

Whitehall

Three
Forks

Chief Joseph
Pass, 7,264

Cardwell

Lost Trail
Pass
7,014

Wisdom

Big Hole Pass
7,360

Silver Star

BIG HOLE

Jackson

Twin Bridges

North
Fork

Badger Pass
6,760

Shoup

Salmon

Bannack

Dillon

Lemhi Pass
7,373

Grant

Clark Canyon
Reservoir

LEMHI PASS

N W E S
20 miles

Summary Data for Three Routes:

	Distance	*Climbing*
Lemhi Pass	460 mi.	15,000 ft.
Big Hole	420 mi.	13,000 ft.
Route 200 Shortcut	170 mi.	7,000 ft.

Great Falls is perhaps *the* critical transition point in the entire Lewis and Clark Trail—both for the original expedition and for today's bicycle tourer—as it is the transition from the plains to the mountains. And not just any mountains; these are *the Rocky Mountains*—actually made up of many different and dramatic interlocking mountain ranges. With 1,800 miles behind you, there are another 1,200 miles to go—600 of which are in the Rocky Mountains.

The Corps of Discovery used three different routes over the Continental Divide, as shown in the map and summary above. On their original westbound journey they crossed over Lemhi Pass. On their return eastbound journey Lewis and Clark split the group and explored two different routes. Clark took his group through the Big Hole and then down the Yellowstone River. Lewis took his group on the more direct route they had learned about from the Indians—about 300 miles shorter than their original westbound route. I call this third option the "Route 200 Shortcut," because it approximates today's Route 200. The two groups rejoined where the Yellowstone River joins the Missouri River near the Montana-North Dakota border.

Which route should you take? I will lay out the advantages and disadvantages of each and let you decide based on what's important to you. All three routes are described in both the Master Plan and the Detailed Plan. This part of Montana is an area where you could put together a great loop trip if you want to park a car someplace and take two of these routes. You could also use these routes along with the state highway map to design your own loop.

The **Lemhi Pass Route** is the original route the Corps of Discovery followed on their westbound trip. It offers historical accuracy and a feeling of discovery and excitement, as you think about Lewis desperately searching for Indians so they could purchase horses before winter set in, and wondering when they would reach the Continental Divide and what the other side would be like. You, too, will wonder about making it over the mountains. This route is the longest at 460 miles, the most challenging, the most beautiful, and has the least traffic. From Great Falls it follows the river south, winding up canyons through the foothills, past the Gates of the Mountains, and into Helena—state capital and great small city. On south to Three Forks, where Lewis and Clark once again agonized over which of the three forks would lead them to the source of the Missouri River. Along the river and up through pretty valleys to Dillon—another good small town for bicycle tourers. This is the only route that includes the following places:

1. Camp Fortunate, where Sacagawea was unexpectedly reunited with her brother, Chief Cameahwait, in an incredibly emotional scene that was probably critical to the success of the expedition. The site is now covered by Clark Canyon Reservoir.

2. The town of Grant, with its population of 35 and the Horse Prairie Hilton Inn—a friendly, reasonably priced B&B with restaurant.

3. Lemhi Pass and the (arguable) source of the Missouri River. You can see what Lewis saw when he first looked across the Continental Divide. He expected an easy portage to a river that would float them down to the Pacific; instead he saw more mountains and mountain ranges than he had ever dreamed of.

4. The town of Salmon, Idaho, a great little active outdoor adventure town, where you can take time off for a whitewater rafting adventure on the Salmon River (also known as the River of No Return). After scouting this river for several days, Lewis and Clark reluctantly decided they could not navigate it.

Before you choose this route, be aware there are two significant disadvantages. First, it includes two major passes instead of one. Lemhi Pass at 7,373 feet is described below. Lost Trail Pass at 7,014 feet includes 3,500 feet of climbing in 23 miles on the south side (or 2,600 feet of climbing in 12 miles if you're travelling eastbound).

Second, it includes 24 miles of fairly rough dirt road. I have done it on my touring bike, because I desperately wanted to do this route; but I will never (well, *probably* never) do it again and can't recommend it. The dirt includes 1,400 feet of climbing in 12 miles on the east side and 2,400 feet in 12 miles on the west side, and the ride *down* the west side is especially rough. After rain, Lemhi Pass can be muddy, slippery, and difficult for four-wheel drive vehicles! There is talk about adding a layer of gravel on top of the dirt, which might make it better in some ways and worse in others.

If you want to ride this route westbound but are concerned about Lemhi Pass, it is always possible to ride as far as Grant, and then make a last-minute decision to ride a pretty good dirt road 12 miles north to Bannack and connect with the Big Hole Route. Eastbound riders don't have this easy option. Once you ride to Salmon, you would have to backtrack 45 miles and 4,000 feet to get back on the Big Hole Route.

The **Big Hole Route** is almost as long (420 miles) as the Lemhi Route, all paved, almost as beautiful, almost as free of traffic, and almost as hilly. Historically, this follows Clark's return

Can you find the cyclist climbing Lemhi Pass?

route pretty closely between Lolo and Bannack and between Dillon and Great Falls. You can choose to follow Clark's route by taking the dirt road between Bannack and Grant, and using the Lemhi Pass Route between Grant and Dillon. (see summary map above) This route does *not* follow Clark's route up the Yellowstone River, because this would involve several hundred miles on I-94.

This is the only route that includes the following places:

1. The Big Hole, a gorgeous high valley with dramatic mountains on both sides. There are many prosperous (and mostly invisible) ranches here using the unique Beaverslide (see photo with Wisdom, MT) to collect and store hay.

2. The cute, tiny town of Jackson with its motel, restaurant, hot springs, and bar.

3. The Big Hole National Battlefield and Visitors Center. It is definitely worth an hour or two to both see and hear the tragic and heroic story of Chief Joseph and the Nez Perce Indians.

The third option is the **Route 200 Shortcut** between Great Falls and Missoula. This approximates the eastbound return route of Lewis and nine men in 1806, as they followed the well-worn Indian trail up the "River of the Road to the Buffalo" (today's Blackfoot River). About ten miles east of Lincoln, they followed the trail over the divide, at what is now called Lewis and Clark Pass—about five miles north of today's Route 200 crossing at Roger's Pass. Lewis followed the trail east—close to today's Augusta—and picked up the Sun River to Great Falls.

This general route was also followed in 1859 when John Mullan constructed the Mullan Road so the U.S. Army could transport military

The Big Hole near Jackson, MT

Approaching the Divide on the Route 200 Shortcut

supplies over 600 miles from the Missouri River at Fort Benton to the Columbia River at Wallula—both places we pass on the Lewis & Clark Trail. The road was completed in only one year, although there was a 130% cost overrun and the quality of the road left something to be desired.

The major (only?) advantage of this route is that it's shorter with less climbing. If you have a tight schedule, or need to make up time, this route can help. If Lewis and Clark had known about this route, they could have saved about 45 days and continued over the Bitterroots in the summer weather of early August.

Route 200 also has several disadvantages. First, because it is more direct, it carries more and faster traffic—including trucks—than the other routes. Second, although this route involves less climbing, the climbing is less pleasant. Especially between Simms and Lincoln, the highway tends to be straight with lots of big ups and downs. Third, Lincoln, at about the halfway point, is the only significant town on this 165-mile stretch. If you don't want to do two long days, you can detour through Augusta, stop in Ovando, or camp in pleasant Forest Service campgrounds. Finally, although the scenery is beautiful, it's not as spectacular as the other routes; and you miss a lot of great towns.

LEMHI PASS AND BIG HOLE ROUTE

Cascade, MT

Population: 730

Cascade is a pleasant small town for an overnight stop, and especially convenient if you don't want to do the whole 88 hilly miles to Helena in a single day. There are two possible areas to stay. There is camping, motels, food shopping, and a café right in town. There is also camping with a full restaurant and bar near Hardy, about nine miles south (towards Helena) from the downtown area.

Zip: 59421

🛏 1) Badger Motel & Café ($), 1st St., 406-468-9330

   2) A&C Motel ($), 308 1 Ave. N, 406-468-2513

▲ 1) Atkinson Park, 3rd Ave. N, next to I-15, good grass, no shade, restrooms, showers at pool next door

   2) Missouri Inn, 9 mi. south of Cascade, camping behind restaurant, restrooms with showers, some shade, be aware of possible conflict with weekend flea market on summer weekends, 406-468-9884

Wolf Creek, MT

Population: 150

Wolf Creek is a very small fishing town right on the river in the beautiful Wolf Creek Canyon. There are two motels, a restaurant, café, and bar. Pleasant and convenient as this town is, the motels are usually filled by fishermen on a weekly basis during the summer. Call ahead for reservations. There are also two primitive National Forest Service campgrounds north (towards Cascade) of Wolf Creek.

Zip: 59648

1) Montana River Outfitters Cabins ($–$$), 800-800-4350

2) Frenchy's Motel ($), 406-235-4251

▲ 1) NFS Campground, 11 mi. north (towards Cascade), on river, rough ground, no water, pit toilet

2) NFS Campground, 3 mi. north (towards Cascade), on river, rough ground, no water, pit toilet

Helena, MT

Pop 30,000

Nestled in the foothills of the Elkhorn Mountains, Helena is the capital of Montana. There was nothing here in 1864 when four discouraged miners decided to take one last chance to find gold on their way home to Georgia. They struck it rich, and the population exploded. The name "Last Chance Gulch" stuck, and today you can visit shops and restaurants along a pleasant pedestrian mall in the gulch. Bicycle tourers can minimize hills and avoid traffic by skirting the city to the north and east, but you miss a lot if you don't tackle some of the hills and see the sights.

Helena is a very appealing small city. It's big enough to have a variety of services, but small enough to get around without too much traffic. The nearby mountains, river, and lake offer great opportunities for year round outdoor recreation. There is an active community of both road and mountain bikers. Finally, it is a well-educated and sophisticated small city with lots of music and art.

There are clusters of motels and restaurants near the I-15 interchanges and in the downtown area. You can find camping either five miles east or five miles north of the city, although food shopping is much better north of the city. Remember that east of the city means heading westbound on our route, and north of the city means heading eastbound.

The Capitol offers both guided and self-guided tours. Note that the dome is gilded with copper instead of the more typical gold, once again reminding us what made this state. The building contains several historical paintings, including the famous mural of "Lewis and Clark Meeting the Flathead Indians at Ross' Hole" by Charles Russell. Across the street the Montana Historical Society Museum has exhibits of Montana history, plus a gallery of Russell art. The Last Chance Tour Train leaves from the museum for an overview tour of the city, including the pedestrian mall in Last Chance Gulch, the cathedral, and the elegant Victorian mansions built with the wealth from gold mining.

Seventeen miles north of Helena, and down a 2.7-mile steep hill from its own exit on I-15, is the beautiful two-hour boat trip along a three-mile stretch of the Missouri River with 1,200-foot cliffs through the Gates of the Rocky Mountains (406-458-5241, www.gatesofthemountains.org). Although it may be difficult to fit this into your riding plan (it almost requires either an overnight stop in Wolf Creek or an extra day in Helena), this is a spectacular section of the river.

On July 19 Lewis wrote, *"wherever we get a view of the lofty summits of the mountains the snow presents itself, altho' we are almost suffocated in this confined vally with heat . . . this evening we entered much the most remarkable clifts that we have yet seen. these clifts rise from the waters edge on either side perpendicularly to the hight of 1200 feet. every object here wears a dark and gloomy aspect . . . the river appears to have forced it's way through this immence body of solid rock for the distance of 5 3/4 miles and where it makes it's exit below has thrown on either side vast collumns of rocks mountains high . . . from the singular appearance of this place I called it the gates of the rocky mountains."*

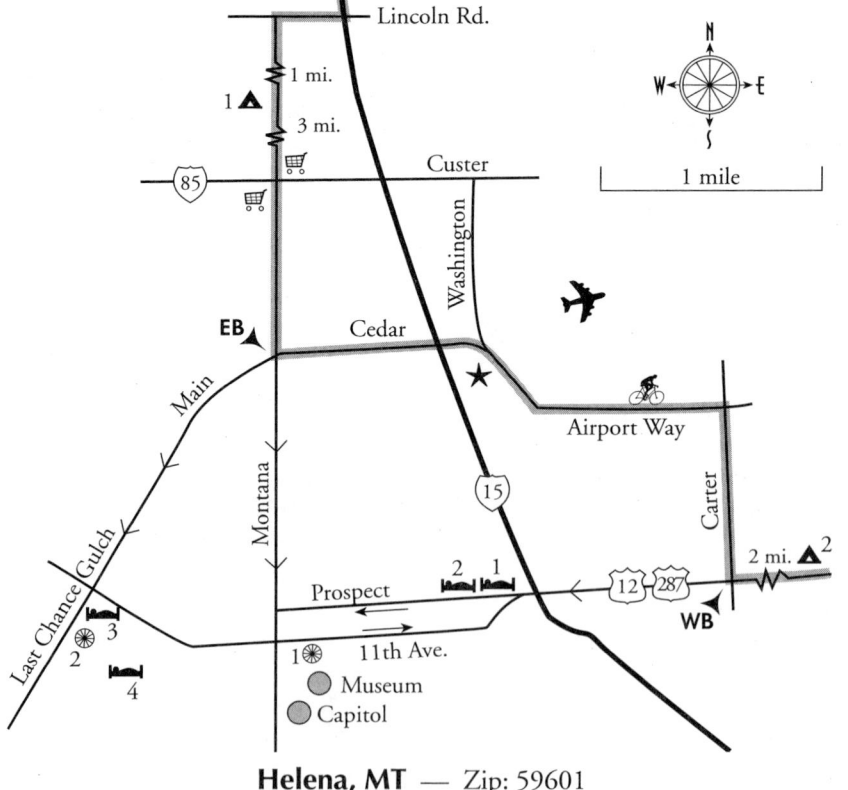

Helena, MT — Zip: 59601

Gates of the Mountains, near Helena, MT

★ **Chamber of Commerce:** 225 Cruse, 800-743-5362, www.helenachamber.com, hchamber@initco.net

▬ The Chamber of Commerce can provide a listing of 20 motels and 8 B&Bs. Listed below are a few convenient ones from different price categories.

1) Motel 6 ($), 800 N Oregon, 406-442-9990

2) Holiday Inn Express ($$), 701 Washington, 800-465-4329

3) Budget Inn ($$), 524 N Last Chance, 800-862-1334

4) St. James B&B ($$$), 114 N Hoback, 406-449-2623

▲ 1) Helena Campground and RV Park, 5820 N Montana, 406-458-4714, 5 mi. north, former KOA campground, quiet, good grass sites with shade, excellent restrooms with showers, pool, hot tub, laundry, camp store, relatively expensive tenting, excellent food shopping 3 flat mi. south

2) Buzz In RV Park and Campground, 3699 Hwy 12, 406-449-1291, 5 mi. east, open, near highway, grass, some shade, showers, laundry

✷ 1) Big Sky Cyclery, 1419 11th Ave., 406-442-4644

2) Great Divide Cyclery, 336 N Jackson, 406-443-5188

Townsend, MT

Population: 1,650

Townsend is a pleasant small town with motels, campgrounds, restaurants, and good food shopping. If you plan to camp, wait until you arrive and make your choice based on your priorities.

Zip: 59644

★ **Townsend Area Chamber of Commerce:** Box 947, 406-266-3911

🏨 Mustang Motel ($) and Lake Townsend Motel ($), 406-266-3491

▲ 1) Indian Road CG, 1 mi. north, grass, shade, water, pit toilet, no shower

2) Roadrunner RV CG, .6 mi. north, on road, some grass, open, no shade

Along the Jefferson River, Three Forks, MT

Three Forks, MT

Population: 1,200

As its name suggests, Three Forks is where the Missouri River splits into three rivers. Confirming what they already suspected when they left Fort Mandan, Lewis and Clark believed the westward branch was the most promising, and they named it the Jefferson, after their president and sponsor. They diplomatically named the others the Madison (Secretary of State) and the Gallatin (Secretary of Treasury).

This small town requires a flat 2.5-mile detour southeast from Route 287. It includes a small market, a couple of restaurants, two motels, and the attractively restored Sacajawea Inn. There is also a motel and campground located directly on Route 287 near the intersection with I-90. The nearby Wheat Montana Bakery and Deli offers a limited, but very good, menu. Although I hesitate to mention restaurants because they change periodically, I have to tell you we had a memorable creative dinner at the Historic Headwaters Restaurant on Main Street.

Another six flat miles east and north of town is the Missouri Headwaters State Park, where the river actually splits. This is a flat area, and it is difficult to see the actual split of the rivers unless you cross the river and climb the limestone cliff (as Lewis did) or go up in an airplane and get a wonderful overview. It's a pleasant place with a primitive campground, but there is little to see or do here.

In 1805 Sacagawea recognized their campsite as the place where her Shoshoni group had been camping when they were attacked by a Hidatsa hunting party four years earlier. Several were killed, and several boys and women were taken as prisoners and slaves.

The area around Three Forks was rich in beaver, and three men from the Corps of Discovery later found their way back as guides and trappers. Four years later John Potts was killed by Blackfeet Indians, and a year after that George Drouillard had both his scalp and his head taken off.

John Colter also returned to the area to trap, trade, and fight. He was the first white man to wander through the thermal pools and geysers that are now part of Yellowstone National Park, but were originally called Colter's Hell. He was with Potts when Potts was killed, but the Blackfeet had a special punishment for Colter. He was stripped naked and given a headstart, running barefoot over the needle grass and prickly pear. The Blackfeet then started chasing him for a human hunt. The Indians must have been furious when Colter outran all but one of them, then turned and killed him. They kept chasing Colter across the flat land, but he hid in a pile of driftwood in the Gallatin River. During the night he stole away, and over the next week managed to travel 200 miles to safety.

Back on Route 287, five miles farther south is Lewis and Clark Caverns State Park (see camping below). Although the campground is convenient to the highway, the caverns require a three-mile ride up a 1,400 foot hill. It takes about two hours to walk the two-mile tour of the caverns.

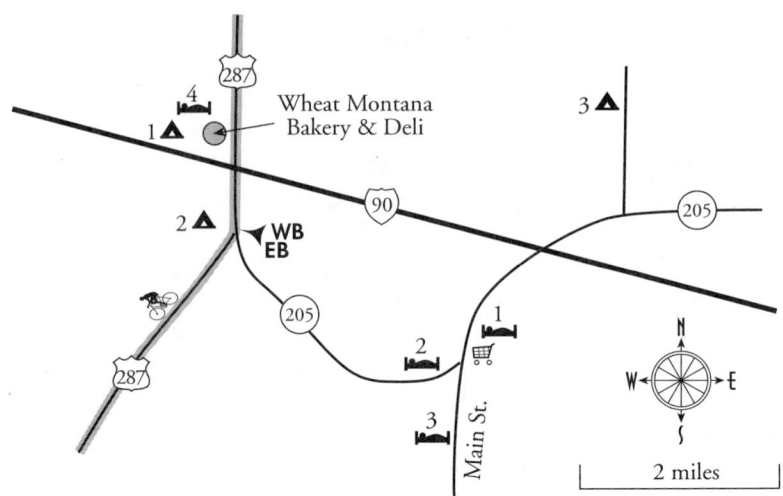

Three Forks, MT — Zip: 59752

★   **Three Forks Chamber of Commerce:** Box 1103, 406-285-4753, www.threeforksmontana.com

🛏 1) Sacajawea Inn ($$), 5 N Main, 800-821-7326

2) Broken Spur Motel ($-$$), 124 W Elm 406-285-3277

3) Lewis and Clark Sportsman's Lodge ($$), 510 S Main, 406-285-3454

4) Fort Three Forks Motel ($$), on Route 287 near I-90, 406-285-3233

▲ 1) Fort Three Forks RV Park and Campground, grass, no shade, windy, good restrooms with showers, 406-285-3233

2) KOA Campground, Route 287 just below I-90, 406-285-3611

3) Missouri Headwaters State Park Campground, no water, pit toilets, flat, near river, 6 mi. east and north of town

4) Lewis and Clark Caverns State Park, Route 287 4.8 mi. south of Route 205 intersection, sloping ground, pretty canyon, no shade, little privacy, good restrooms with showers

Special Events

> Rodeo, 3rd weekend in July
> Lewis and Clark Rendevous, last weekend in July
> Antique Aircraft Show, first weekend in August

Cardwell, MT

Pop 35

Cardwell Store is an interchange on I-90 that offers a convenience store and inexpensive cabins, tepees, and camping area.

Zip: 59721

▲ Cardwell Store, camping behind store, grass, some shade, restrooms with showers

Whitehall, MT

Pop 1,100

Whitehall offers good food shopping and a variety of motels and restaurants in the small downtown area and near the I-90 interchange a half mile from downtown.

Zip: 59759

🛏 1) Whitehall Creek Motel ($), Legion St., 406-287-5315

2) Chief Motel ($), Legion St., 406-287-3921

3) Rice Motel ($), Legion St., 406-287-3895

4) Super 8 Motel ($$), I-90 Interchange, 406-287-3055

Silver Star, MT

Population: 50

This pleasant tiny town offers a country store, café, and, two miles farther down the route, a fishing resort with cabins, rooms, and campground.

Zip: 59751

🛏 & ▲ Jefferson River Cabins and Campground, 406-684-5225

Twin Bridges, MT

Population: 375

In Twin Bridges the Jefferson River splits again into three rivers. Lewis and Clark named the westernmost river the Wisdom (now the Big Hole River that flows through the town of Wisdom), and the central river the Philanthropy (now the Beaverhead). Although tempted by the larger volume and western direction of the Wisdom, they chose the Philanthropy because it was warmer—deducing that it must flow from a greater distance into the mountains. The easternmost river, the Ruby, was never a temptation. Its source, at the Continental Divide near Yellowstone National Park, was later determined to be the most distant source of the Missouri River.

Be sure to notice the Beaverhead River just north and west of town and think about the Corps of Discovery dragging their canoes up this river. On August 4 Clark wrote, *"the method we are compelled to take to get on is fatigueing & laborious in the extreen, haul the Canoes over the rapids, which Suckceed each other every two or three hundred yards and between the water rapid oblige to towe & walke on stones the whole day except when we have poleing men wet all day Sore feet &c."*

Lewis was struggling on ahead of the main party at this point, trying ever more desperately, as summer turned into fall and the river continued to peter out, to locate Indians who could provide them with horses for travel over the mountains. At this time they still believed it would be a one-day portage over the mountains to a new river that would carry them to the Pacific. Clark was following behind with the main group—several of whom were sick and injured, and all of whom were becoming discouraged by the ever dwindling river and increasing difficulty of making mileage towards the mountains.

About ten miles upriver (south) from Twin Bridges Sacagawea recognized the "Beaver's Head" rock formation off to the right, and the captains felt reassured they were heading in the right direction to find the Shoshoni and horses. Many people today question how appropriate the name is for this rock formation. I think it's a valid question if you just view it from the main road, but I've found the formation actually looks more like a beaver if you explore farther north and east off the main road—as the Native Americans would have done in their normal daily life.

Today Twin Bridges offers cabins, a motel, small restaurants, grocery store, and a rest area with water and restrooms on the river.

Beaverhead Rock Monument,
Twin Bridges, MT

Historical Association
Twin Bridges, MT

Zip: 59754

★ **Chamber of Commerce:** PO Box 134

1) Hemingway's Cabins and Fly Shop ($$), 406-684-5648

2) King's Motel ($), 800-222-5510

▲ Hemingway's Cabins and Fly Shop, lawn with bath house and showers, 406-684-5648

Dillon, MT

Population: 4,000

Located in the southwestern corner of the state, Dillon is the county seat of Beaverhead County and the home of Western Montana College of the University of Montana. Named after Sydney Dillon, president of the Union Pacific Railroad, the town was built as the railroad pushed north in 1880 to haul gold from Butte. Notice the attractive architecture of the courthouse, railroad station (now the visitor center), and Western Montana College (south end of town).

Today agriculture is the main industry in this area, and Dillon seems to be a young and active town. Although it's a little too large to walk around, it's flat and easy to ride anywhere on your bicycle. There is a good selection of motels, restaurants, food shopping, and campgrounds.

Kids love fire drills in Dillon, MT.

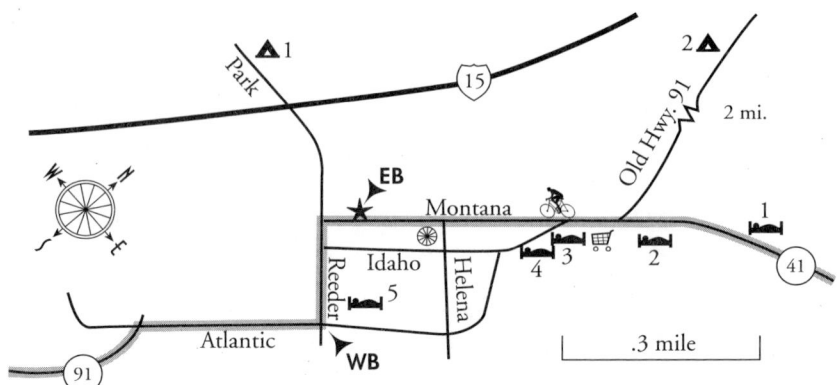

Dillon, MT — Zip: 59725

★ **Chamber of Commerce:** Box 425, 406-683-5511,
www.bmt.net/~chamber, chamber@bmt.net

🛏 1) Sacagawea Motel ($), 775 N Montana, 406-683-2381

2) Best Western Paradise Inn ($$), 650 N Montana, 406-683-4214

3) Super 8 Motel ($$), 550 N Montana, 800-800-8000

4) Sundowner Motel ($), 500 N Montana, 800-524-9746

5) Centennial Inn B&B ($$), 122 S Washington, 406-683-4454

▲ 1) KOA, E Park St. (from Reeder St.), convenient, pool, 406-683-2749.
If mosquitoes are a problem, try the drier Skyline (see 2 below).

2) Skyline RV Park, 2.5 relatively flat mi. north on Old Hwy. 91, sloping dry
ground, not much grass or shade, good restrooms with showers, laundry,
406-683-4692

✳ Bad Beaver Bike and Ski, 25 E Helena, 406-683-9292

Special Events

Jaycee Rodeo and Concert, Labor Day weekend
Beaverhead County Fair, week before Labor Day

*Montana
traffic jam*

LEMHI PASS ROUTE

Clark Canyon Reservoir and Dam

Twenty miles upriver (south) from Dillon, Clark Canyon Reservoir offers two possibilities for camping. This is the general location of Camp Fortunate for the Corps of Discovery, although the actual site is now buried under the reservoir.

The story of Lewis forging ahead with a small party to find the source of Horse Prairie Creek, cross the Continental Divide at Lemhi Pass, drink from the headwaters of the Columbia River, and finally make contact with the Shoshonis is a spectacular adventure—especially as told by Stephen Ambrose in *Undaunted Courage*. Ever more desperate to find Indians and horses as the river petered out, the mountains loomed, and winter approached, Lewis and a small band of men finally saw an Indian scout, who ran away from them. Later that day Lewis caught up with two Indian women, convinced them he was friendly, and finally met with the Shoshoni leaders.

Although the Indians suspected that Lewis was leading them into a trap, they finally followed their leader, Chief Cameahwait back over Lemhi Pass to find the rest of the Corps of Discovery and help transport their baggage over the pass. The story of the emotional meeting of Chief Cameahwait and Sacagawea back at Camp Fortunate—when they discovered they were brother and sister—is one more incredible example of truth being stranger than fiction. Although these Indians were frightened and poor in all resources, they offered everything they had for the success of the Corps of Discovery. Even though the expedition was sometimes clobbered by bad luck, this was a case of incredibly good luck—hence the name of Camp Fortunate.

▲ 1) Clark Canyon Reservoir NFS Campground, 19 mi. south of Dillon and 12 mi. east of Grant, off I-15 on Lemhi Pass route, pretty location on lake, windy, no shade/grass/privacy, covered picnic tables, water, pit toilets

2) Armstead Campground, 19 mi. south of Dillon and 12 mi. east of Grant, east side of I-15 across from Clark Canyon Reservoir, 406-683-4199, more sheltered, grass, showers, laundry

Grant, MT

Population: 35

Twelve miles farther west is the "town" of Grant, a road intersection and a former stagecoach stop on the Dillon-Salmon run. Later it was a stop on the Gilmore and Pittsburgh Railroad, whose Galloping Goose rail-bus is still parked here. The Horse Prairie Hilton is a rustic rambling B&B with a "big sky" view all around.

Zip: 59725

▬ & **▲** Horse Prairie Hilton ($–$$), Hwy. 324, 406-681-3144; restored ranch house and former stagecoach stop; bar and lounge; hot tub; accommodations include B&B rooms, kitchenette unit, hunters' lodge, and tenting; full breakfast; dinner available; reservations recommended.

Horse Prairie Hilton at the stage stop, Grant, MT

LEMHI PASS, MONTANA/IDAHO BORDER

If you made it to the top of the Continental Divide here, you deserve some time for rest and reflection. Lewis arrived here with a small party on August 12, 1805. Revel in your accomplishment, as Lewis did on August 12. *"After refreshing ourselves we proceeded on to the top of the dividing ridge from which I discovered immence ranges of high mountains still to the West of us with their tops partially covered with snow. I now decended the mountain about 3/4 of a mile which I found much steeper than on the opposite side, to a handsome bold running Creek of cold Clear water. here I first tasted the water of the great Columbia river. after a short halt we continued our march along the Indian road."*

Although Lewis wrote nothing of his feelings at this moment, most historians speculate that he must have been disappointed to look west and see nothing but a series of massive snow-capped peaks instead of a broad gentle river flowing to the Pacific. I'm not convinced he was discouraged. I have looked both east and west, seen the same view of many confusing mountains, and thought optimistically: If a series of rivers can flow eastward through that tangle of mountains, there's no reason a series of rivers can't flow westward through a similar tangle of mountains.

It's worth a short walk down to the Sacagawea Memorial, where Horse Prairie Creek first emerges from a small spring. Although Lewis and Clark—and some writers—claim this is *the source* of the Missouri River, the source of the Red Rock River (a neighboring tributary of the Ruby/Jefferson/Missouri River) is technically the farthest point from the mouth of the Missouri, and therefore is officially considered *the source*. *"two miles below McNeal had exultingly stood with a foot on each side of this little rivulet and thanked his god that he had lived to bestride the mighty & heretofore deemed endless Missouri." (August 12, Lewis)*

The author also "exultingly stood with a foot on each side of this little rivulet and thanked his god that he had lived to bestride the mighty & heretofore deemed endless Missouri." Below Lemhi Pass, MT

Salmon, ID

Population: 3,000

This delightful town is your reward for climbing over both Lemhi Pass (3,500 feet above you) and Lost Trail Pass (3,500 feet above you). You climbed one to reach Salmon, and you will climb the other to leave. So enjoy yourself here. Salmon has many opportunities for camping, lodging, shopping, and eating; and it is a flat and compact town that is easy to get around.

If you have any dreams of whitewater rafting, the Chamber of Commerce lists 27 outfitters and guides; and this would make a fine resting place for a day or two. What's rewarding to us was extremely disappointing and discouraging to Lewis and Clark. They knew they were on the west side of the Continental Divide, and they thought they would float gently down to the Pacific Ocean; but the Salmon River below here is known as the "River of No Return" for good reasons.

At first they refused to believe the Indians, who told them the Salmon was not navigable. Cameahwait *"added on further enquiry . . . that the river was confined between inacessable mountains, was very rapid and rocky insomuch that it was impossible for us to pass either by land or water down this river to the great lake where the white men lived as he had been informed. this was unwelcome information but I still hoped that this account had been exaggerated."* *(August 13, Lewis)* However, after several days of exploring the river, they reluctantly agreed and set off on foot on the most difficult and dangerous part of their trip—struggling over Lost Trail Pass and Lolo Pass in early fall snowstorms.

In 1805 Lewis and Clark were the first white men to visit this area. In 1832 Captain Bonneville drove the first wagon over the Rockies and built a fort on the Salmon River. In 1855 a Mormon group from Salt Lake City established a fort in this area and named it *Lemhi,* after a person in the Book of Mormon. In 1866 a group of prospectors from Montana discovered gold fourteen miles west of Salmon, and this led to the establishment of Salmon City in a more convenient location in 1867.

*Clark determined the Salmon River
(aka "River of No Return") was not navigable.
Below North Fork, ID*

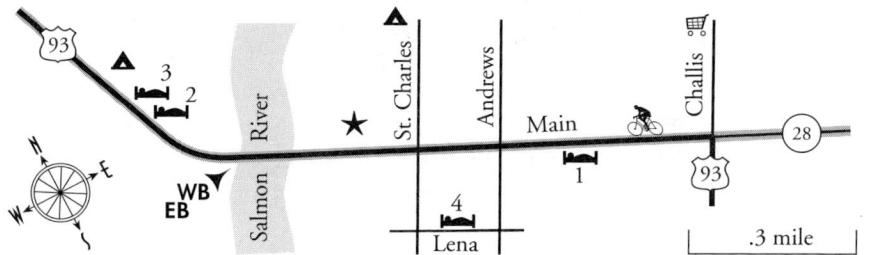

Salmon, ID — Zip: 83467

★ **Chamber of Commerce:** 200 Main, 208-756-2100

🛏 1) Motel DeLuxe ($), 112 S Church, 208-756-2231

2) Stagecoach Inn ($$), 201 Hwy. 93 N, 208-756-2919

3) Wagons West Motel ($$), 503 Hwy. 93 N, 800-756-4281

4) Heritage Inn B&B ($), 510 Lena, 208-756-3174

▲ 1) Century II Campground, 603 Hwy. 93 N, laundry, 208-756-2063

2) Salmon Meadows, St. Charles 3 blocks N of Main, grass, shade, laundry, showers, 208-756-2640

North Fork, ID

Population: 250

Twenty-one miles north of Salmon is the tiny village of North Fork, where the North Fork of the Salmon River joins the main river. There are two motels, two restaurants, and a campground. This is also a staging area for many raft trips on the river.

If you want to take a side detour down the river towards Shoup on 18 miles of paved road along the river, you can get a good idea of the rugged canyon that scared Lewis and Clark. There is a pleasant café with a couple of rustic cabins at Shoup.

Zip: 83466

1) North Fork Motel and Campground ($$), 208-865-2412

2) River's Fork Inn ($$), 208-865-2301

3) Shoup General Store and Cabins ($), 18 mi. west of North Fork on Salmon River Rd., Shoup, 83469, 208-394-2125

4) 100 Acre Wood B&B, 3 mi. north on Route 93, 208-865-2165

1) North Fork Motel and Campground, 208-865-2412

2) Wagon Hammer Springs Campground and RV Park, 1 mi. South on Route 93, 208-865-2477

Former gold rush town and capital of Montana Territory, Bannack, MT

BIG HOLE ROUTE

mile BH-262

Bannack, MT

Population: ghosts

Once a wild and booming gold mining town in the 1860s, Bannack was the first capital of the Montana Territory. Clark and his party passed right by millions of dollars of gold in Grasshopper Creek on their return trip in 1806. Too bad they weren't looking for minerals as well as flora and fauna. Bannack was gradually abandoned during the 1900s, until the state park service took it over and started restoring buildings and offering guided tours. Today it is a fascinating collection of 60 buildings that are only partially restored. It is a true ghost town with no commercialization.

Bannack is located 4 miles south of Route 278 about 21 miles west of Dillon. The access road is paved for 3 miles and pretty good dirt for the last mile.

Jackson, MT

Population: 75

Jackson is an oasis 48 miles west of Dillon and 21 miles south of Wisdom. The tiny town exists to take advantage of the hot springs here, and you can find a room at the lodge and meals at the lodge or across the street at Rose's Cantina. If you missed the chance to get a Stetson in St. Joseph, you can get a custom made cowboy hat from Buffalo Gal in the converted church here.

The Big Hole Valley is a high valley bordered by the Bitterroot Mountains to the west. Although not obvious from the road, this valley is the home of many large and prosperous cattle ranches.

Zip: 59736

Jackson Hot Springs Lodge, 406-834-3151

Antelope and cattle sharing high pasture in the Big Hole, near Wisdom, MT

Wisdom, MT

Population: 135

Wisdom is another oasis located 21 miles north of Jackson and 56 miles east of Darby, the next significant town with services. Located at the intersection of two highways, the town has a campground, a small food market, excellent art gallery, motel and restaurants.

This valley is also known as the Land of 10,000 Haystacks. Many areas in the world have their own ways of stacking and storing hay, and the Beaverslides of this area are unique. The movable racks lift hay onto the top of a large stack, and then a fence is built around the stack.

Zip: 59761

Nez Perce Motel ($), 406-689-3254

1) American Legion Park, 0.3 flat mi. west of town, open, no shade, water, pit toilet

2) May Creek NFS Campground, 17 mi. west on Route 43, pleasant high elevation wooded campground with water and pit toilets, 406-689-2431

Beaverslide and the breadloaf-like mounds of hay it builds,
near Wisdom, MT

BIG HOLE NATIONAL BATTLEFIELD

Located ten miles west of Wisdom on Route 43, the visitor center run by the National Park Service is definitely worth an hour or two. This is the place where Chief Joseph and his "non-treaty" Nez Perce were camped in 1877 near the end of "the Indian Wars" when they were surprised by General Gibbon's army. After the U.S. Army slaughtered many women and children in a surprise early morning attack, the Nez Perce fought bravely—shocking the army by winning the battle. But they eventually lost the war—massively outmanned and outgunned.

The whole story of the Nez Perce, including their kindness to Lewis and Clark in western Idaho, their banishment to a barren reservation, the 90% reduction in size of this reservation when gold was discovered on it, the rabid pursuit of the "non-treaty" group who refused to be mistreated, and their final banishment to an alien reservation in Oklahoma is fascinating, tragic, and moving.
For more information: Box 237, Wisdom, MT, 406-689-3155, www.nps.gov/biho

mile LP-385

RESUME: COMBINED LEMHI PASS AND BIG HOLE ROUTE

Sula, MT

Population: 10

Sula is located at the head of the Bitterroot Valley, 13 miles and 2,000 feet below Lost Trail Pass and the Continental Divide. Today downtown Sula is a compact community that includes a general store, restaurant, campground, and cabins.

Sula was originally known as Ross' Hole, named after Ursula Ross, the first white person born in this area. This is the place where Lewis and Clark met a very different kind of Indian. Their lighter complexion and strange Salish dialect suggested they might be the mythical "Welsh Indians," led to America in 1170 by the Welsh Prince Madoc. Like the myth of the Northwest Passage, the myth of the Welsh Indians took a long time to die. The captains mistakenly called these Indians the

Gorgeous campsite on the Bitterroot River reserved for bicycle tourers, near Sula, MT

"Flatheads," even though they did not press their foreheads into a flattened shape, as Indians farther west on the Columbia actually did.

The view from the Jake Wetzsteon pioneer home in Sula can be seen in the large Charlie Russell mural of "Lewis and Clark Meeting the Flathead Indians at Ross' Hole" in the Montana Capitol building (see Helena).

Zip: 59871

1) Lost Trail Hot Springs Resort, 6 mi. south (east) of Sula, cabins, motel, restaurant, hot mineral pool, hot tub, sauna, 800-825-3574.

2) Camp Creek Inn B&B, 3.5 mi. south (east) of Sula, cabins and rooms in historic ranch house, 406-821-3508.

1) Sula KOA, cabins, cottages, tent sites, hot tub, camp store, restaurant, 800-KOA-9867

2) Spring Gulch NFS Campground, 3 mi. north of Sula, private grassy and wooded sites on the Bitterroot River with water and pit toilets, special area next to river for bicycle campers! (See photo on previous page)

Darby, MT

Population: 800

The Lewis & Clark Trail runs north along the Bitterroot River, and both traffic and population increase as you proceed towards Missoula. Wilderness turns into civilization pretty quickly near Darby. Land is no longer cheap, as people from Missoula and a few rich and famous Californians have spread up this beautiful valley.

After being called Doolittle and then Harrison, Postmaster James Darby renamed the town after himself in 1888, and the name stuck. Darby has experienced several different booms and busts during its history. In the late 1800s it was first a fur trading post and then a mining town. In the early 1900s there was a logging boom for the copper mining industry and then an apple boom. Later came growth in agriculture, ranching, and timber; and more recently outdoor recreation in all seasons. Today Darby provides a surprising amount of services for a population of only 800.

Zip: 59829

1) Wilderness Motel ($), 308 S Main, 800-820-2554

2) Bud & Shirley's Motel ($$), 406-821-3401

3) Honey's Motel ($), 406-821-3111

1) Lick Creek CG, 6 mi. north on Route 93, grass, shade, showers, laundry, 406-821-3840

2) Bitterroot Family Campground, 8 mi. north on Route 93, 406-363-2430

Hamilton, MT

Population: 3,000

The history of Hamilton is very different from most towns in this area. During the 1880s the "immigrant copper king," Marcus Daly, bought several sawmills in the beautiful Bitterroot Valley and decided to design and build a town here. The town was named after James Hamilton, one of the developers Daly brought in from Minnesota.

Rocky Mountain Spotted Fever was first detected here in 1873, and the Rocky Mountain Laboratory researched this disease for many years. It took 33 years to discover the disease was spread by ticks and then develop vaccinations and medicines to control it.

As traffic and population continue to increase on the approach to Missoula, it is pleasant to get off the main highway (Route 93) and ride down the Eastside Highway between Hamilton and Florence. Two miles north of Hamilton on the Eastside Highway, Marcus Daly built himself a 42-room Georgian mansion with gorgeous views in all directions. The Daly Mansion is worth at least a quick stop to look around, and perhaps a more detailed tour.

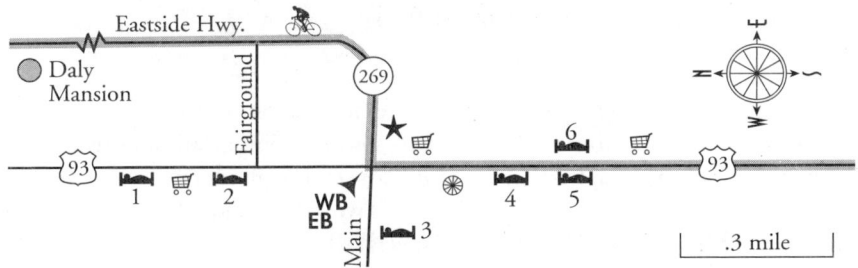

Hamilton, MT — Zip: 59840

★ **Bitterroot Valley Chamber of Commerce:** 105 E Main, 363-2400, www.bvchamber.com, localinfo@bvchamber.com

🛏 1) Super 8 Motel ($$), 1325 N 1st, 800-800-8000

2) Comfort Inn ($$), 1113 N 1st, 800-442-INNS

3) City Center Motel ($), 415 W Main, 406-363-1651

4) Deffy's Motel ($), 321 S 1st, 800-363-1305

5) Best Western Hamilton Inn ($$), 409 S 1st, 800-426-4586

6) Bitterroot Motel ($), 408 S 1st, 406-363-1142

▲ Angler's Roost, 3.5 flat mi. south of Hamilton, next to river, poor grass, good shade, clean bathrooms with showers, camp store.

✳ Valley Bike & Ski, 219 S 1st, 406-363-4428

mile LP-420

Stevensville, MT

Population: 1,300

About halfway between Hamilton and Missoula, Stevensville is the home of St. Mary's Mission Church, the first church established in Montana. After several Flathead delegations to St. Louis requested that "the black robes" come to their area, the Jesuits responded by sending Father deSmet to build a mission in 1841. Although things went well for almost ten years, the fathers never quite realized that they were primarily wanted for their magical powers to help the Flatheads succeed in hunting and fighting other tribes. When things went sour for the Flatheads, they gradually drove the missionaries out of the area. The church is well worth a quick visit—only a few blocks west of our route on 4th Street.

In 1863 John Winslett and J.K. Houk established a store here. A year later the settlers named the town after Isaac Stevens, the first governor of the Washington Territory. Are you surprised to learn that this area was once part of the Washington Territory?

Lolo, MT

Population: 2,800

Although technically a town, Lolo appears more like a series of strip malls at a major intersection on our route. This has always been an important intersection—the start of the trail (now highway) over Lolo Pass. Although it's possible to find most of the services you need in Lolo, I think it's worth it to ride the ten relatively easy miles into Missoula to enjoy that very special town.

Lolo was an important stop for Lewis and Clark. They camped here on September 9 and 10 and named it Traveller's Rest, as they rested and made final preparations for their journey over the mountains. This is where they learned that the Indian hunting parties travelled to the eastern plains using a route directly eastward through Missoula. The Indians told them they could get to the Gates of the Mountains (just downriver from Helena) in four days. Although you can imagine how Lewis and Clark must have felt—having just travelled 52 days from the Gates of the Mountains, and now facing winter conditions in the Bitterroots—there is no mention of disappointment or discouragement in their journals.

Zip: 59847

▭   Day's Inn ($$), 406-721-2121

▲   Bitterroot Gateway RV Park, mostly permanent RVs, off highway, grass, shade, showers, 406-273-6034

Missoula, MT

Population: 52,000

Missoula is both the cultural and commercial center of western Montana. The hometown of the University of Montana attracts many well educated people who want to take advantage of both the university and the myriad of year round recreational opportunities here. The area still produces timber and paper products, and some light manufacturing and medical companies have grown up around the university.

Although Missoula is not directly on two of our bicycle routes, it is only a ten-mile relatively flat side trip from Lolo, and well worth the effort if time permits. In fact, it's a great place for a rest day. There is good camping, a wide variety of lodging and restaurants, and many bicycle shops. If you have any suspicions about your equipment, this is the place to get it checked or fixed. It's a long way in either direction before you will see this level of expertise and availability of parts.

The city is flat, but it's large enough that you will want your bike for getting around. Although traffic can be heavy on the main roads, there are many opportunities to take parallel roads with much lighter traffic. The older and very pleasant downtown area just north of the river contains some inexpensive motels and a wide variety of good restaurants, bars, and shops. Entering town from the southwest, Route 93 turns into Brooks, where there are several newer motels, malls, chain restaurants, and stores. The University of Montana campus and residential area are on the east side of town, just south of the river.

Check the Visitors Bureau for many interesting things to do in town. A few ideas: The U.S Forest Service offers tours of the Smokejumper's Center just beyond the airport on Route 93. Ride and walk around the University and hike up to the "M" for some exercise and a great view. Visit Adventure Cycling's headquarters in an old church on Pine St. downtown. Check a bike shop to learn about mountain biking in Rattlesnake Canyon just north of town. Do laundry!

To learn more about the history of the area, visit the Historical Museum at Fort Missoula. The U.S. Army arrived in Lolo to try to stop Chief Joseph and the Nez Perce in 1877 (see Fort Fizzle, page 176). They then constructed Fort Missoula at the current more strategic location. In the late 1890s this fort was the home of a black army bicycle corps that rode 2,000 miles to St. Louis to demonstrate the effectiveness of infantry troops on bicycles. The army was not impressed.

In earlier pre-history this convergence of five valleys was once the bottom of Lake Missoula, covered by 2,000 feet of water. That's well above the "M" on the hill by the university.

Although Clark never made it to Missoula, Lewis passed through what is now the downtown area on his eastbound return trip. On their westbound trip they went down the Bitterroot River and camped for two days at Traveller's Rest (now called Lolo) in preparation for the dreaded trip across the Bitterroot Mountains. Today it is one of the most beautiful sections of our route.

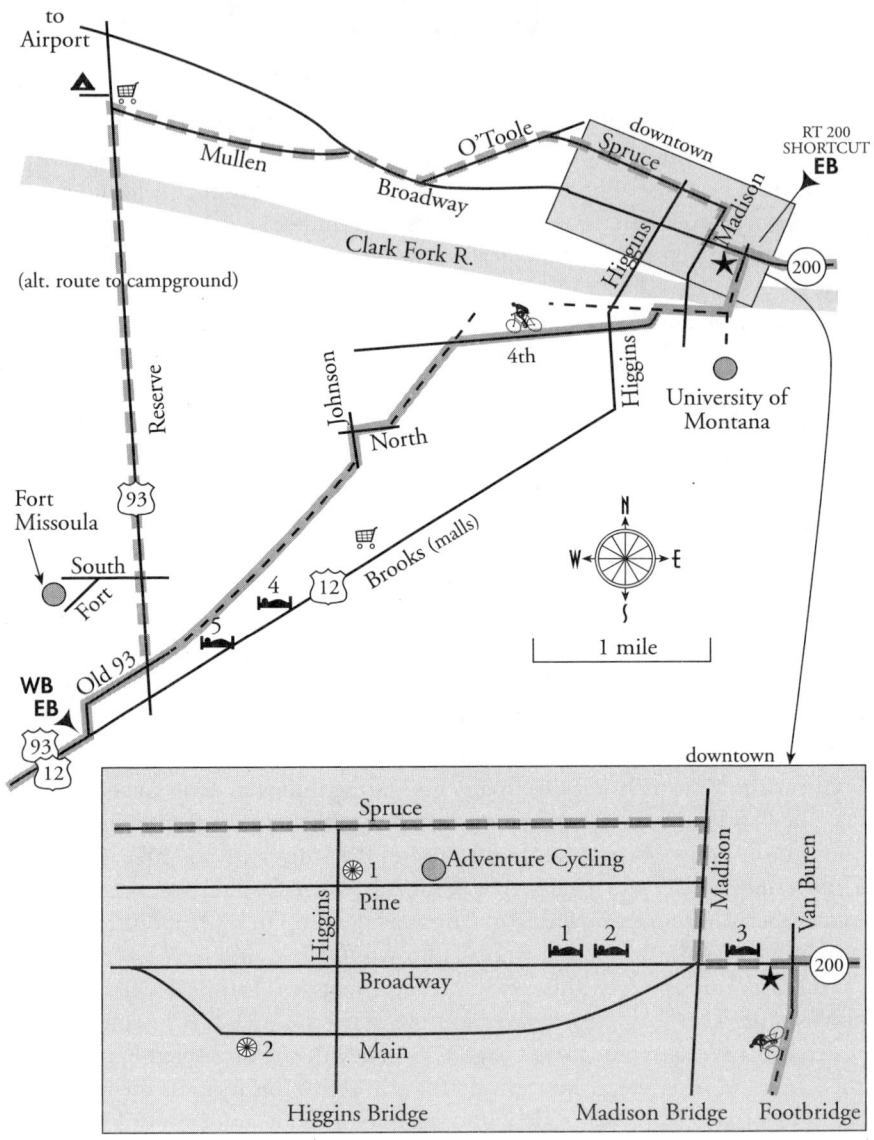

Missoula, MT — Zip: 59801

★ **Convention and Visitor's Bureau:** 825 E Front, 406-543-6623, www.missoulachamber.com

🛏 The Visitor's Bureau lists 41 motels and 5 B&Bs. A small sample in convenient locations:

  1) Bel Aire Motel ($$), 300 E Broadway, 800-543-3184

2) City Center Motel ($), 338 E Broadway, 406-543-3193

3) Creekside Motel ($$$), 630 E Broadway, 800-551-2387

4) Brooks Motor Inn ($$), 3333 Brooks, 800-538-3260

5) Super 8 Motel ($$), 3901 Brooks, 888-900-9022

▲   Missoula KOA, 3695 Tina (off Reserve), 800-562-5366

✷ 1) Bike Doctor, 420 N Higgins, 721-5357

   2) Missoula Bicycle Works, 113 W Main

ROUTE 200 SHORTCUT ROUTE

Augusta, MT

Population: 300

Although it adds 21 miles to the distance between Great Falls and Lincoln, some people may want to detour through this small town to break up the trip and avoid some hills and traffic.

Zip: 59410

1) Wagons West Motel ($), 406-562-3295

2) Bunkhouse Inn ($), 406-562-3780

Lincoln, MT

Population: 530

At an elevation of 4,500 feet, Lincoln is a cool oasis about halfway between Great Falls and Missoula. If you're not camping, it's a "must" overnight stop, and fortunately, it's a good stop for everyone. This is a "western" town designed for both residents and tourists who enjoy an active outdoor life—hunting, fishing, snowmobiling, hiking, mountain biking, cross-country skiing, horseback riding. Many buildings are solid and rustic log cabin style, and restaurants serve hearty steak dinners—32-ounce T-bone and 16-ounce filet mignon.

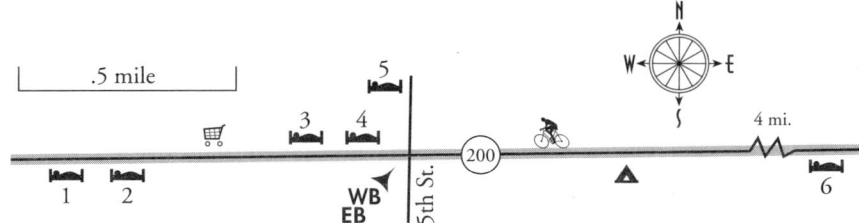

Lincoln, MT — Zip: 59639

★   **Lincoln Valley Chamber of Commerce:** Box 985, 406-362-4949

1) Leeper's Ponderosa Motel ($), 888-362-2976

2) Three Bears Motel ($), 800-838-9771

3) Blue Sky Motel ($), 800-293-4521

4) Snowie Pines Inn Motel ($), 800-809-2463

5) Hotel Lincoln ($), 877-362-8814

6) 7-Up Ranch and Supper Club ($), cabins, motel, and restaurant 5 mi. east on Hwy. 200, 406-362-4255

▲ Hooper Park and Campground, quiet off road, shady, satisfactory restroom, no shower

Special Events

Rodeo, July 4
Fine Arts Festival, early August
Fiddler's Contest, late August
Golf Tournament, Labor Day

Ovando, MT

Population: 100

It's possible to spend a night in this tiny town a half mile off the main highway. When you make reservations, I recommend checking the hours of the one restaurant in town.

Zip: 59854

▙ Blackfoot Commercial Co. B&B ($), 406-793-5555

▲ Camping is allowed behind the museum. There is an outhouse, and water is available at Blackfoot Commercial Co. across the street.

I. Over the Bitterroots

Missoula, MT to Lewiston, ID

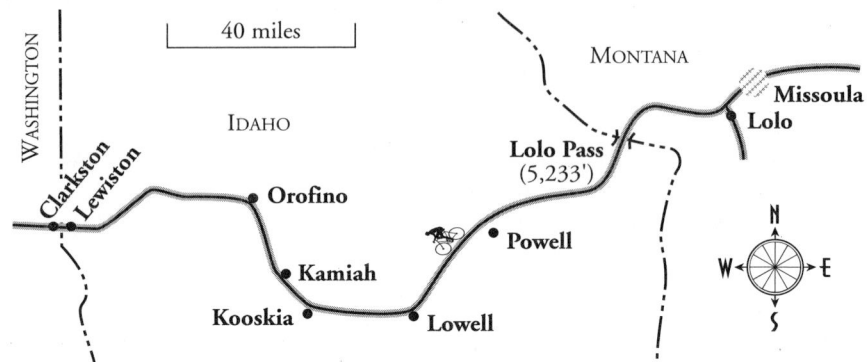

Although September days can sometimes be warm and beautiful in the Rockies, the Corps of Discovery encountered an early snowstorm that almost wiped them out. The twelve days from Traveller's Rest (Lolo, MT) to the Weippe Prairie (Weippe, ID; pronounced Wee-ipe) were the most difficult of the entire expedition. Today this part of the Trail is arguably the most beautiful.

In 1854 John Mullan considered Lolo Pass for the Army road he built across the Rockies, but instead he decided to follow the Clark Fork River northwest from Missoula. When the railroad came, it also followed the Clark Fork, and the highway later followed the railroad.

It wasn't until the 1930s and the Great Depression that the Civilian Conservation Corps built a single-lane dirt road across Lolo Pass. They mostly followed an ancient trail along the ridges known to the Nez Perce as "the road to buffalo country," and to the Montana Salish as "the trail to the Nez Perce." This is the trail followed by Lewis and Clark, and it is now called the Lolo Motorway (Road 500). Even today this is a rough single-lane dirt road, often clear of snow for only a couple of months each year. It is accessible to four-wheel drive vehicles and mountain bikers prepared for several days of remote wilderness. Contact the Forest Service (Powell Ranger Station below) if you want to pursue this route, since access will be limited during the coming bicentennial years.

Our route along Highway 12, which follows the Lochsa (meaning "rough water") River, was not completed until 1962. Once you cross Lolo Pass, it's 77 miles of glorious downhill and spectacular scenery along the rushing river.

But it was different for the Corps of Discovery. Instead of leading the group along the established Native American trails that followed the ridges, Old Toby, the Shoshoni guide, led them down the steep slopes to the river in the rugged canyon.

The expedition struggled along the south side of the canyon and camped near Powell on September 14. Clark wrote, *"Here we wer compelled to kill a Colt for our men & Selves to eat for the want of meat & we named the South fork Colt killed Creek . . . The Mountains which we passed to day much worst than yesterday the last excessively bad & Thickly Strowed with falling timber & Pine Spruc fur Hackmatak & Tamerack, Steep & Stoney our men and horses much fatigued."*

By this time, the captains knew they couldn't make it on the route along the river. Near Whitehouse Pond they climbed 2,000 feet back up to the ridge and camped September 15 at Snowbank Camp on what is now the 500 Road.

On September 16 they struggled along the ridge all day in a snowstorm. Clark wrote, *"I have been wet and as cold in every part as I ever was in my life, indeed I was at one time fearfull my feet would freeze in the thin mockersons which I wore."* That night they killed a second horse for dinner at Lonesome Cove Camp.

On September 17 they awoke to find their horses scattered, and they couldn't get started until 1 pm. Another horse for dinner.

By September 18 they were desperate, and they decided that Clark should go ahead with some hunters. Lewis and the main party ate a concoction of portable soup, bear oil, and twenty pounds of candles. Unappealing as this sounds, keep in mind that candles were made from animal tallow, and they contained at least some nourishment. On this day Clark's party ate nothing, but they came upon a place where they could view a plain in the distance. They named this spot Spirit Revival Ridge. It took two more miserable days to reach the Nez Perce village on the Weippe Prairie. Clark was able to send food back to the main party on September 21, and the next day the main party arrived at Weippe.

After their twelve-day ordeal, the men stumbled into the Nez Perce village more dead than alive. Gorging themselves on an unfamiliar diet of roots and fish compounded their starvation with massive dysentery.

According to oral legend, the Nez Perce held a council to decide what to do with these pathetically weak strangers. Living too far to the west to trade with white Americans, the Nez Perce had only a few old guns and iron goods, like pots, pans, and tools. They were constantly harassed by every surrounding tribe—all of whom were better armed and equipped. The modern guns and ammunition of the Lewis and Clark expedition would make them the best armed tribe west

June in the Bitterroots near Darby, MT

of the Mississippi River, and the horses and other equipment and supplies would be a bonus.

Their decision was easy, quick, and rational; kill the strangers and take their equipment. However, before they could execute this decision, a respected elderly woman named Watkuweis (meaning "returned from a far country") stepped forward and convinced the chiefs to treat the strangers well. She had previously been kidnapped by Blackfeet Indians and later treated well by white men.

Watkuweis carried the day, and the Nez Perce became loyal and helpful friends to the expedition—resupplying them and holding their horses until they returned the next Spring. Once again, the expedition was saved by a woman. A related tragic irony of this happy experience is the terrible way the United States treated the Nez Perce 70 years later—a story that can be seen and heard at both the Big Hole National Battlefield near Wisdom, Montana, and the Nez Perce National Historical Park near Lewiston, Idaho.

Fort Fizzle, MT

About five miles west of Lolo is a sign commemorating Fort Fizzle. It was here that Captain Rawn of the U.S. Army, along with some reluctant recruits from Missoula, erected a barricade to stop Chief Joseph and his Nez Perce band of warriors, women, and children in their attempt to escape to Canada.

When the Indians became aware of this, they climbed over the ridge to the north and proceeded down the next valley—neatly bypassing the barricade and the soldiers. Hence the name, "Fort Fizzle."

Lolo Hot Springs, MT

Population: 20

Lolo Hot Springs consists of a huge parking lot, natural hot spring pools, restaurant, convenience store, motel, RV park, and campground. It is attractive to many cyclists because of its hot springs and its convenient location 25 miles west of Lolo and 20 miles east of Powell.

Zip: 59847

🛏 1) The Fort at Lolo Hot Springs Motel ($$), 406-273-2290

▲ 1) Lewis and Clark NFS Campground, 10 mi. east of Lolo Hot Springs; woods, privacy, water, pit toilets

2) Lolo Hot Springs RV Park and Campground, 406-273-2290

3) Lee Creek NFS Campground, 1.4 mi. west of Lolo Hot Springs; woods, privacy, water, pit toilets

Powell Ranger Station

Although Powell Ranger Station is not an official town in Idaho, it's a valuable place for cyclists because of its strategic location and the services it offers. If you're not camping, the next indoor lodging is 68 miles west in Lowell. Even if you choose to camp at one of the many National Forest Service campgrounds along the river (listed below), the store and restaurant at Lochsa Lodge are the only ones for many miles.

Zip: 59847

★ Powell Ranger District, Lolo, MT 59847, 208-942-3113

🛏 Lochsa Lodge ($), restaurant, motel rooms, cabins, 208-942-3405

▲ NFS campgrounds below have water and pit toilets. More information can be obtained at the Powell Ranger Station (208-942-3113):

1) Powell, near river and Lochsa Lodge

2) Whitehouse, on river 3 mi. west of Powell

3) Wendover, on river 4 mi. west of Powell

4) Jerry Johnson, north side of road 11 mi. west of Powell

5) Wilderness Gateway, across river 38 mi. west of Powell

6) Apgar, on river 57 mi. west of Powell

Special Attraction

Lewis and Clark Trail Adventures, Box 9051, Missoula, MT 59801, 406-728-7609, 1–6 day raft trips on Lochsa and Salmon rivers; mountain bike, driving, and hiking trips on the Lolo Trail

Lochsa Lodge, Powell Ranger Station, MT

Lowell, ID

Population: 25

Lowell is the spot where the Selway (meaning "calm water") River meets the Lochsa (meaning "rough water") River to form the Clearwater River. Although there is no town as such, you will find a thriving community offering many services for cyclists just across the bridge at the Three Rivers Resort. You can shop or eat, stay in a cabin or camp, swim or soak, or arrange for a raft trip on the river. (Three Rivers Rafting, 888-926-4430, www.threeriversrafting.com, info@threeriversrafting.com)

Zip: 83539

1) Three Rivers Resort ($$), Box 61, 208-926-4430,
http://adventuresports.com/asap/resort/threerivers/welcome.htm; resort on the river with camping, motel rooms, and log cabins; pool and jacuzzis; full restaurant and camp store; raft trips available.

2) Ryan's Wilderness Inn Motel ($), 208-926-4706

1) Three Rivers Resort, see Lodging above

2) Wild Goose NFS CG, 2 mi. west of Lowell on river, water, pit toilets, 208-926-4275

Rafting on the Lochsa River near Lowell, MT

Kooskia, ID

Population: 700

Kooskia is a working town with a motel, restaurant, and medium size food market. Our bicycle route crosses the river twice to swing by the edge of downtown, although it's possible to stay on Route 12 and skip the town.

mile 2392

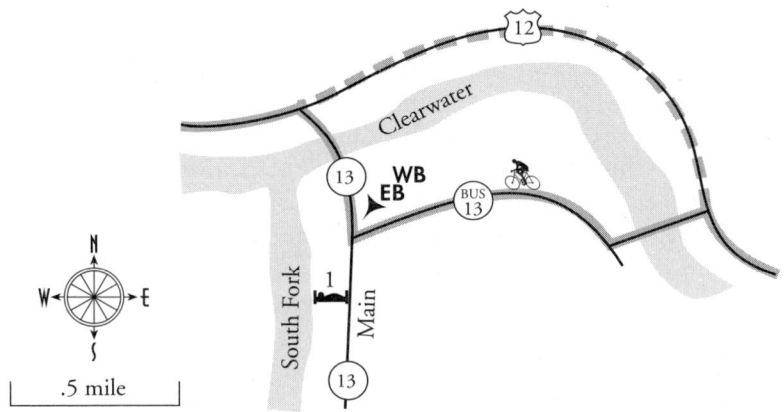

Kooskia, ID — Zip: 83539

1) Mt. Stuart Inn Motel ($), Main, 208-926-0166

2) Looking Glass Lodge B&B ($$), 208-926-0855, 9 mi. east on Route 12

3) Bear Hollow B&B ($$$), 800-831-3713, 5 mi. east on Route 12

Clearwater River near Greer, ID

Kamiah, ID

Population: 1,200

Legend says that the Heart of the Monster rock outcrop here was the source of all people. Coyote wrestled with the monster, killed it, and flung the parts all over, making all Native American tribes. Since there were no people here, he squeezed blood from the heart to make the Ne-Me-Poo (Nez Perce people).

Near Kamiah (pronounced Kam'-ee-eye) on Highway 12 is a sign commemorating the Long Camp, where Lewis and Clark camped from May 7 to June 10, 1806, on their return trip while they waited impatiently for the snow to melt in the Bitterroots so the Nez Perce could lead them back to the plains. Historians now believe the actual site of this camp was on the north side of the river just west of Kamiah, but the other facts are correct. It was a long time to sit around and wait, and they occupied their time preparing for the journey and engaging in various athletic contests with the friendly Indians. The wait was exacerbated by their lack of trade goods, for they were down to trading buttons, clothes, and other personal items for basic food.

Kamiah today has several motels, a private campground, several restaurants, and good food shopping.

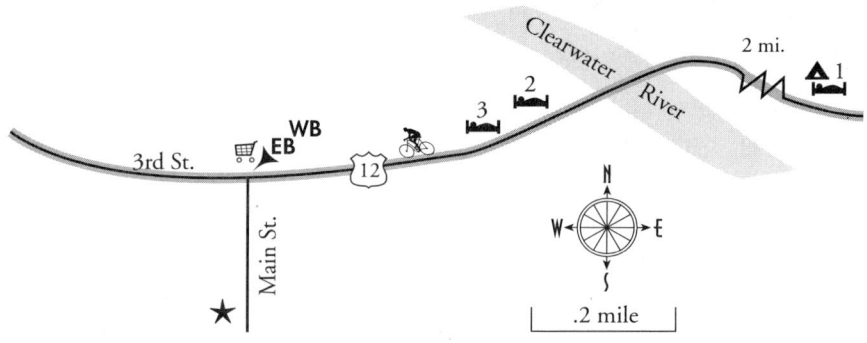

Kamiah, ID — Zip: 83536

★   **Chamber of Commerce:** 518 Main, 208-935-2290

🛏 1) Lewis Clark Resort ($$), Hwy. 12, 800-264-9943

2) Clearwater 12 Motel ($), Hwy. 12, 208-935-2671

3) Kamiah Inn Motel ($), Hwy. 12, 208-935-0040

▲   Lewis Clark Resort and RV Park, Hwy. 12, showers, pool, hot tub, 800-264-9943

Orofino, ID

Population: 3,000

The area along Orofino Creek where it joins the Clearwater River languished for 50 years after Lewis and Clark passed through. In 1836 Henry Spalding founded the Nez Perce Indian Mission at Lapwai and printed the first Bible in the Northwest. In 1848 the area became part of the Oregon Territory, and then in 1855 the Walla Walla Treaty made it part of the Nez Perce Indian Reservation.

Everything changed in 1860, when gold was discovered on Orofino Creek, leading to the establishment of the town of Pierce. "Oro fino" means "fine gold" in Spanish. Always rich in natural resources, the area later turned to logging, and the railroad was extended upriver from Lewiston in 1899. In 1972 the Dworshak Dam was built to block off the North Fork of the Clearwater River, thereby creating the 53-mile Dworshak Reservoir. This is the highest "straight-axis concrete gravity dam in the Western World" and the "largest ever constructed by the Army Corps of Engineers." Have you ever noticed that almost every dam is the biggest and the best if you define its category carefully? As usual, it is surrounded by many boat ramps and remote camping areas, but these campgrounds are too distant to be useful to bicycle tourers.

At the confluence of the North Fork and the main Clearwater River, four miles west of town on the north side of the river, is the huge Dworshak National Fish Hatchery. This is the "largest combination producer of steelhead trout and spring chinook salmon in the world." Another three miles beyond and up a steep hill is the dam (not damn!) visitor center, with displays, a tour of the dam, and fantastic views of the dam and reservoir. Then it's seven miles back to town to return to the

Dugout replica at Canoe Camp, Orofino, ID

main route. If you're wondering whether it's worth the trek, the Chamber of Commerce in town has additional information to help you decide.

While Lewis and some of the men were recovering their health and energy with the Nez Perce on the Weippe Prairie, Clark and the rest of the party moved down to Twisted Hair's River Camp on the Clearwater River near present day Orofino. Four miles downstream, at the confluence with the North Fork, they established their Canoe Camp, where they spent ten days burning and digging out five large logs to make canoes. Today there is a pleasant park at this site on the south side of the river, displaying an example of a dugout canoe. As you continue your ride down the river, ponder what it must have been like shooting the rapids in long, narrow, heavy dugout canoes.

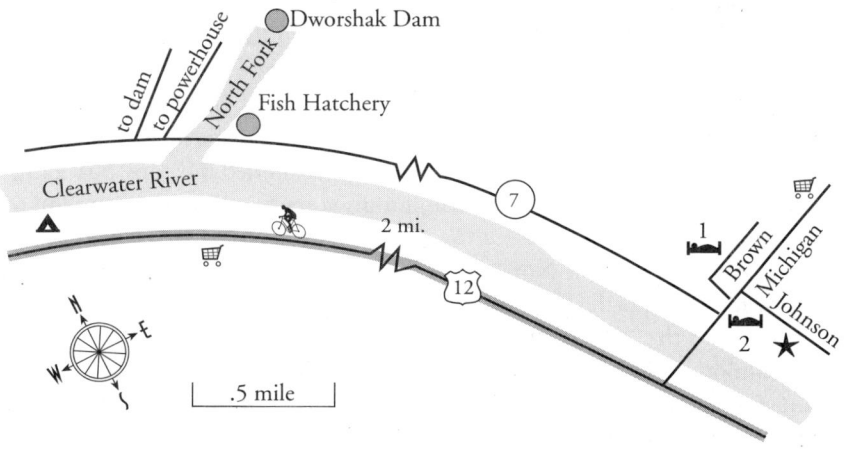

Orofino, ID — Zip: 83544

★   **Orofino Chamber of Commerce**
     217 1st, 208-476-4335, orofinochamber@clearwater.net

🛏 1) White Pine Motel ($), 222 Brown, 208-476-7093

   2) Hegelson Place Hotel ($), 125 Johnson Ave., 208-476-5729

▲   Pink House Recreation Site, RVs and tenting, showers (under construction in 2000)

Lewiston, ID, Clarkston, WA

Populations: 31,000 — 7,000

mile 2465

Located where the Clearwater River joins the Snake River at Idaho's western boundary with Washington, Lewiston is the only seaport in Idaho. Timber, grain, and other agricultural products are still carried downriver to the Pacific by barge. Today Potlach is the largest employer in Lewiston, producing timber and paper products.

Tourism is another important industry, and Lewiston is the gateway to the Hells Canyon National Recreation Area and all its activities. Along the Idaho-Oregon border the Snake River cuts the deepest gorge in the United States for over 70 miles. More than 8,000 feet deep, it is deeper than the Grand Canyon. Although it is possible to drive around its edges for several hundred miles and catch glimpses of its majesty, or hike some of the 1,000 miles of wilderness trails, the best way for cyclists to experience it is on a 1–2 day jet boat trip or a 1–6 day raft trip. Advance reservations are a good idea, although it is sometimes possible to get last minute bookings on trips. This is a great time and place to take a break from the bike for an unforgettable experience. The Chamber of Commerce is happy to provide more information—either in advance or after you arrive.

Originally called Tsceminicum, the Nez Perce long used this sheltered canyon area as a place to spend winters. Lewis and Clark arrived here on October 10, 1805, and traded with the Indians to get more dogs. All but Clark learned to enjoy dogs as food, and they preferred this to the plentiful salmon. After their long stay upriver at Canoe Camp, they were happy to make good time racing down the river towards the Pacific. Their journals suggest they were taking more risks than usual through the many difficult rapids.

The first steam-powered sternwheeler made it up through the rapids of the Columbia and Snake all the way to Lenore in June, 1861. However, as the river level dropped during the summer, boats could only make it to Lewiston, and that's how it became the major inland port for goods transported between Portland and the mines farther upriver. It's interesting that miners came to this area from the west rather than from the east.

Clarkston started out as Jawbone Flats, the ferry landing across the river from its big sister, Lewiston. Later it was developed as a planned, irrigated agricultural

Jet boat on the Snake River in Hell's Canyon, near Lewiston, ID

community by big money from New England. Its name was later changed to Concord, and finally to Clarkston to honor William Clark. Although you might expect twin cities that face each other across both a river and a state line to be rivals, they feel more like a single town. In two visits I have yet to sense the kind of rivalry evident in other similar situations.

Twelve miles east of Lewiston is the Nez Perce National Historical Park (Box 100, Spalding, ID 83450, 208-843-2261, www.nps.gov/nepe). It's only a mile off our route, and well worth at least an hour to see their summary movie about the history of the Nez Perce, an example of a dugout canoe, and other interesting exhibits.

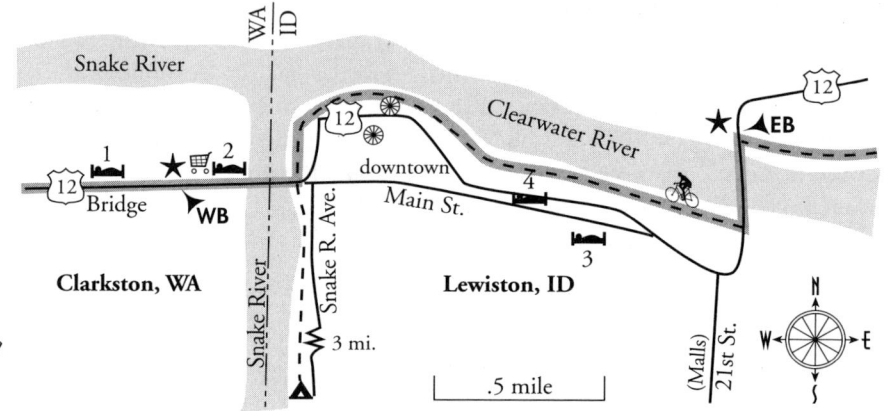

Lewiston, ID — Zip: 83051, **Clarkston, WA** — Zip: 99403

★   **Lewiston Chamber of Commerce**
     111 Main, seasonal visitor center north of Clearwater River bridge,
     800-473-3543, www.lewistonchamber.com

     Clarkston Chamber of Commerce: 502 Bridge St., 509-758-7712,
     www.clarkston.com

🛏 1) Hacienda Lodge Motel ($), 812 Bridge, Clarkston,

     2) Motel 6 ($), 222 Bridge, Clarkston, 800-466-8356

     3) Riverview Inn ($$), 1325 Main, Lewiston, 800-806-ROOM

     4) Howard Johnson's Motel ($$), 1716 Main, Lewiston, 800-IGO-HOJO

▲ 1) Hells Gate State Park, 4 mi. south of Lewiston on Snake River Ave., shade, grass, showers, 208-799-5015

     2) Chief Timothy State Park, 8 mi. west of Clarkston on Hwy. 12, swimming beach, 509-758-9580

✺   Follet's Mountain Sports, 714 D St., 208-743-4200

     Pedals-N-Spokes, 829 D St., 208-743-656

🚲 J. INLAND EMPIRE

LEWISTON, ID TO UMATILLA, OR

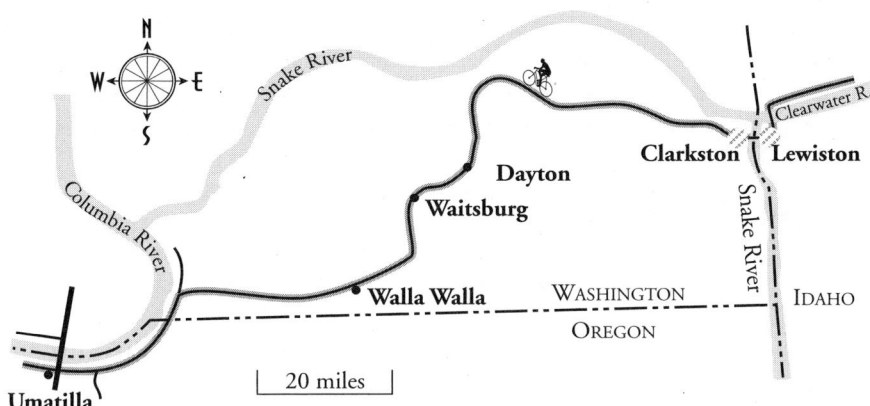

The name "Inland Empire" was originally coined in 1883 by newspaper editor Frank Dallam to attract people to the area around Spokane. Although there is no official definition of this name, most people believe it covers the area between the Cascade Mountains on the west and the Bitterroot Mountains at the border of Idaho and Montana on the east, and from the Canadian border on the north down to the Blue Mountains near the Oregon border.

The Columbia-Snake River system is very much at the center of this region, and it had much to do with forming the geological and cultural character of the area. Although the Inland Empire includes mountains and forests, it is primarily a rich agricultural area.

The hilly country between Lewiston and Walla Walla is also known as the Palouse. This name may come from the French word "pelous," meaning grass-covered hills, or from an old Native American village named "Palus." Although these hills challenge farmers, the soil is too rich to ignore. In fact, the thick layer of humus laden

Rolling wheat country in the Inland Empire, near Pomeroy, WA

loess soil is one of the defining characteristics. Primarily wheat farms cover this area, and the contour farming on the hills produces beautiful patterns of different colors and shades. You may be surprised to learn that eastern Washington produces 10% of the wheat in the United States. Other crops, like onions and fruit are also important, and there are a number of excellent wineries.

Downriver from Clarkston the Snake River loops around to the north through the Snake River Canyon, which is now a lake backed up by a dam. Since there are no roads along the canyon, about ten miles west of Clarkston our route heads inland, following approximately the overland route Lewis and Clark used on their return trip in 1806.

There are more hills than you might expect in this 120-mile stretch to the Columbia River. It's a 2,200-foot climb to Alpowa Summit before dropping into the lush farmland of the Tucannon Valley. Then it's another 1,500 feet of climbing to Dayton, another 800 feet to Walla Walla, and a final 400 feet to the Columbia. You can see that it gets less hilly as you head farther west. If you're heading eastward, the opposite is true; it gets hillier until you crest Alpowa Summit.

From Dayton to Waitsburg, our route follows the Touchet River Valley, very close to the return route of Lewis and Clark in 1806. From Walla Walla we follow the Walla Walla River Valley down to its confluence with the Columbia River— about 12 miles below the mouth of the Snake River. Then most of the last 27 miles to Umatilla is right along the Columbia River as it makes its big curve around to the west.

*Columbia County
Courthouse,
Dayton, WA*

Dayton, WA

Population: 2,600

mile 2533

Often called "historic Dayton," this pleasant small town boasts 90 buildings on the National Register of Historic Places. Along with a very attractive county courthouse on Main Street and the oldest Washington railroad depot a block north on Commercial Street, there are many attractive homes within an easy downtown walking area. The Chamber of Commerce offers helpful descriptive maps for walking tours.

There are several good options for lodging, and the Patit Creek restaurant has a reputation throughout the state. Since Dayton is a popular weekend retreat with several wineries nearby, it's a good idea to make reservations.

Lewis and Clark camped just east of town on Patit Creek on their return trip in 1806. The surrounding land was first used for grazing in the 1860s, but it was soon converted to growing wheat and other grains because of the good soil and rainfall. Today it is still primarily a wheat growing area, although Seneca foods claims that it cans 37% of the world's asparagus here.

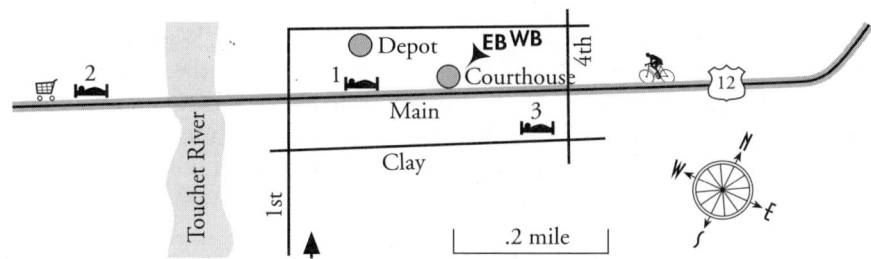

Dayton, WA — Zip: 99328

★ **Dayton Chamber of Commerce:** 166 E Main, 800-882-6299, www.historicdayton.com

🏨 1) Weinhard Hotel ($$), 235 E Main, 509-382-4032

2) Blue Mountain Motel ($), 414 W Main, 509-382-3040

3) Purple House B&B ($$), 415 E Clay, 800-486-2574

▲ Lewis and Clark Trail State Park, 5 mi. west of Dayton, 509-337-6457, wooded private sites, water, no showers

Special Events

All Wheels Weekend, Fathers' Day Weekend (car show, races, dance)
Summer Hoopla, mid-July (basketball, parade)
Columbia County Fair, 2nd weekend in Sept.

Waitsburg, WA

Population: 1,000

Waitsburg is worth at least a quick detour and is only a few blocks from Route 12. The downtown area was rebuilt entirely in brick after a disastrous fire in 1880. The Bruce Memorial Museum at 318 Main St. (509-337-6582) is only open weekends and by special appointment, but you can always ride by and enjoy the exterior.

The Corps of Discovery camped on the bank of the Touchet River near town on May 1, 1806, on their return journey. Today there is a motel, restaurant, and grocery store if you decide you'd like to stay.

Zip: 99361

▄▄▄   Waitsburg Inn Motel ($), 509-337-8455

Walla Walla, WA

Population: 30,000

"A town so lovely, they named it twice" is the local legend. The Walla Walla Valley was originally the home of several Native American tribes, and the name means "small rapid streams" or "many waters." In 1818 the North West Company built Fort Nez Perce at the mouth of the Walla Walla River. This fertile area has produced a wide variety of agricultural products, although wheat is king today.

In 1836 Marcus and Narcissa Whitman, early pioneers on the Oregon Trail, established a mission among the Cayuse Indians eight miles west of town at a place called Waiilatpu (place of the rye grass). For many years they taught the Indians about farming as well as Christianity. This was also an important stop for many pioneers on the Oregon Trail.

As in many mission ventures, there was misunderstanding. While the white missionaries wanted to civilize the natives and convert them to Christianity, the Indians cared more about the white man's magic in growing food and defeating enemies than about religion. When a measles epidemic killed many Indians, but very few whites eleven years later, the Indians blamed the missionaries and slaughtered the Whitmans and ten others. The restored Mission can be visited today to learn about pioneer life in this area.

In 1853 the Washington Territory was established, and Walla Walla was the center of activity. Governor Isaac Stevens negotiated the Treaty of 1855 with the local Indian tribes, which set aside reservations for the Indians and most of the best land for American settlers. In 1859 Fort Walla Walla was built by the U.S. Army, and for 50 years it was the center of pioneer life in this area.

Today Walla Walla offers a wide variety of motels, restaurants, and shopping, but no camping. There is an older pleasant downtown and a newer area of malls east of town on Isaacs Ave. You may choose to ride on busy Isaacs to take advantage of the services there, or you can follow the quieter and more pleasant bypass bicycle route shown on the town map. The Route 12 bypass to the north of town carries a lot of fast traffic and should be avoided.

mile 2565

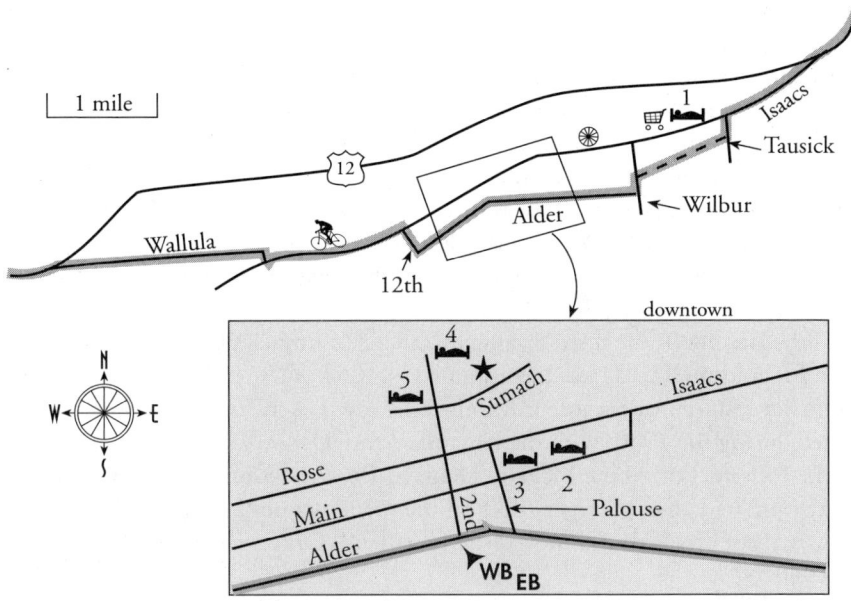

Walla Walla, WA — Zip: 99362

★ **Walla Walla Valley Chamber of Commerce**
29 E Sumach, 509-525-0850, 877-WWVISIT,
www.wwchamber.com, info@wwchamber.com

▰ The Chamber of Commerce lists 5 B&Bs and 13 motels and hotels. A small sample is listed below:

1) Colonial Motel ($), 2279 Isaacs, 509-529-1220

2) Travelodge ($$), 421 E Main, 509-529-4940

3) City Center Motel ($$), 627 W Main, 800-453-3160

4) Best Western ($$), 7 E Oak, 800-448-5544

5) Budget Inn Motel ($), 305 N 2nd, 888-529-4161

▲ Pierce's Green Valley Campground, 24676 Hwy. 12, Touchet, 24 mi. west of Walla Walla, 509-394-2387; grass, little shade, water, porta-potties, no showers or privacy

✹ Bicycle Barn, 1503 E Isaacs, 509-529-7860

Umatilla, OR

Population: 3,200

When Lewis and Clark passed through here in 1805, they were slowed down as they negotiated the Muscleshell Rapids. They found a Native American village alongside the river, since this area was used as a river crossing and place of commerce. There is evidence that this site has been occupied since about 470 BCE.

Today this is still an important river crossing and a crossroads of interstate highways and railroads that continue to provide some commerce. The rapids are gone, having been used as the base for the McNary Dam in the 1950s. In fact, most of the lower Columbia River today is really a series of lakes created by dams. Only in pictures and visitor centers can you get an idea what the river was like 200 years ago.

In the late 1800s the town, originally called Columbia, was a freight transfer station for gold mining. It was incorporated in 1864 as Umatilla Landing and became the county seat because it was the only town in the county. The town boomed during the 1940s with the Umatilla Army Depot, and again in the 1950s with the construction of the McNary Dam. In 1963 the John Day Dam, 40 miles downstream, had an even larger effect on the town by flooding much of the original town, most of which was moved to higher land. Only a few buildings are older than 1940.

At McNary Dam there is a visitor center that emphasizes how fish are transported around dams in both directions. You can also visit the fish ladder and watch fish struggling upstream.

If you are camping, there is beautiful camping right in town. You should also consider camping at Crow Butte, another beautiful campground 27 miles west of here, to break up the long stretch to Biggs Junction.

Navigating the Columbia River today

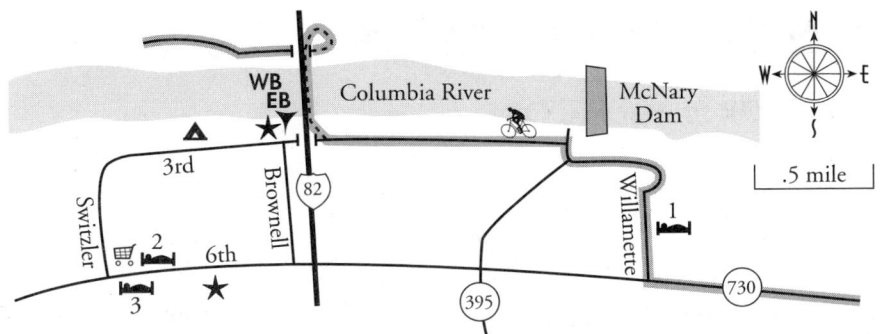

Umatilla, OR — Zip: 97882

★ **Umatilla Chamber of Commerce:** 1530 6th St., 800-542-4944

Oregon Visitor Center: 3rd St. just west of I-82

🛏 1) Desert River Inn ($$), 705 Willamette Ave., 877-922-1000

2) Tillicum Inn ($), 1481 6th St., 541-922-3236

3) Rest A Bit Motel ($), 1370 6th St., 800-423-9913

▲ 1) Umatilla Marina RV Park, 1710 Quincy, 541-922-3939, grass, shade, showers

2) Hat Rock CG, opposite Hat Rock SP, 8 mi. east of Umatilla on Hwy. 730, 503-567-4188, private, grass, shade, pool, showers

3) Crow Butte State Park, Box 217, Paterson, WA 99345, 509-875-2644, 27 mi. west of Umatilla on Hwy. 14, 2 flat mi. off highway, beautiful grass, shade, showers

🚲 K. DOWN THE COLUMBIA RIVER

UMATILLA, OR TO ASTORIA, OR

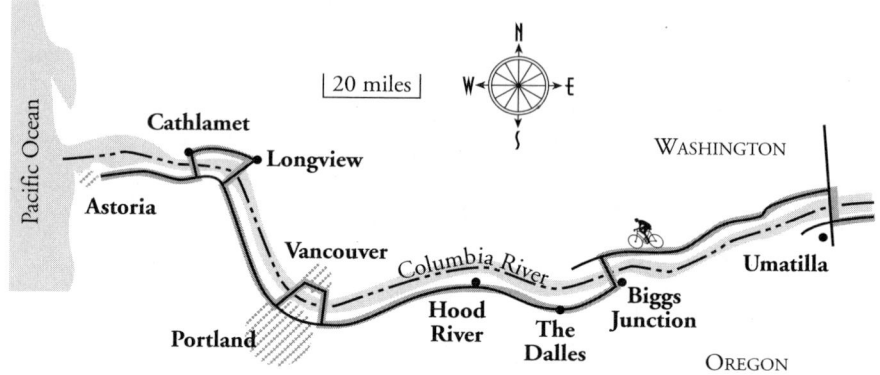

By the time the Corps of Discovery hit the Columbia River, they must have felt that the end was in sight—at least figuratively if not literally. Although the Columbia had yet to be explored and mapped above Portland, they knew they were on the Columbia River. Very soon they spotted a large volcano they took to be Mt. St. Helens, although it was actually her neighbor volcano—Mt. Adams. On October 19 Clark wrote, *"I ascended a high clift about 200 feet above the water from the top of which is a leavel plain extending up the river and off for a great extent . . . from this place I descovered a high mountain of emence hight covered with Snow, this must be one of the mountains laid down by Vancouver, as Seen from the mouth of the Columbia River, from the Course which it bears which is West I take it to be Mt. St. Helens, destant 156 miles."* Shortly they would spot and recognize the magnificent Mt. Hood.

They must have also felt good about travelling rapidly downstream after fifteen months of struggling upstream and two months of even more difficult struggling over the mountains. In fact, the final 630 miles down the rivers took only one month. There are many stories of the expedition taking significant risks shooting the rapids in their awkward dugout canoes. Sometimes the Indians lined the banks to watch them, perhaps hoping to pick up the spoils from their wrecks.

Lewis and Clark found a big change in both the landscape and the Indians as they moved down the river. The change in the landscape is still very visible today. East of the Columbia River Gorge, around The Dalles, the Columbia Plateau is a relatively dry area. Fourteen inches of rainfall per year is only enough to grow wheat and other crops with the help of irrigation. Thirty five miles west of The Dalles the rainfall is 65 inches per year, and the vegetation is green and lush all the way to the Pacific.

Lewis and Clark also found a big change in the Indians, due partly to the natural barrier formed by the Columbia River Gorge, and partly to the influence of white men. East of the gorge the Nez Perce were honest, friendly, and helpful. The Gorge prevented them from travelling easily to the west, and they had no previous contact with white men.

The Chinooks, who lived west of the Gorge, were similarly prevented from travelling east. The two groups had developed quite independently and spoke very different languages. Furthermore, the Chinooks had had previous contact and experience with white traders, and they expected much more from the Corps of Discovery. Their culture also seemed to allow petty thievery, and this caused many problems for the captains—especially since they were running low on many supplies and trading goods. Several times on the return trip Lewis came close to losing his temper and perhaps taking drastic action against the Indians, which all would have regretted later.

The Columbia River Gorge—designated a "national scenic area" in 1986—is a spectacular stretch that includes about 80 miles between The Dalles and Troutdale. One of the best places to learn more about the Gorge is the Columbia Gorge Discovery Center in The Dalles.

It was difficult deciding which side of the river to use as a bicycle route, but I finally chose the Oregon side for two reasons: the availability of services and camping is more evenly spaced; and the bike trails and sections of the Historic Columbia River Highway provide beautiful riding—especially the new stretch through the Mosier Twin Tunnels that is now open only to bicycles and pedestrians. The trade-off is that it requires 30 miles (three stretches of 5, 15, and 10 miles) of riding on I-84. Although riding the interstate shoulder is noisy, sometimes dirty, and not that pleasant, it is beautiful along the river, flatter, and arguably safer than riding Route 14 on the Washington side as traffic increases towards Vancouver and Portland.

Maryhill Museum, high above the Columbia River, across from Biggs Junction, OR

Biggs Junction, OR

Although Biggs Junction is little more than an interchange on I-84, you may be very happy to find the services it offers after riding 84 miles from Umatilla. Perhaps surprisingly, this is the longest stretch without overnight services on our whole route. One way to break it up is to camp at Crow Butte State Park 27 miles west of Umatilla (see Camping under Umatilla). Biggs Junction offers several motels, restaurants, and excellent camping at Maryhill State Park just across the river in Washington.

One other little surprise that Biggs offers is an amazing look at the *original* Oregon Trail. Look for a small roadside sign on the south side of the Frontage Road two miles west of Biggs, and walk along the ruts of the old trail parallel to the road. Since this land is not good for commercial development, farming, or grazing, the trail looks very much as it did 150 years ago. Ponder what it must have been like hauling huge Conestoga wagons through this rugged terrain.

Another attraction nearby is Maryhill Museum of Art and the Stonehenge Memorial (509-773-3733). Maryhill was originally built as a family mansion by railroad baron Sam Hill as the start of a Quaker community in 1914. Since he was unable to attract others—including his wife—to the remote location, he abandoned the idea. Later he was convinced to turn it into an art museum, and it finally opened in 1940—eleven years after his death. Stonehenge is a replica of the English monument and is dedicated to local men who lost their lives in World War I. Both are located on Route 14 on the Washington side of the river. It's important to understand they are on the plateau about 500 feet above the river, so plan your visit accordingly. If you're not fascinated by original art, you may be satisfied to enjoy the view of Maryhill from our route along the Oregon side.

The bridge across the Columbia here is about a half-mile long and narrow without any sidewalk. Fortunately, traffic is light, and you can claim your lane for the short distance across.

Wagon tracks on the Oregon Trail, near Biggs Junction, OR

Zip: 97065

mile 2723

1) Dinty's Motor Inn ($), 541-739-2596

2) Riviera Best Western ($$), 541-739-2501

▲ 1) Maryhill State Park, Maryhill, WA, 800-233-0321; on river, grass, shade, showers

2) Deschutes River State Park, 4.5 mi. west of Biggs on Frontage Rd., 541-739-2322, on river, grass, shade, no showers

The Dalles, OR

Population: 11,000

After navigating a difficult stretch of river they named the Short Narrows and the Long Narrows, the expedition camped *"on a high point of rocks, which forms a kind of fortification."* They spent the next two days here, resting, hunting, and repairing the dugout canoes.

Later French traders named this town The Dalles (rhymes with "pals") because of the flat flagstones that created the rapids in this area. These rapids, as well as the magnificent Celilo Falls upriver, are now all covered by the lake created above The Dalles Dam. You can visit the dam and see both pictures and a three-dimensional model of the area before the dam was built. The dam also offers a short train ride to view the fish ladders and power plant. West of town is the Columbia Gorge Discovery Center with many exhibits on the geology, history, and culture of this area.

Today's downtown area includes motels and restaurants within walking distance. Near the center of this area are several large interesting murals on the sides of buildings that depict different historical scenes. If you need malls, big food supermarkets, chain restaurants, and more motels, head northwest out 6th St. (Route 30 west of downtown).

Lewis & Clark at Rock Fort *by Robert Thomas. One of several murals adorning the walls of businesses in The Dalles, OR*

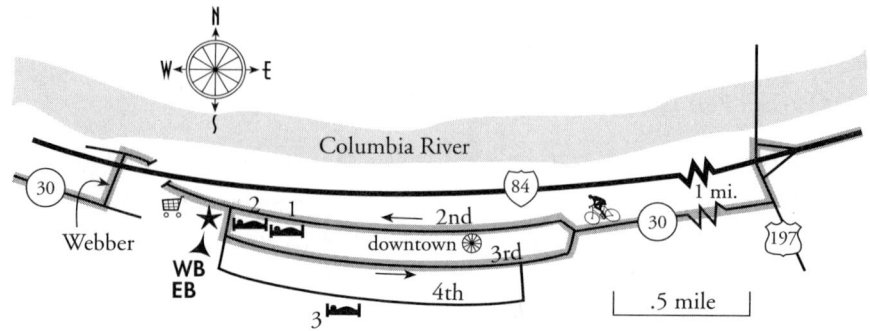

The Dalles, OR — Zip: 97058

★ **The Dalles Area Chamber of Commerce:** 404 W 2nd, 541-296-2231, 800-255-3385, www.gorge.net/tdacc

The Chamber of Commerce lists 16 motels and B&Bs in and near The Dalles. Below is a sample of convenient downtown locations:

1) Best Western Umatilla House ($$), 112 W 2nd, 800-722-8277

2) Oregon Motor Motel ($), 200 W 2nd, 541-296-9111

3) Budget Inn ($), 118 W 4th, 541-296-5464

⊕ Life Cycles, 418 E 2nd, 541-296-9588

Special Attraction: Columbia Gorge Discovery Center, 5000 Discovery Drive (541-296-8600)

Mount Hood towering over the Columbia River

Hood River, OR

Population: 4,600

The town of Hood River is located where the Hood River flows into the Columbia. Above town the river formed a large fertile valley now famous for fruit—especially pears. Farther up is forest rich with timber. Above the forest rises the snow-capped peak of Mt. Hood—a magnificent landmark volcano.

After Lewis and Clark came through here, fur trappers and traders roamed the area before it was permanently settled in the 1850s. Although fruit and timber are still the dominant industries, tourism continues to grow. The wind howling through the confines of the Gorge has made Hood River the wind-surfing capital of the west coast. It is fun to watch them on a windy weekend. Count on a stiff west wind through the gorge during the summer, but sometimes in spring and fall you get a big easterly wind.

The growth of tourism has brought many restaurants and other services to town, and has also raised prices and made reservations more important—especially on weekends. Much as I hesitate to recommend restaurants, we had an excellent creative Italian dinner at the North Oak Brasserie.

If you have thoughts of crossing the Hood River Bridge to Washington, think long and hard. The bridge is very narrow, and almost a mile long with open grate decking. I crossed it once because I felt I had no options, but I will never do it again. It is the most unpleasant and dangerous bridge I have ever experienced, and it's even more dangerous when it is wet and windy.

Doing flips in a moderate breeze, near Hood River, OR

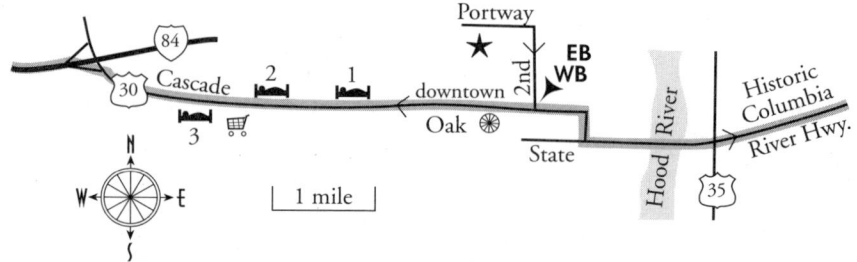

Hood River, OR — Zip: 97031

★   **Hood River County Chamber of Commerce:** 405 Portway Ave.,
    800-366-3530, www.gorge.net/hrccc

🛏   The Chamber of Commerce lists 11 motels/hotels and 7 B&Bs. A sample
    of convenient locations:

1) Prater's Motel ($$), 1306 Oak, 541-386-3566

2) Sunset Motel ($$), 2300 Cascade, 541-386-6027

3) Lone Pine Motel ($), 2429 Cascade, 541-386-8882

▲   Viento State Park, 6 mi. west of Hood River, wooded, showers,
    hiker-biker area

⊕   Discover Bicycles, 205 Oak, 541-386-4820

Historic Columbia River Highway

Cascade Locks, OR

Population: 850

mile 2768

The village of Cascade Locks is located in a beautiful place on the banks of the Columbia, where you will find motels, campground, restaurants, and food shopping. During the summer the sternwheeler *Columbia Gorge* offers two-hour cruises on the river (503-223-3928).

Native American legend claims the Great Spirit once built a bridge of stone across the Columbia here. Scientists think a nearby mountain may have collapsed about 1,000 years ago, damming up the river. The river eventually tunnelled under the dam and created a bridge of stone. Unfortunately, it's all long gone. Today's Bridge of the Gods is a graceful steel structure built in the 1920s for $600,000. In the 1990s it was repainted for $800,000. It is a long narrow toll bridge not recommended for cyclists.

Zip: 97014

★ **Cascade Locks Tourism:** Box 355, 541-374-8619

🛏 1) Columbia River Inn ($$), 800-595-7108

   2) Bridge of the Gods Motel ($$), 541-374-8628

   3) Econo Inn ($$), 877-374-8417

▲ 1) KOA Campground, 1 mi. east of Cascade Locks on Forest Lane Road

   2) Ainsworth State Park, 9 mi. west of Cascade Locks, wooded, showers, hiker-biker area

Troutdale, OR

Population: 8,000

Troutdale is located at the boundary between the scenic Columbia River Gorge and greater metropolitan Portland. The town includes a downtown with trendy shops, art galleries, restaurants, and a helpful Chamber of Commerce. Although the town is mostly residential, there are several motels and chain restaurants around Exit 17 of I-84 (intersection with 257th St.).

Zip: 97060

★ **Chamber of Commerce:** Box 245, 338 E Historic Columbia River Highway, 503-669-7473, stateoforegon.com/troutdale/tacc

🛏 Located at Intersection of I-84 and 257th St.

   1) Motel 6 ($), 503-665-2254

   2) Phoenix Inn ($$), 800-824-6824

   3) Inn America ($$), 800-469-4667

VANCOUVER, WASHINGTON, AND PORTLAND, OREGON

When the Corps of Discovery visited this area in 1805, they found scattered Native American villages along both sides of the river that both traded and occasionally fought with each other. The same might be said about the two modern cities of Vancouver and Portland today.

The first white people to establish a settlement here were from the British Hudson's Bay Trading Company, who wanted to expand their fur trading operations inland from the coast. Fort Vancouver was originally built as a trading post, as opposed to a military fortification. Searching upriver from their base in Astoria, the British chose the first relatively flat and open expanse of land they could find on the north side of the river, expecting the Columbia River to become the natural boundary between the British and American empires.

Americans came to this area in the 1840s for very different reasons. They had heard about the fertile farmland in the Willamette Valley, south of today's Portland; and they travelled out the Oregon Trail with their families as permanent farmers and settlers. By 1846 over 5,000 had settled in this area.

In 1846 the international boundary was peacefully agreed to be the 49th parallel, where it still is today; and the British in Vancouver were replaced by Americans. The wide expanse of fertile land south of the river and the limited land north of the river started the trend towards the large city of Portland and the small city of Vancouver. In 1883 the decision of the Northern Pacific to build the railroad on the Oregon side further accelerated this trend. Today greater Portland has almost ten times the population of Vancouver—for better or worse, depending on your point of view.

Portland believes in bicycles! Bike Trail on I-205 bridge

mile 2819

Our bicycle route, as shown in the overview map, seeks to offer a scenic and convenient way to travel through this heavily populated area. Vancouver offers cycling with lower traffic and a compact downtown area with a B&B, motels, and restaurants. It is very easy to stay in Vancouver and take a bus to downtown Portland, which provides a great area for walking.

It is also possible to ride into Portland from Vancouver, or directly through Portland on the Oregon side. Portland has two youth hostels, lots of microbreweries, night clubs, and other activities that may be very appealing to some people. If you want to ride in and/or through Portland, I strongly recommend Metro Regional Services' (www.metro-region.org or 503-797-1510) *Bike There* map for $6. Portland can be very friendly to cyclists—IF you know what you're doing.

Although Portland is about 100 miles from the end of the Lewis and Clark Trail, it is the logical commercial transportation hub for the western end of the route. The airport is relatively convenient and friendly to bicycles, as shown on the overview map (page 204). Union Station downtown provides Amtrak service both up and down the west coast, and also through Spokane and northern Montana (along the Hi-Line route we follow) to Chicago. Next door to Union Station is the Greyhound terminal.

O.O. Howard house in Fort Vancouver Historic Site

Vancouver, WA

Population: 135,000

Although Vancouver has a large population, it is very spread out. The relatively compact downtown area on the river near the I-5 bridge makes it seem like a much smaller town. There is a B&B, several motels, and several restaurants within walking distance in the pleasant downtown area. North along I-5 and east along Mill Plain are newer areas with malls and franchise restaurants.

A short bike ride away—and large enough that a bicycle is ideal for getting around—is Fort Vancouver National Historic Site. Originally established by the British as a fur trading post, this site has since been the home of Ulysses S. Grant, American troops training for World War I and II, pioneer aviation work, Henry Kaiser's massive ship-building effort for World War II, and current Army and National Guard units. Today you can visit the old stockade, air museum, and restored homes along Officers' Row to get a feel for the rich and varied history of this location.

Lewis and Clark camped downriver from the present site of the I-5 bridge on the night of November 3, 1805. Although they were opposite the mouth of the Willamette River, there was a large island (today's Hayden Island) in the way and they never noticed the river. On their way home the next spring, after they had paddled more than ten miles past today's Portland and Vancouver, Indians told them they had missed the river again, even though they had been looking for it. Clark then took a small group and returned to explore the river for several miles. He wrote in his journal that this flat rich farmland could support 40,000–50,000 souls. By 1850 more than 13,000 people had braved the rigors of the Oregon Trail to settle in the Willamette Valley.

Doris Hale and her Vintage Inn, Vancouver, WA

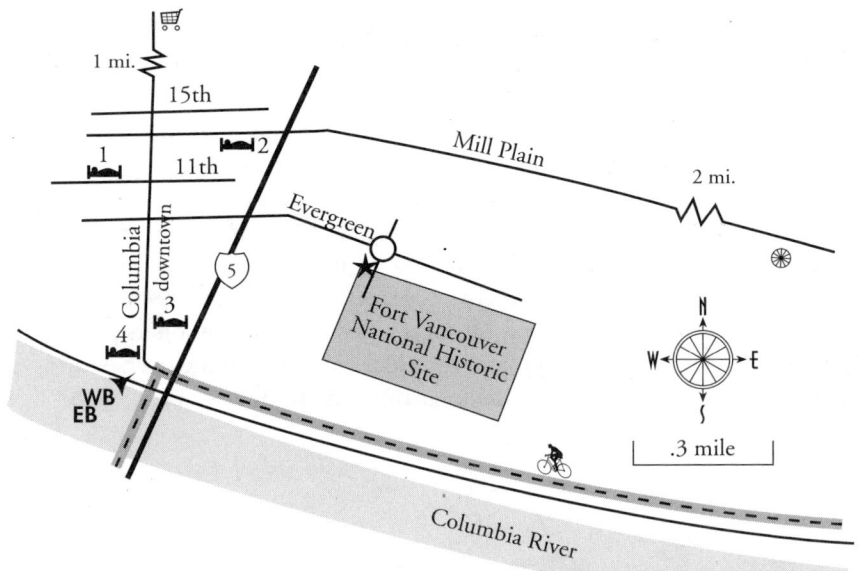

mile 2819

Vancouver, WA — Zip: 98663

★ **Southwest Washington Visitors Bureau:** 101 E 8th St., 877-600-0800, www.southwestwashington.com, info@southwestwashington.com

O.O. Howard House Information Center: 750 Anderson St., located in Fort Vancouver National Historic Site

🛏 The Chamber of Commerce lists 1 B&B and 14 motels and hotels in Vancouver. A small sample of convenient downtown locations is listed below:

1) Vintage Inn B&B ($$), 310 W 11th, 888-693-6635, www.vintage-inn.com; restored 1903 mansion filled with elegant antiques; walking distance to downtown restaurants and historic attractions; 4 large rooms with queen beds and shared bath; full breakfast.

2) Shilo Inn ($$), 401 E 13th, 800-888-2244

3) Vancouver Lodge ($), 601 Broadway, 360-693-3668

4) Red Lion Hotel at the Quay ($$$), 100 Columbia, 800-222-8733

✹ Chain Reaction Cyclery, 6503 E Mill Plain, 360-696-9234

Special Events

International Discovery Walk, 3rd weekend in April

Fort Vancouver July 4th (largest fireworks west of the Mississippi draws 80,000 people)

Wine and Jazz Festival, late August

Portland, OR

Population: 500,000

In 1844 the first two settlers each wanted to name their new town after their hometown back east—Boston and Portland. Portland won in a coin toss. If you're ending or beginning your trip by air, Portland Airport is ideal—good airline connections, convenient location, and reasonable traffic on the access roads for cyclists.

Today the city straddles the Willamette River just south of its confluence with the Columbia River. Major industries include manufacturing and electronics.

The downtown area on the west side of the Willamette River offers pleasant walking along the river and shopping in the blocks just west of the river. Saturdays bring an active crafts market to the area near Burnside Bridge, which is a good bridge for bicycles to cross.

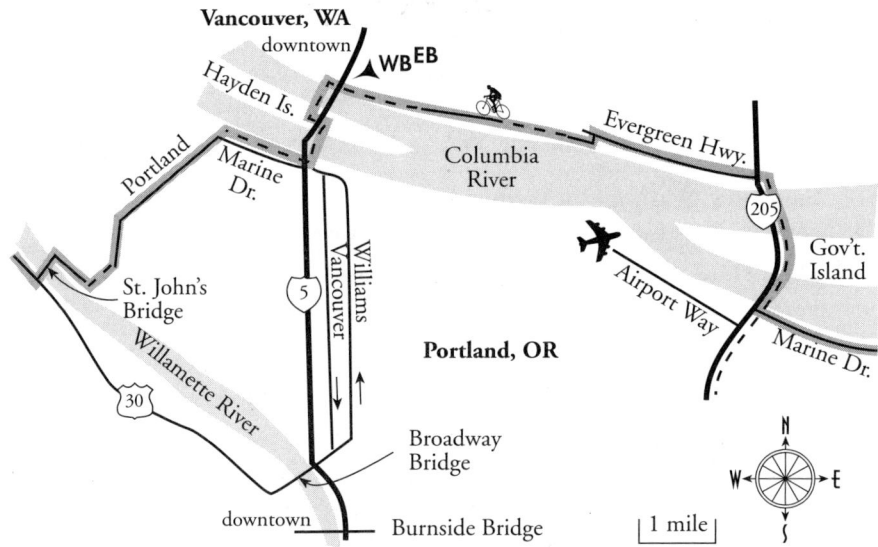

Portland Overview

★   **Portland Visitors Association:** 877-678-5263,
     www.travelportland.com

Hostels

1) Northwest Portland International Hostel ($), 1818 NW Glissan,
   503-241-2783

2) Portland International Hostel ($), 3031 SE Hawthorne, 503-236-3380

   Motels near Airport

3) EconoLodge Airport ($$), 9520 NE Sandy, 503-252-6666

4) Super 8 Motel Airport ($$), 11011 NE Holman, 800-800-8000

5) Travelodge Airport ($$), 9727 NE Sandy, 800-621-4358

Special Events: Portland Rose Festival, month of June (www.rosefestival.org)

mile 2867

Rainier, OR

Population: 1,700

Rainier is located on the south side of the Columbia River opposite Longview. There are a couple of restaurants, a medium supermarket, and one motel. If you're in a hurry, you could spend a night here, stay on Route 30 on the Oregon side to Westport, and save 12 miles plus a ferry ride.

Zip: 97048

Rainier Budget Inn Motel ($), 120 A St., 503-556-4231

Longview, WA

Population: 32,000

Longview is a relatively new city, planned and developed from scratch by the Long-Bell Lumber Company in 1919. Long-Bell, already well established in Kansas City, wanted to build a large mill in a seaport so they could export lumber from their newly purchased timber lands in southwest Washington. Chairman Robert A. Long's friend, J.C. Nichols, convinced the company to plan and build a beautiful city as a home for their new lumber mill. Hence the name "Longview."

While walking your bike across the sidewalk of the high Lewis and Clark Bridge, you can see that paper, lumber, and shipping are still important parts of life

Lewis & Clark Bridge into Longview, WA

in Longview. The city spreads out with boulevards, esplanades, and wide avenues from its central core in R. A. Long Square. Animal lovers will want to check out the Nutty Narrows Squirrel Bridge across Olympia Way near the northwest corner of the square. To the east of Long Square is the commercial area. To the south is the industrial area and the seaport on the river. To the west is mostly residential, built around natural looking parklands and Lake Sacajawea, also planned and developed from a marsh area known as Fowler's Slough.

I had been to Longview twice before and never understood or appreciated that it was a planned city with definite organizing principles. The Chamber of Commerce has excellent information and a walking map of the central city.

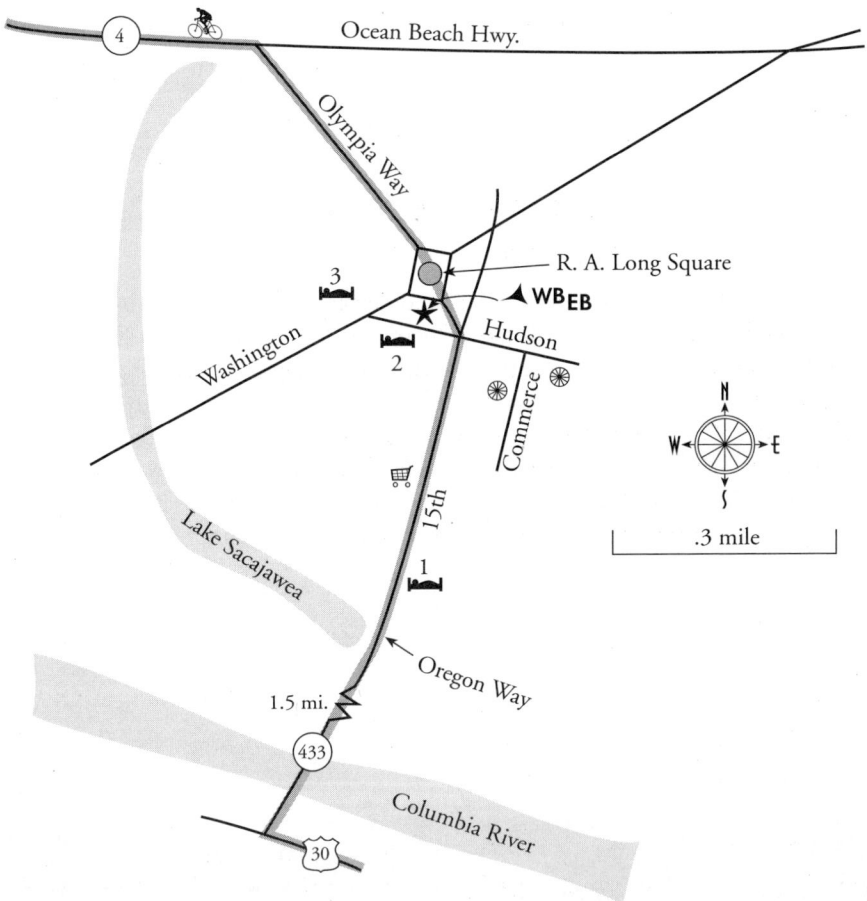

Longview, WA — Zip: 98632

★ **Longview Area Chamber of Commerce**
1563 Olympia Way, 360-423-8400, www.ci.longview.wa.us

🛏 The Chamber of Commerce lists 8 motels and 2 B&Bs. Below is a sample of convenient locations:

1) Travelodge ($$), 838 15th, 800-578-7878

2) Hudson Manor Hotel ($), 1616 Hudson, 360-425-1100

3) Town Chalet ($), 1822 Washington Way, 360-423-2020

✹ 1) Byman's Bikes, 1156 Commerce, 360-577-4481

2) Bob's Pedal Power, 1111 Hudson, 360-425-3870

Cathlamet, WA

Population: 550

Originally the home of the Kathlamet Indians, part of the Chinook tribe, the name comes from the word "calamet," meaning "stone." This stretch of river with a rocky river bed was first sighted by the British Lieutenant William Broughton in 1792, while he was verifying the American Captain Robert Gray's earlier discovery of the Columbia River. Legend has it that Lewis and Clark drank from Queen Sally's Well (180 South 2nd St.), but their journals suggest they were in a hurry by this time of their trip, smelling the salt water and the end of their journey.

The first permanent white settler was James Birnie of the Hudson's Bay Company, who established a trading post at Birnie's Retreat in 1846. Today Cathlamet is the county seat of Wahkiakum County. A very pleasant town of 550, it has many services because it serves as a regional center. There are several restaurants, and the Wahkiakum County Historical Museum (65 River St.) is a small museum that tells many stories of this area.

Just south of town is Puget Island, named by Broughton for his friend, Lt. Peter Puget. This flat two- by five-mile island is sometimes called "Little Norway," because it was settled by Scandinavians in 1884. A fifteen minute ferry ride connects the island with Westport, Oregon. The ferry leaves Puget Island every hour on the hour and leaves Westport every hour at fifteen minutes past the hour.

Puget Island ferry

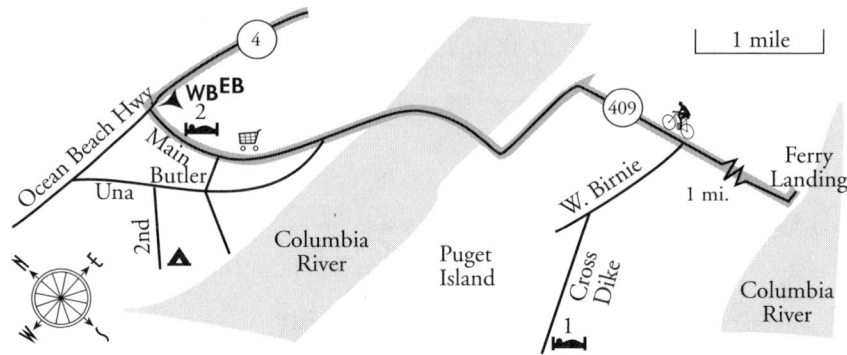

Cathlamet, WA — Zip: 98612

★ **Lower Columbia Economic Development Council**
Skamokawa, 98647, 360-795-3996, lcedc@tdn.com

🛏 1) Redfern Farm B&B ($$), 277 Cross Dike Rd., Puget Island,
360-849-4108; quiet rural farm four flat mi. from town and ferry;
two rooms with queen beds and private baths; full breakfast;
best call 4-6 pm.

  2) Bradley House B&B, 61 Main, 800-551-1691

▲   Elochman Slough Marina, RV, Camping, 500 2nd St., 360-795-3501; open
camping near marina, little privacy or shade, clean restrooms with showers,
easy walk to downtown.

Skamokawa, WA

Skamokawa, WA
Population: 400

Skamokawa is a tiny hamlet on a sheltered estuary 4.5 easy miles west of Cath-lamet. Although not really on our route, it's well worth considering a detour here to the Skamokawa Center (www.skamokawapaddle.com, 888-920-2777), which includes a B&B, general store, café for breakfast and lunch, and a kayak operation. It's possible to rent kayaks or join a tour to explore miles of sheltered waters and see many birds among the islands in the Columbia River. Among their many kayak offerings is a moonlight tour and a two-day Lewis and Clark tour. An easy walk east, the Duck Inn serves dinners.

Skamokawa Vista Park (206-795-8605) is a quarter mile farther west on the river. It offers pleasant camping with shade, a beach, and clean restrooms without showers.

Westport, OR
Population: 75

Westport is an intersection where the road from the ferry landing connects with Route 30 on the Oregon side. There is a motel, restaurant, deli, and grocery store, and it's possible to spend a night here.

Zip: 97016

🛏 Westport Motel ($), 503-455-2212

Astoria, OR
Population: 10,000

"Ocian in view! O! the joy." (*Nov. 7, 1805, Clark*) You, too, can experience the joy of reaching your goal—the Pacific Ocean. Although the Corps of Discovery was still almost twenty miles from the actual ocean when Clark wrote this in his journal at Pillar Rock, near Altoona, Washington, this was the goal they had all been working toward. They were tantalizingly close, but it would be another month of struggling in and around the mouth of the Columbia River before they set up their winter quarters at Fort Clatsop—six miles south of Astoria.

What they really saw that day was the broad expanse of the Columbia River near its mouth. Over the next fifteen days the expedition spent most of the time pinned down by wind, waves, and terrible weather at two campsites near the north end of today's Astoria Bridge. On November 28 Clark wrote, *"This is our present Situation,! truly disagreeable. aded to this the robes of our Selves and men are all rotten from being Continually wet, and we Cannot precure others, or blankets in their places . . . at maney times it blew for 15 or 20 minits with Such violence that I expected every moment to See trees taken up by the roots, Some were blown down. Those Squals were Suckceeded by rain, O! how Tremendious is the day."*

During this period they were able to walk overland to Cape Disappointment and what is now Fort Canby State Park on the north side of the mouth of the river. They explored this area and several miles up the coast near Long Beach, Washington, always hoping to find a ship from back home. A ship could have replenished their supplies and equipment, provided them with manufactured goods for trading, and offered transportation home for their journals, specimens, and some or all of their men.

Finding no sign of trading ships, little game for food, and paying high prices to Chinooks for basics, they voted to search for winter quarters on the south side of the river, where the Clatsops were more friendly, there were more elk, they could make salt, and they could keep a lookout for a trading ship. Much has been made of this decision—where everyone had an equal vote, even a black slave and an Indian woman. They worked their way back upriver to find a safer place to cross, and then spent ten days camped on today's Tongue Point (just east of downtown Astoria) while searching for a good location for their winter camp.

On December 7, one month after their joyous arrival, they arrived at the site of Fort Clatsop and began building their home for the winter. The Native Americans in this area were indeed friendly, in fact sometimes too friendly. They liked to hang around the fort, trade food for manufactured goods, and occasionally steal something. The captains revived the army discipline of standing watch and closing the fort each night.

The expedition remained at Fort Clatsop until March 23, always hoping to hail a ship near the mouth of the river while waiting for the snow to melt in Idaho and Montana so they could re-cross the Rockies. It was another difficult winter, but much different from the previous winter at Fort Mandan. Instead of cold weather, they had wet weather; it rained almost every day. Clothing rotted, fleas infested their bedding, and many men were suffering from a variety of diseases. Game was scarce, their goods available for trading were running low, and their days were filled with monotony. The previous winter they were excited about proceeding westward from Fort Mandan; this winter it must have been difficult wondering if this was the end of their journey or only the halfway point.

Although it was difficult for everyone, it was also a very productive period for the captains. They wrote a great deal in their journals, Clark updated his maps, and they made important decisions about their return routes.

Thirteen years before Lewis and Clark, the American Captain Robert Gray was the first white man to discover the Columbia River. The British, Spanish, and Russians were also sailing this part of the coast and making rival claims to the land. Lewis and Clark were the first white men to arrive by land in 1805. In 1811 John Jacob Astor's group of fur traders arrived by sea and established the first American settlement here. Their fort was sold to the North West Company of Montreal when the British arrived during the War of 1812, but it was returned to the Americans for good in 1818.

Astoria languished in the shadow of Fort Vancouver farther upriver, until the American-British boundary was established along the 49th parallel, and the British started moving out of Vancouver. As the Oregon Territorial government was established, American pioneers were pushing farther west from the Willamette Valley to settle permanently in this area.

In 1864 the first salmon cannery was built, and a new industry developed. The area prospered from salmon canneries until the 1960s. It has also been a port for grain and lumber exports, and more recently tourism has become an important industry.

Today Astoria is the home of the excellent Columbia River Maritime Museum, many pleasant Victorian homes and B&Bs, and several interesting restaurants. Some local favorites that have been around a while: Home Spirit Bakery (1585 Exchange) serves homemade bread and scones, and lunches and dinners by reservation. The Columbian Café (1114 Marine) serves unique breakfasts and lunches. The Rio Café (125 9th St.) offers good value in creative Mexican food.

For a better view of the whole area, you can ride 600 feet up Coxcomb Hill, just south of downtown, and walk up the 125-foot Astoria Column. Wound around the outside wall of the column is a spiral mural depicting the history of the lower Columbia River area. From here you can look southwest over Youngs Bay to the Fort Clatsop area, west to Warrenton and Fort Stevens, and northwest over the mouth of the Columbia River and "the bar"— graveyard for more than 200 ships.

Astoria Bridge at the mouth of the Columbia River, Astoria, OR

Although Astoria is the official end of our bicycle route, you will probably want to spend at least a day or two here to savor your accomplishment and enjoy the Lewis and Clark sites and other special attractions in this area. Stop at the Astoria Chamber of Commerce to get more details about each site and riding directions.

About six miles from Astoria is Fort Clatsop (www.nps.gov/focl, 503-861-2871), where the local residents built a replica of the original fort. The National Park Service operates a very informative visitor center there. If you're lucky, you might visit on a rainy day and get a feel for what it must have been like living there during a wet winter.

About eighteen miles north and west from Astoria is the Lewis and Clark Interpretive Center in Fort Canby State Park, Washington (www.parks.wa.gov/ftcamby, 360-642-3029). They have a good overview of the entire expedition, and a spectacular view of the Pacific Ocean and the mouth of the Columbia River from high on the cliffs. This excursion requires riding over the four-mile Astoria bridge, which demands both competence and confidence because of its length. Just east of the north end of the bridge is the spot where the Corps of Discovery was trapped by weather from November 10–15, 1805. If you make the decision to cross the bridge, you might consider combining this trip with a return trip up the Washington side of the river to Cathlamet.

About sixteen miles southwest of Astoria is Seaside—and a reconstruction of the site where Lewis and Clark established their Salt Works. You might also consider combining this trip with a ride farther down the spectacular Oregon coast and a loop back to Portland by another route.

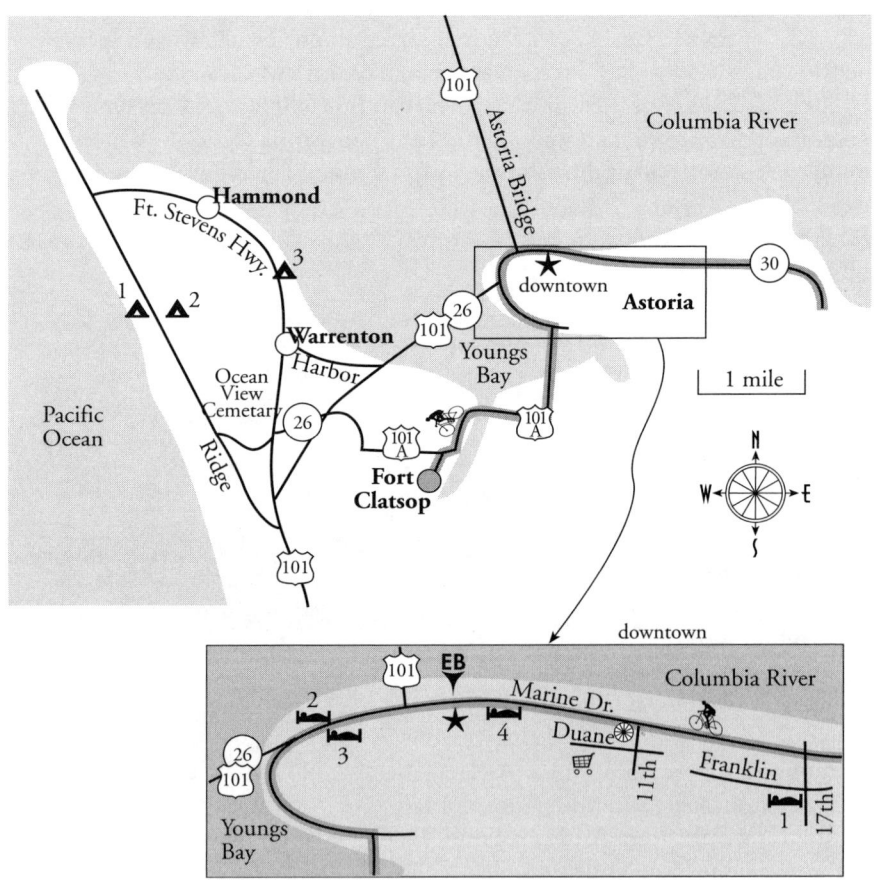

Astoria, OR — Zip: 97103

★ **Chamber of Commerce:** 111 W Marine Dr., 503-325-6311, www.oldoregon.com

mile 2927

▬ The Chamber of Commerce lists 8 B&Bs and 10 motels. A small sample of convenient locations is shown below:

1) Columbia River Inn ($$), 1681 Franklin, 800-953-5044, www. moriah.com/Columbia; restored 1870 Victorian "Painted Lady" with river views; walk to downtown; 4 rooms with queen beds, private baths, and various special amenities; bike storage; full breakfast.

2) Dunes Motel ($$), 288 W Marine, 800-441-3319

3) Lamplighter Motel ($$), 131 W Marine, 800-845-8847

4) Economy Lodge ($), 495 Marine, 503-325-4211

▲ This area is very popular for camping during the summer. Call for reservations!

1) Fort Stevens State Park, Warrenton (97146), 800-452-5687

2) KOA Campground, 1100 NW Ridge, Hammond (97121), 800-KOA-8506

3) Kampers West Kampground, 1140 NW Warrenton, Warrenton (97146), 503-861-1814, primarily for RVs, expensive for tenters

✳ Bikes & Beyond, 1089 Marine, 503-325-2961

Fort Clatsop, near Astoria, OR

5

DETAILED ROUTE:
INTERTOWN MAPS AND CUE SHEETS

Sometimes the route is well marked.

This chapter includes cue sheets (detailed directions) and less detailed maps for routes between towns. These maps are *not* to scale and are *not* intended for detailed navigation. They are intended to be pictures to illustrate and support the cue sheets. Although the collection of maps in this book is sufficient for riding the entire Lewis & Clark Trail, most people will want to supplement these maps with state highway maps, easy to get in advance from state tourism offices (listed in Appendix E), or from visitor centers along the way.

Intertown maps are broken into sections to fit the format of the book and be a reasonable size to tear out and carry in a handlebar bag or pocket. Since each individual defines "a day's ride" differently, these sections are *not* intended to be a day's worth of riding. Compass directions have been added in parentheses to help clarify some turns and provide confirmation. Key roads have been printed in bold to help you focus on them quickly.

I recommend that you tear out any sections you don't want to make the book smaller and lighter. You may also want to tear out individual sheets each day and carry them in your handlebar bag or pocket for easy reference while riding between towns.

Below each cue map in this section is a more detailed description of hills than that found in the Master Plan (Chapter 3) or the overview descriptions for each section in Chapter 4. The Master Plan tells you what you need to know for planning (for example, the average climb is 30 feet per mile); the cue sheet descriptions will tell you what to expect during each ride (for example, it's flat for 30 miles with two big hills near the end).

Directions		**Compass**	
St	Straight	(N)	North
R	Right	(S)	South
L	Left	(E)	East
BR	Bear Right	(W)	West
BL	Bear Left		
MR	Merge Right		
ML	Merge Left		
(n/s)	No sign		

Detailed Directions — Westbound

Cum	Leg	Dir	Road

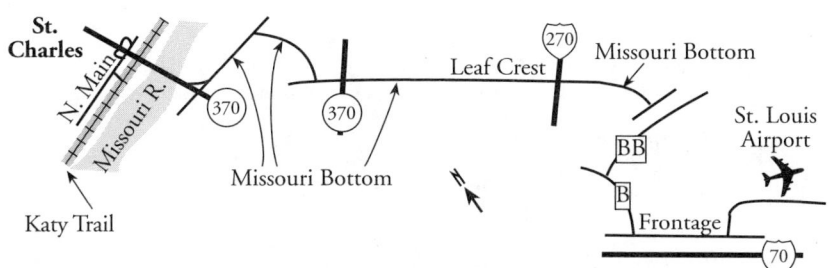

Easy hills on Missouri Bottom and 370 bridge. Traffic can be heavy.

Cum	Leg	Dir	Road
0.0		R (W)	**Airport Rd.** from Main Airport Building Exit (map p. 41)
0.2	0.2	R (W)	**Frontage Rd.** toward I-70, LT Park
1.1	0.9	R	**Route B** at light
1.7	0.6	R	**Route BB**
2.0	0.3	L	walk through gate opposite 1st runway across 50 feet of grass to main highway
2.1	0.1	L (N)	**Missouri Bottom** at light
3.6	1.5	St	across I-270
4.0	0.4	St	**Leaf Crest**
4.3	0.3	St	**Missouri Bottom**
4.8	0.5	R	Missouri Bottom (n/s) after Route 370 overpass
6.2	1.4	L	Missouri Bottom at T
7.3	1.1	R	**Frontage Rd.** just before Route 370 entrance; sign says "NO OUTLET"
7.9	0.6	L	**Bike Trail** up onto 370 bridge, across river
8.5	0.6	R	down Bike Trail ramp at end of bridge to N Main
8.7	0.2	R (W)	**N Main**
8.8	0.1	L,R	**Katy Bike Trail** parallel to N Main
10.3	1.5		Visitor's Bureau (on right)
10.5	0.2		Lewis & Clark Center, right on Perry St.
10.6	0.1		Frontier Park in St. Charles (map p. 42)

Cum	Leg	Dir	Road

Scenic flat riding on hard-packed crushed limestone rail trail.

Cum	Leg	Dir	Road
0.0		West	**Katy Trail** from Frontier Park in St. Charles (map p. 43)
6.2	6.2		Greens Bottom Rd.: restroom
16.5	10.3		Weldon Springs: restroom
21.1	4.6		Matson: restroom
26.8	5.7		Augusta (map p. 44)
34.3	7.5		Dutzow: conv. store, 4-mile spur to Washington (map p. 45)
38.0	3.7		Marthasville: bike shop, restrooms, water, restaurants
61.1	23.1		McKittrick: 3-mile spur to Hermann (map p. 46)
71.3	10.2		Bluffton (p. 48)
76.4	5.1		Portland: café, bar
85.5	9.1		Mokane: restroom, bar, grill, market
91.5	6.0		Tebbetts: restroom, Mrs. Turner's Store
103.6	12.1		N Jefferson: 2-mile spur to Jefferson City (p. 48)
114.0	10.4		Hartsburg (p. 49)
117.9	3.9		Wilton: water, restroom
139.9	12.0		McBaine: 9-mile spur to Columbia (p. 50)
138.8	8.9		Rocheport (map p. 50)
148.7	9.9		New Franklin (p. 52)
149.5	.8		Franklin (p. 52)
152.2	2.7		Boonville (map p. 53)

Cum	Leg	Dir	Road

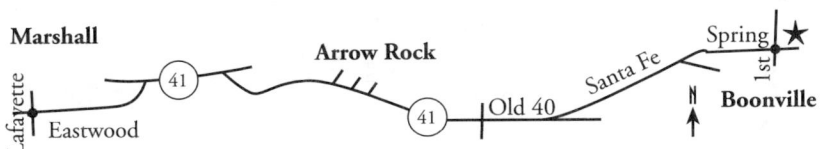

Mostly short gentle to moderate hills through farm country.

0.0		West	**Spring St.** from Visitor Center in Boonville (map p. 53)
0.3	0.3	MR	**Santa Fe Trail**
6.1	5.8	MR (W)	**Old Route 40**
6.5	0.4	St	**Route 41**
18.8	12.3		Arrow Rock State Historical Site Campground on right
19.1	0.3		Arrow Rock State Historical Site Museum on right
19.3	0.2		Arrow Rock on right (map p. 56)
29.6	10.3	L (W)	**Route 41**
31.4	1.8	L	**Eastwood Rd.** (n/s; watch mileage)
33.9	2.5		Lafayette at Visitor Center in Marshall (map p. 58)

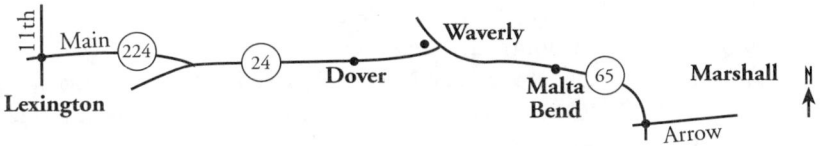

Mostly short gentle to moderate hills through farm country.

0.0		North	**Route 65** from Arrow in Marshall (map p. 58)
10.1	10.1		Malta Bend: conv. store
14.6	4.5		Grand Pass: no services
18.5	3.9	L (W)	**Route 24** in Waverly: small store, restaurant
28.5	10.0		Dover: conv. store
36.9	8.4	BR (W)	**Route 224** into Lexington
39.0	2.1		Main at 11th in Lexington (map p. 59)

mile 152

Cum	Leg	Dir	Road

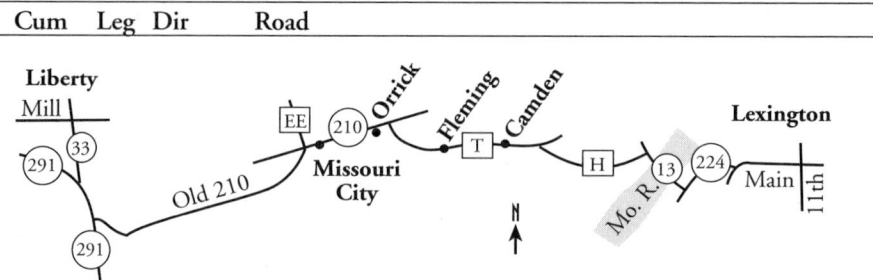

Downhill to cross river. Flat bottomland with few short hills around Camden and Fleming. Busy traffic and hill by Missouri City. Flat on Old 210 with gentle hills into Liberty.

Cum	Leg	Dir	Road
0.0		West	**Main** from 11th in Lexington (map p. 59)
0.2	0.2	BR	**Route 224** down hill
0.6	0.4	R (N)	**Route 13** (over narrow .6 mile bridge)
5.1	4.5	L (W)	**Route H** in Henrietta: café, covered picnic tables, water
9.8	4.7	L (W)	**Route T**
11.2	1.4		Camden: no services
13.7	2.5		Fleming: no services
16.4	2.7	L (W)	**Route 210**
17.4	1.0		Orrick, .5 mi. off to left
26.7	9.3		Missouri City: no services
28.1	1.4	L	**Old Route 210** (n/s) at intersection for Route EE north
33.7	5.6	MR (N)	**Route 291** (ride frontage road or bike trail on west side)
36.1	2.4	BR (N)	**Route 33** (Leonard St.)
36.8	0.7	St (N)	**Lightburne** across Mill in Liberty (map p. 60)
36.9	0.1		back of Visitor Center on left

Spur Route to Independence

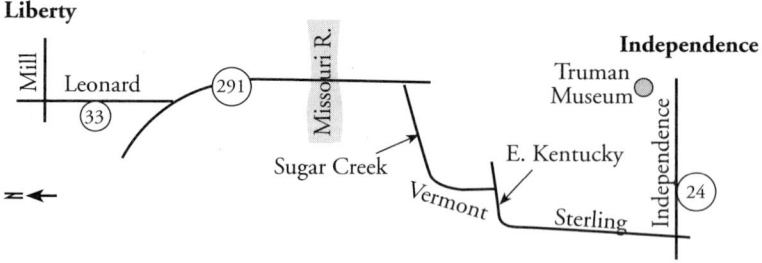

Long gentle hills, big road, and light traffic to river. Quiet back road with long significant hill up to Independence Ave.

Cum	Leg	Dir	Road
0.0		South	**Leonard** from Mill in Liberty (map p. 60)
.7	.7	ML	**Route 291**, bike trail on west side
6.1	5.4	R	**Sugar Creek**, becomes Vermont

Cum	Leg	Dir	Road
10.0	3.9	R	**E Kentucky**
10.2	.2	L	**Sterling**
11.4	1.2	L	**Independence Ave.** (Route 24)
12.6	1.2		Truman Museum on left

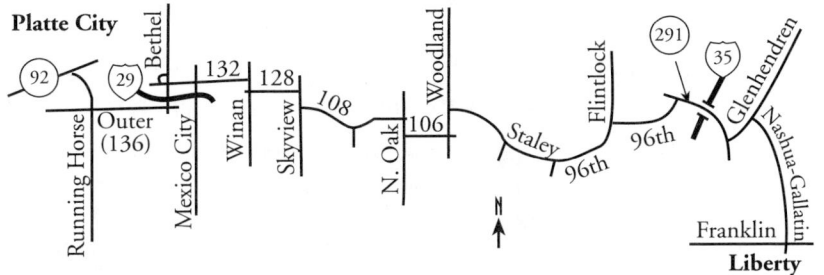

This whole section is moderately hilly with mostly short ups and downs through farm country and suburban neighborhoods.

0.0		North	**Gallatin** from Franklin in Liberty (map p. 60)
2.0	2.0	L	**Glenhendren**
2.3	0.3	R	**Route 291**, across I-35
2.8	0.5	L (S)	**96th**
3.4	0.6	L (S)	**Flintlock,** becomes 96th again
6.0	2.6	St	across I-435
6.5	0.5	BR (W)	**Staley**
7.5	1.0	BR	Staley
9.5	2.0	L	**Woodland** (n/s)
9.7	0.2	R	**106th**
10.7	1.0	R	**North Oak**
11.0	0.3	L	**108th**
11.5	0.5	St	across Route 169
13.9	2.4	BR	**108th**
15.1	1.2	R	**Skyview**
16.6	1.5	St	Skyview, across I-435 and LP Cookingham
17.6	1.0	L	**128th**
18.6	1.0		cross Interurban Rd.
20.1	1.5	R	**Winan**
20.6	0.5	L	**132nd**
21.4	0.8	St	across Mexico City Rd. (n/s) onto Outer Rd.; airport 2 mi. south on Mexico City Rd.
22.9	1.5	R,R (S)	**Bethel** (across I-29)
23.1	0.2	R (W)	**Outer Rd.,** becomes 136th
24.6	1.5	R (N)	**Running Horse**
25.7	1.1	L (W)	**Route 92** in Platte City (map p. 66)

mile 262

Cum	Leg	Dir	Road

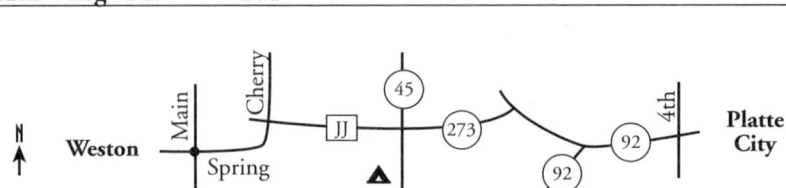

Mostly farm country with moderate rolling hills and occasional short steep hills near Weston. There are long climbs up to Route 45 from both directions.

0.0		St (W)	**Route 92** from 4th St. in Platte City (map p. 66)
1.0	1.0	St	to Route 273 (Route 92 goes left)
1.3	0.3	L	**Route 273**
5.2	3.9	St	**Route JJ** (Weston Bend State Park & CG .4 mi. South)
7.2	2.0	L	**Cherry**
7.5	0.3		Spring at Main in Weston (map p. 67)

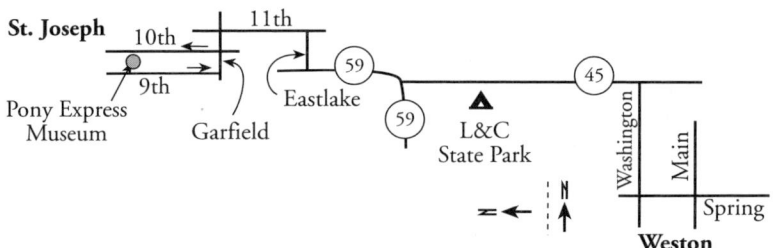

After a few gentle hills out of Weston, lots of flat bottomland.

0.0		St (W)	**Spring** from Main St. in Weston (map p. 67)
0.1	0.1	R	**Washington**
0.8	0.7	L	**Route 45**
12.4	11.6		Lewis & Clark State Park (p. 68)
13.5	1.1	St	**Route 59**
28.1	14.6	St	Route 59 across Route 752
29.3	1.2	ML	Route 59
29.9	0.6	R	**Eastlake**
30.3	0.4	L	**11th**
30.8	0.5	L	**Garfield**
30.9	0.1	R	**10th**
31.9	1.0		10th at Pony Express Museum in St. Joseph (map p. 69)

Cum	Leg	Dir	Road

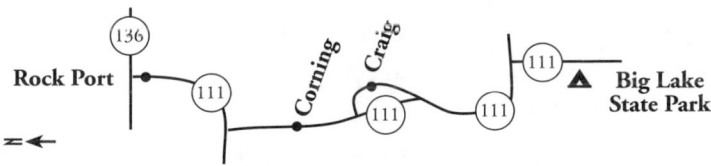

First 6 miles from St. Joseph has moderate hills through suburbs. Beyond Amazonia is flat bottomland, except for 8 short (60 ft) nuisance hills on dirt Road 400.

Cum	Leg	Dir	Road
0.0		North	**Noyes** from Frederick in St. Joseph (map p. 69)
0.2	0.2	L	**Sherman**
0.2	0.0	BR	**Corby Parkway**
0.6	0.4	BR	**Northeast Parkway**
0.8	0.2	BL	**Northwest Parkway**
2.3	1.5	R	**St. Joseph Ave.** (Route 59)
3.4	1.1	BL	**Route K**
9.4	6.0	L	**Route T** in Amazonia: covered picnic tables, water
13.9	4.5		Pavement ends in Nodaway
14.0	0.1	L	**Road 400** (dirt) — **CRITICAL TURN !**
17.9	3.9		Pavement resumes
28.4	10.5	L	**Route 111**
28.7	0.3		Forest City: bar, diner
33.8	5.1	L	**Route 111/159**
39.2	5.4	R	**Route 111**
41.6	2.4	L	Big Lake State Park (p. 72)

Flat bottomland with final gentle 3-mile climb up to Rock Port.

Cum	Leg	Dir	Road
0.0		North	**Route 111** from Big Lake State Park (p. 72)
2.1	2.1	L	Route 111 (at Route 118 intersection)
8.3	6.2	BL	Route 111; Craig .2 mi. on right: café
8.7	0.4	ML	Route 111
16.5	7.8		Corning: no services
26.4	9.9	R	Route 111 at T; cross I-29
			(Left to Brownville; see p. 73 for map and description)
30.3	3.9	R (E)	Route 136 in Rock Port (map p. 72)

Cum	Leg	Dir	Road

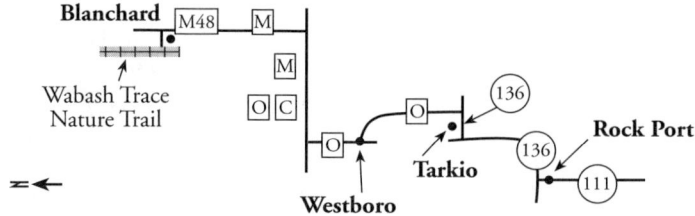

Lots of short ups and downs (some steep) through rich farm country.

Cum	Leg	Dir	Road
0.0		East	**Route 136** from Route 111 in Rock Port (map p. 72)
7.8	7.8	R (E)	Route 136 in Tarkio (p. 74)
8.8	1.0	L (N)	**Route O**
18.2	9.4	R (N)	Route O in Westboro: no services
18.4	0.2	R (E)	**Routes C/O**
18.6	0.2	St	Route C
22.7	4.1	St	Routes C, M
23.5	0.8	L (N)	**Route M**
26.4	2.9	St	M 48 across state line and stop sign in Blanchard
26.6	0.2	L (W)	dirt road (n/s) (last street in town)
26.8	0.2	R (N)	Wabash Trace Nature Trail

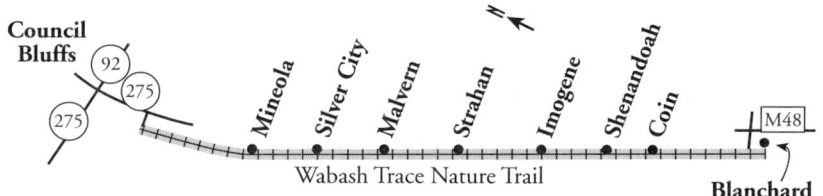

Mostly level with some long gentle ups and downs on this former railroad. Hard-packed crushed limestone surface.

Cum	Leg	Dir	Road
0.0		North	**Wabash Trace Nature Trail** from Blanchard
5.6	5.6		Coin
16.6	11.0		Shenandoah (map p. 74)
25.6	9.0		Imogene
31.8	6.2		Strahan
37.6	5.8		Malvern
46.2	8.6		Silver City
51.8	5.6		Mineola
61.4	9.6	L (N)	**Route 275** from parking lot at end of bike trail
61.8	0.4		**Route 92/275** in Council Bluffs (map p. 76)

Cum	Leg	Dir	Road

mile 490

Moderate Loess hills first 8 miles to Crescent. Then all flat bottomland.

Cum	Leg	Dir	Road
0.0	0.8	North	**N Broadway** (Route 183) from Broadway in Council Bluffs (map p. 76)
7.0	7.0	St	Route 183 in Crescent: 3 small restaurants, conv. store
17.6	10.6	St	Route 183 in Loveland: café
17.8	0.2		Intersection G14: Wilson Island CG 7 mi. west (See map p. 82 for detour to Wilson Island State Park Campground and DeSoto National Wildlife Refuge)
21.9	4.1	L (W)	**Erie** (Route 183) in Missouri Valley (map p. 82)
22.2	0.3	R (N)	**Route 183**
26.4	4.2	L(W)	**Route F50** (270th St.)
32.5	6.1	R (N)	**K45** in Modale: small restaurant, conv. store
39.4	6.9		Mondamin: conv. store, bar, grill
46.0	6.6		Little Sioux: no services
55.4	9.4		Blencoe: conv. store
62.2	6.8		Main St. (Route 175) in Onawa (map p. 83)

Cum	Leg	Dir	Road

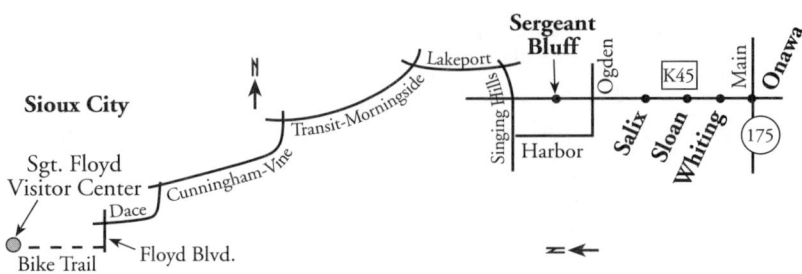

Flat bottomland with one 300 foot significant climb on Singing Hills between K45 and Lakeport. The recommended detour on Harbor is flat and avoids a heavy traffic stretch on K45.

Cum	Leg	Dir	Road
0.0		North	**K45** (10th St.) from Main St. in Onawa (map p. 83)
7.7	7.7		Whiting on left: conv. store, bar, café, small market
15.9	8.2		Sloan: bar, café, small market
21.9	6.0		Salix on left: bar
29.2	7.3	L	**Ogden** (n/s, 1st traffic light, just before grain elevators)
30.0	0.8	R	**Harbor** after I-29: motels
32.5	2.5	R	**Singing Hills** (n/s): motels
34.2	1.7	L	**Lakeport** at top of hill: motels
36.5	2.3	L	**Morningside**, becomes Transit
38.4	1.9	L	**Vine**, becomes Cunningham
39.3	0.9	L	**Dace**; cross Sgt. Floyd River
39.7	0.4	L	**Floyd Blvd.,** ride under I-29
40.0	0.3	R	**River Bike Trail**; hug river on left
41.4	1.4		Sgt. Floyd Visitor Center in Sioux City (map p. 85)

Cum	Leg	Dir	Road

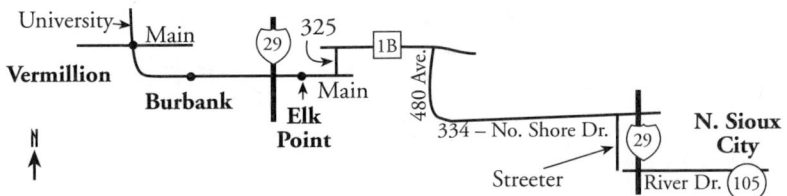

All flat bottomland with a short climb up to Vermillion at the end.

Cum	Leg	Dir	Road
0.0		West	**Bike Trail** from Sgt. Floyd Visitor Center in Sioux City (use town map on p. 87 for first 6 miles)
3.1	3.1	St	Council Oaks (n/s) through Riverside Park
3.5	0.4	L (N)	**Riverside Blvd.**
4.9	1.4	L	**Military Rd.**
5.3	0.4	L	**Route 105 South** (River Drive) after river
6.3	1.0	R (N)	**Streeter** (frontage rd.) after I-29: motels
8.4	2.1	L	**Bike Trail** along North Shore Drive
9.2	0.8	St	**North Shore Drive** (334th St.) after school
13.3	4.1	R	**480 Ave.**
17.3	4.0	St	across 330th St. (CR 6)
18.8	1.5	St	across I-29
19.4	0.6	L	**CR 1B**
23.5	4.1	L	**325th St.**
23.6	0.1	R	**Main St.**
24.8	1.2		Elk Point (p. 88)
33.2	8.4		Burbank: bar
39.4	6.2		University at Main St. in Vermillion (map p. 88)

mile 594

Cum	Leg	Dir	Road

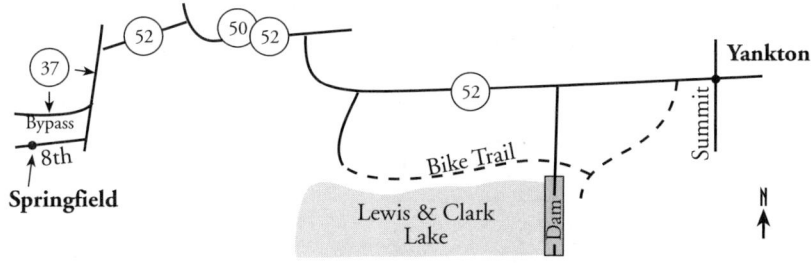

Short downhill from Vermillion to flat bottomland the rest of the way.

Cum	Leg	Dir	Road
0.0		West	**Cherry** from Stanford in Vermillion (map p. 88)
1.0	1.0	L (W)	**Timber**
9.3	8.3	R (N)	**454 Ave.** (paved road)
14.3	5.0	L (W)	**Route 50**
28.7	14.4		Route 50 at Broadway in Yankton (map p. 90)

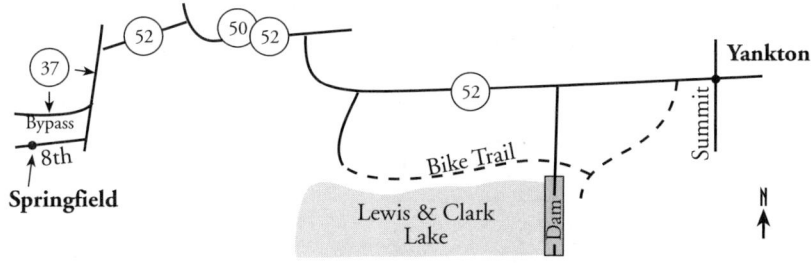

Long steep hill up 52 from lake. Long gentle to moderate hills, mostly down.

Cum	Leg	Dir	Road
0.0		West	**8th St.** (Route 52) from Summit in Yankton (map p. 90)
3.5	3.5	L	**Bike Trail** on south side of road at Fish Hatchery, follow up north end of dam
4.3	0.8	St (W)	Bike Trail across dam road. A side trip left (south) 3.1 mi. across dam takes you up hill to Visitor Center.
4.7	0.4	St	Pass marina, restaurant, and cabins. Bike trail winds along the north side of Lewis & Clark Lake past several excellent picnic areas and campgrounds (see Yankton p. 90).
8.1	3.4		Beach, rest rooms, water. Follow exit road north and east out of park.
8.8	0.7	L (W)	**Route 52** up big hill
12.3	3.5	L (W)	Route 50/52
17.2	4.9	L (W)	Route 52
29.4	12.2	L (S)	**Route 37**
32.1	2.7	BR (W)	Route 37 at east access road to Springfield (map p. 95)

Cum	Leg	Dir	Road

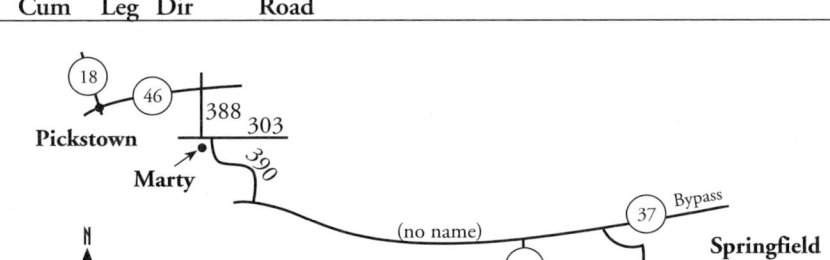

Long gentle to moderate hills. Long significant hill up to Marty and Route 46.

33.2	1.1	West	Route 37 at west access road to Springfield
37.4	4.2	St (W)	Nameless road where Route 37 turns left
40.4	3.0	St (W)	across CR 18 (Avon Rd.)
60.1	19.7	R (N)	**390 Ave.** in Greenwood: abandoned town
67.0	6.9	L (W)	**303 St.** at Marty Indian School
67.1	0.1	R (N)	**388 Ave.** (CR 21)
73.2	6.1	L (W)	**Route 46**
75.7	2.5		Fort Randall Casino/Hotel/Restaurant
78.5	2.8		Route 18/281 in Pickstown (map p. 96)

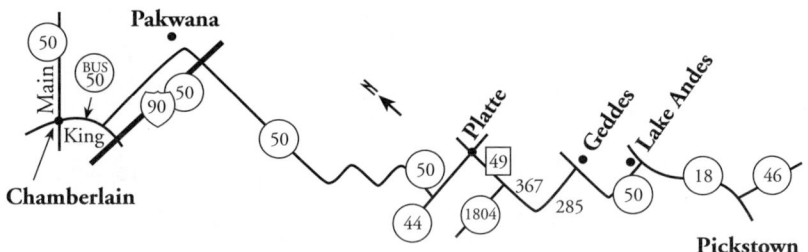

Many long moderate hills through dry farm country away from river.

0.0		North	**Route18/281** from Route 46 in Pickstown (map p. 96)
5.7	5.7	BL	**Route 50** in Lake Andes (p. 97)
6.0	0.3	L (W)	Route 50
20.4	14.4	L (W)	**285 St.** (CR 34); Geddes on right: bar, café
27.3	6.9	R (N)	**367 Ave.** (CR 49)
30.3	3.0	St(N)	367 Ave. (Route 1804 goes left/west)
36.3	6.0	L (W)	**Route 44** (7th St.) in Platte (Map. p 98)
46.3	10.0	R (N)	**Route 50**
53.1	6.8		Academy: no services
78.1	25.0	St (N)	across I-90 towards Pukwana
79.4	1.3	BL (W)	main road (n/s) in Pukwana
85.9	6.5	R (N)	Route 50 (becomes King St.)
88.9	3.2	R (N)	Main (Route 50) in Chamberlain (map p. 98)

Cum	Leg	Dir	Road

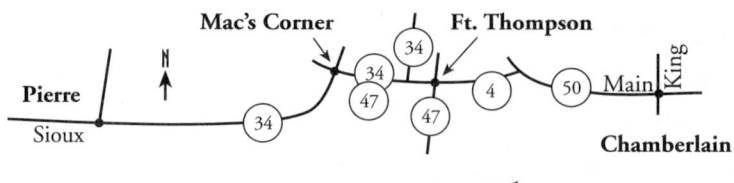

Long tough hill out of Chamberlain. Long moderate hills to Pierre.

Cum	Leg	Dir	Road
0.0		North	**Main** (Route 50) from King in Chamberlain (map p. 98)
0.6	0.6		American Creek Campground
14.7	14.1	L (W)	**Route 4**
22.3	7.6	St (N)	**Route 47** in Fort Thompson (p. 100)
22.9	0.6	St (N)	Route 34/47
35.2	12.3	L (W)	**Route 34** at Mac's Corner: conv. store
78.5	43.3		Farm Island Recreation Area (p. 100)
80.4	1.9		Route 34 at Route 14 in Pierre (map p. 100)

Cum	Leg	Dir	Road

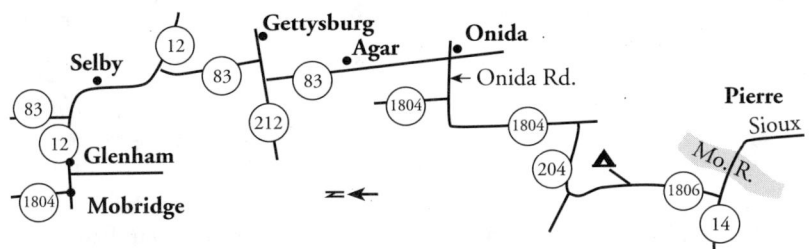

Long moderate, and some significant, hills. One big hill west of Glenham.

Cum	Leg	Dir	Road
0.0		West	**Route 14** Sidewalk (eastbound side) across Missouri River from Riverside Bike Trail in Pierre (map p. 100)
0.4	0.4	St (S)	onto **Frontage Rd.** towards Fort Pierre
0.9	0.5	R (W)	across Deadwood onto **Stanley**
1.1	0.2	R (N)	**Sale Barn Rd.**
1.5	0.4	L (W)	**Route 14/34**
2.1	0.6	R (N)	**Route 1806**
6.0	3.9	BL	Route 1806
7.2	1.2	St (E)	**Route 204** across dam
9.3	2.1	L (N)	**Route 1804** at Oahe Dam Visitor Center: water, restroom, exhibits
28.3	19.0	R (E)	Route 1804
34.3	6.0	St (E)	**Onida Rd.** (Route 1804 goes Left/North)
46.3	12.0	L (N)	**Route 83** in Onida (p. 103)
55.3	9.0		Agar on right: bar/restaurant
67.2	11.9	St (E)	**Route 212**
68.1	0.9	L (N)	**Route 83**, Gettysburg (map p. 104) is 5.2 mi. east on Route 212
98.7	30.6	L (N)	Route 83/12
102.6	3.9		Selby on right (p. 105)
105.3	2.7	St (W)	**Route 12** at intersection with Route 83
115.2	9.9		Glenham
118.8	3.6	St (W)	Route 12 at Route 1804 South intersection
122.7	3.9		Route 12 at 4th (Route 1804) in Mobridge (map p. 106)

Cum	Leg	Dir	Road

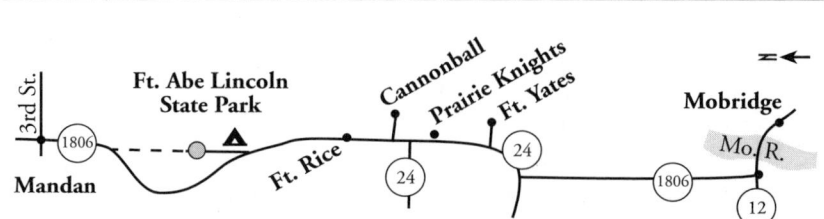

Long moderate hills to Fort Abraham Lincoln. Gentle hills into Mandan.

Cum	Leg	Dir	Road
0.0		North	**Route 1806** from Route 12 in Mobridge (map p. 106
22.1	22.1		Kenel: conv. store
41.2	19.1	R	Route 1806/24
43.6	2.4		Fort Yates 2 mi. to right: Headquarters for Standing Rock Nation; bar, restaurant
57.1	13.5		Prairie Knights Casino/Hotel/Restaurants
63.9	6.8	St (N)	Route 1806, where Route 24 goes Left/West
64.9	1.0		Cannonball 2 mi. on right: conv. store
75.9	11.0		Fort Rice: conv. store
83.5	7.6		Huff: no services
96.7	13.2	BR	**Fort Abraham Lincoln** (p. 111)
97.7	1.0		Visitor Center, Campground; continue straight (north) on park road
99.7	2.0	MR (N)	**Route 1806**
102.2	2.5		Route 1806 at 3rd St. in Mandan (map p. 109)

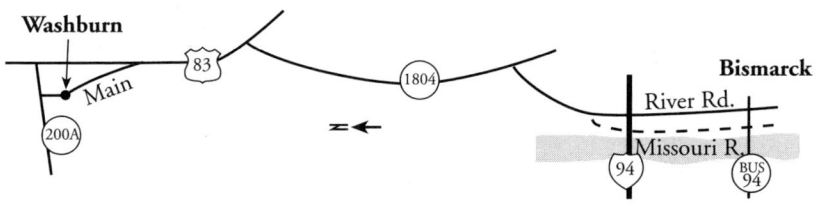

Gentle hills along river with some moderate hills.

Cum	Leg	Dir	Road
0.0		North	**Bike Trail** along River Rd. from Main Ave. (Bus. 94) in Bismarck (map p. 109)
1.7	1.7	ML (N)	onto **River Rd.** at Pioneer Park at end of Bike Trail
5.9	4.2	L (N)	**Route1804**
32.0	26.1	L (N)	**Route 83**
37.1	5.1	L	**Main** in Washburn (map p. 114)

Cum	Leg	Dir	Road

Gentle hills to Stanton. Longer moderate hills to Killdeer. Significant hills west of Killdeer to Route 85. Long tough climb north from Roosevelt Park.

Cum	Leg	Dir	Road
0.0		L (W)	**Route 200A** from Main St. in Washburn (map p. 114)
20.1	20.1	St (W)	200A; Stanton is 1.2 mi. R (N) on Route 31(p. 117)
24.9	4.8	St (W)	**Route 200**
30.9	6.0		4th Ave. in Hazen (p. 117)
32.4	1.5		Main St. in Hazen
38.0	5.6		Beulah 2.9 mi. L (S) on Route 21 (map p. 118)
39.0	1.0		Beulah (west access road)
45.2	6.2		Zap .3 mi. on left (p. 118)
46.0	0.8		Zap (west access road)
52.1	6.1		Golden Valley .4 mi. on left (p. 118)
52.6	0.5		Golden Valley (west access road)
58.9	6.3		Dodge: conv. store, bar
67.1	8.2		Halliday 1.0 mi. on right (p. 119)
80.5	13.4		Dunn Center on right: small restaurant, bar
87.1	6.6		Killdeer (p. 119) 1 mi. on right
107.3	20.2	R (N)	**Route 85/200**
111.9	4.6		Grassy Butte on left: conv. store
125.7	13.8		National Grasslands CG (p. 120)
125.9	0.2		cross Little Missouri River
126.4	0.5		Theodore Roosevelt National Park (p. 120)
141.4	15.0		Watford City (map p. 121)

mile 1186

Cum	Leg	Dir	Road

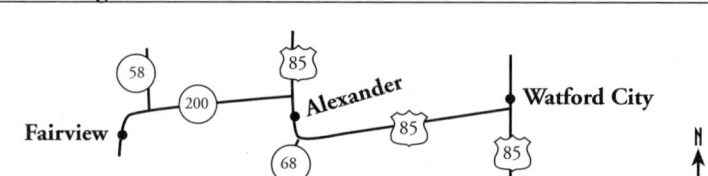

Long gentle to moderate hills all the way.

0.0		West	**Route 85/200** from in Watford City (map p. 121)
7.2	7.2		Arnegard on right
17.0	9.8	St (N)	Route 85/200
19.6	2.6		Alexander (p. 122)
22.0	2.4	L (W)	**Route 200**
37.1	15.1		cross Yellowstone River
40.2	3.1	St (W)	Route 200 at intersection with Route 58
41.1	0.9		Route 200 at Route 201 in Fairview (p. 122)

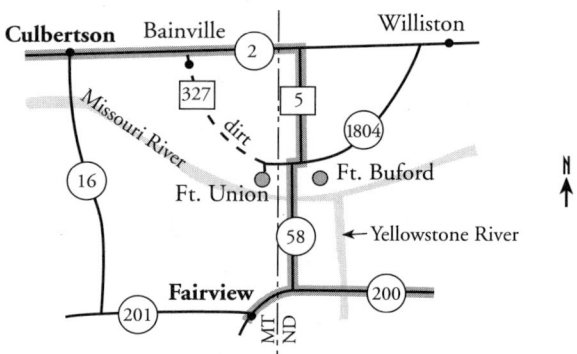

Flat on 58. Long tough climb on CR 5. Route 2 is gentle to moderate hills.

0.0		North	**Route 200** from Route 201 in Fairview (p. 122)
0.9	0.9	L (N)	**Route 58**
9.5	8.6		cross Missouri River
10.8	1.3	R (E)	**Route 1804**; Fort Union 2 mi. on left (p. 125); Fort Buford on right (p. 125)
11.3	0.5	L (N)	**153rd Ave.** (County Route 5)
21.3	10.0	L (W)	**Route 2**
32.0	10.7		Bainville on left
46.4	14.4		Culbertson (map p. 127)

Cum	Leg	Dir	Road

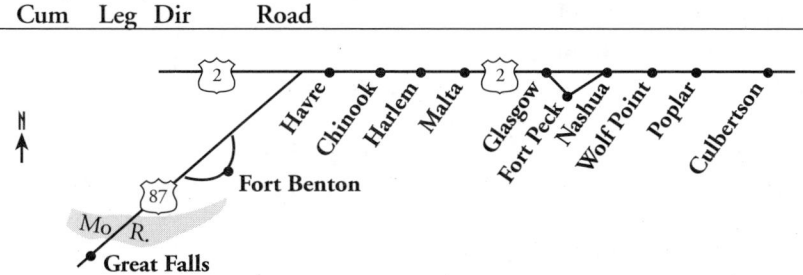

Fort Benton

Great Falls

Route 2 has lots of gentle to moderate hills with some flat riding. The Master Plan in Chapter 3 shows which segments are flatter and which are hillier. There is a big climb to the plateau west of Havre, then more gentle to moderate hills on the plateau. Drop 250 feet into Fort Benton on the river and climb back up to the plateau. Finally a long drop into Great Falls.

mile 1413

Cum	Leg	Dir	Road
0.0		West	**Route 2** from Broadway in Culbertson (map p. 127)
18.8	18.8		Brockton: conv. store
32.6	13.8		Poplar (p. 127)
53.9	21.3		Wolf Point (map p. 128)
72.7	18.8		Frazer on left: no services
88.6	15.9		Nashua: Bergie's homemade ice cream! conv. store, (Fort Peck side trip: p. 130)
102.8	14.2		Glasgow (map p. 129)
116.8	14.0		Rest Area: restrooms, water, shade, covered tables
131.5	14.7		Hinsdale on right: conv. store, small grocery, saloon
145.0	13.5		Saco (p. 131)
154.8	9.8		Sleeping Buffalo Hot Springs Resort on right (p. 131)
172.5	17.7		Malta (map p. 132)
190.0	17.5		Dodson on left: small grocery store, café
214.7	24.7		Fort Belknap Agency: café, conv. store, rest area with restrooms and water
218.2	3.5		Harlem on right (p. 133)
230.2	12.0		Zurich on right: conv. store ?
239.3	9.1		Chinook (map p. 133)
256.7	21.4		Havre (map p. 135)
264.0	3.3	L (S)	**Route 87**
285.0	21.0		Box Elder: conv. store
295.6	10.6		Big Sandy (p. 136)
322.5	26.9		Loma (p. 136)
331.3	8.8	L	**Route 387** down big hill, becomes St. Charles St.
333.7	2.4	L	**21st**
334.1	0.4	R	**Front St.** in Fort Benton (map p. 137)
334.7	0.6	R	**13th St.**
335.0	0.3	L	**St. Charles St.** (Route 386) up big hill

Cum	Leg	Dir	Road
336.5	1.5	L (W)	**Route 87**
348.2	11.7		Carter on left: no services
372.2	24.0	BR	**Route 89N, 200W**
373.1	0.9	St	towards City Center, cross bridge
373.6	0.5		cross Missouri River into Great Falls (map p. 139)

LEMHI PASS AND BIG HOLE ROUTES

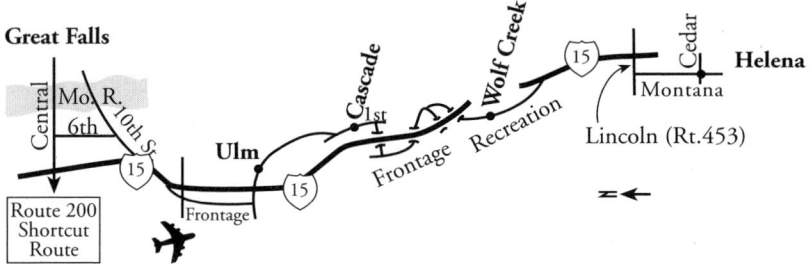

After a 350-foot climb out of Great Falls, gentle hills to Cascade. Then 1,200 feet of steady gentle to moderate climbing along the river to Wolf Creek. Finally 1,600 feet of climbing over two big hills on I-15 before swooping down to Helena.

0.0		West	**1st Ave. North** at River Edge Bike Trail in Great Falls (map p. 139)
0.2	0.2		cross Missouri River on Central Ave. Bridge
0.6	0.4	L (S)	**6th St. SW**
1.9	1.3	R (W)	**10th Ave.** (Route 89, 200, 3, to I-15)
2.5	0.6	St	**I-15 South** towards Helena
3.6	1.1	BR	**Exit 277** to Airport
3.9	0.3	R,L (S)	**Frontage Rd.** (n/s)
11.2	7.3	L	**Ulm-Vaughn Rd.** through Ulm: conv. store, pizza, restaurant
25.6	14.4	ML	**1st St.** (n/s, at baseball field) in Cascade (p. 146)
26.8	1.2	R (W)	**under I-15** (n/s, watch mileage)
26.9	0.1	L (S)	**Frontage Rd.** (n/s)
31.4	4.5	L	Frontage Rd. before I-15
34.2	2.8	St	under I-15 onto Recreation Rd. (n/s)
46.5	12.3		Stickney Creek NFS Campground (p. 147)
54.9	8.4		Wolf Creek NFS Campground (p. 147)
57.9	3.0		Wolf Creek (p. 147)
65.6	7.7	St	**onto I-15**
75.7	10.1		Exit 209 for Gates of the Mountains (p. 148)
84.7	9.0	R (W)	**Exit 200**, Lincoln Rd.
85.1	0.4	L	**Montana Ave.** (n/s)
91.8	6.7		Montana Ave. at Cedar in Helena (map p. 147)

Cum	Leg	Dir	Road

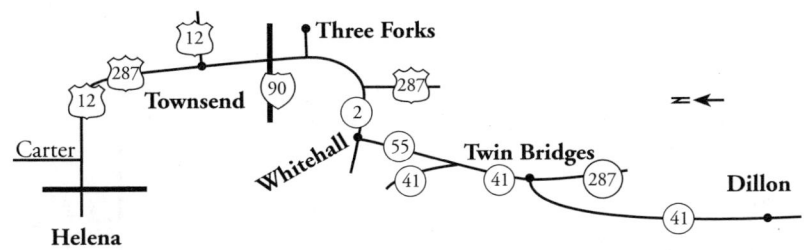

Long gentle to moderate, mostly down, hills to Three Forks. Then shorter moderate and significant hills through canyon to Cardwell. Gentle to moderate long, mostly up, hills to Dillon.

Cum	Leg	Dir	Road
0.0		East!!	**Route 12/287** from Carter Rd. in Helena (map p. 147)
19.2	19.2		Winston: conv. store
31.6	12.4		Townsend (p. 150)
62.0	30.4		cross I-90: Wheat Mountain Bakery & Deli
63.3	1.3	St (S)	Route 287; Three Forks 2.6 mi. left (map p. 151)
73.2	9.9	St (W)	**Route 2** (Route 287 goes south)
78.2	5.0		Lewis & Clark State Park Caverns and CG (p. 151)
85.3	7.1		Cardwell (p. 153)
85.6	0.3	R	**Route 359** (n/s) under I-90
93.0	7.4		Whitehall (p. 153)
93.4	0.4	L (S)	**Route 55**
109.3	15.9		Silverstar (p. 153)
119.8	10.5	R (W)	**Route 41** in Twin Bridges (p. 153)
147.8	28.0		Visitor Center on Montana Ave. (Route 41) in Dillon (map p. 155)

Cum	Leg	Dir	Road

LEMHI PASS ROUTE

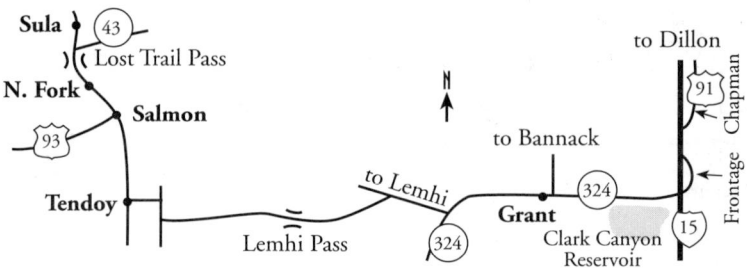

Mostly gentle hills to Clark Canyon Reservoir. Moderate and significant hills climb 1,000 feet to Grant. Then it's about 1,000 feet in 10 miles to the dirt road, and a final 1,600 feet in 12 miles to the pass. It's steep and rough going down 2,600 feet on the west side, and then another 800-foot gentle drop on pavement to Salmon. Along the river to North Fork are gentle grades. Climbing begins gradually with 800 feet to Gibbonsville, and then gets serious with 2,400 feet to Lost Trail Pass. Then a steep downhill to Sula.

Cum	Leg	Dir	Road
0.0		South	**Atlantic** from Reeder in Dillon (5,100 ft) (map p. 155)
0.5	0.5	L	**Chapman**, after Western Montana College; becomes Route 91
4.0	3.5	St (S)	**Frontage Rd.**
7.7	3.7	R	under I-15
7.8	0.1	L	**onto I-15**
12.4	4.6	R	**Exit 51** to Dilys
12.6	0.2	L	under I-15
12.7	0.1	R	**Frontage Rd.**
19.6	6.9	St (W)	**Route 324** across I-15 at Clark Canyon Reservoir (p. 157 for description and campgrounds)
31.9	12.3		Grant (5,800 ft)(p. 158)
41.6	9.7	R	dirt road (sign to **Lemhi Pass**)
43.5	1.9	BL	dirt road (sign to Lemhi Pass)
53.7	10.2	St	cross Lemhi Pass (7,373 ft); .2 mi. walk to Sacajawea Memorial at spring headwater of Missouri River
65.5	11.8	R	**Agency Creek Rd.**
65.8	0.3	L	**Tendoy Lane**
65.9	0.1	R	**Route 28** (pavement) in Tendoy: small store and RV Park
86.4	20.5	St (N)	**Route 93** over Salmon River in Salmon (map p. 160)
107.2	20.8		North Fork (p. 162)
118.0	10.8		Gibbonsville: café, cabins
131.7	13.7	St (N)	Route 93 at Lost Trail Pass (7,000 ft)
144.3	12.6		Sula (p. 165)

Cum	Leg	Dir	Road

(Skip to next page to resume Lemhi Pass and Big Hole Routes in Sula)

BIG HOLE ROUTE

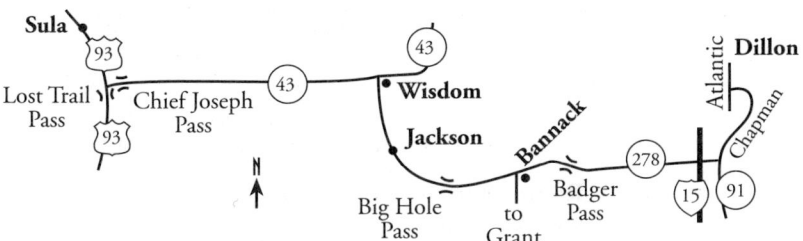

From Dillon it's 1,500 feet of climbing up to Badger Pass and another 1,400 feet to Big Hole Pass. Then a downhill cruise to Jackson and a mostly flat ride to Wisdom. Another 1,400 feet of mostly moderate to steep climbing takes you to Chief Joseph Pass for a great downhill cruise to Sula.

Cum	Leg	Dir	Road
0.0		South	**Atlantic** from Reeder in Dillon (5,100 ft) (map p. 155)
0.5	0.5	L	**Chapman**, after Western Montana College; becomes Route 91
4.0	3.5	R (W)	**Route 278**, under I-15
17.8	13.8		Badger Pass (6,760 ft)
21.4	3.6		intersection Bannack Rd. to Grant (p. 163)
36.4	15.0		Big Hole Pass (7,360 ft)
47.2	10.8		Jackson (p. 163)
65.1	17.9	L (W)	**Route 43** in Wisdom (map p. 164)
74.7	9.6		Big Hole National Battlefield (p. 165)
81.9	7.2		May Creek NFS Campground (p. 164)
90.1	8.2		Chief Joseph Pass (7,240 ft)
91.2	1.1	R (N)	**Route 93** at Lost Trail Pass (7,000 ft)
103.8	12.6		Sula (p. 165)

Cum	Leg	Dir	Road

Resume: Lemhi Pass and Big Hole Routes

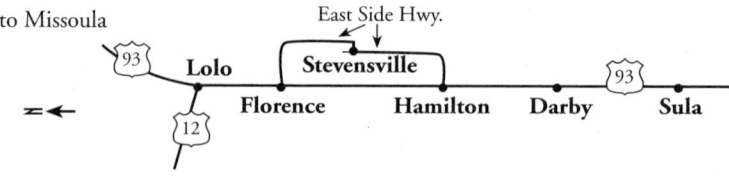

Gentle downhill to Darby with long gentle hills all the way to Missoula.

Cum	Leg	Dir	Road
0.0		North	**Route 93** from Sula (p. 165)
2.9	2.9		Spring Gulch NFS CG (p. 166)
17.8	14.9		Darby (p. 166)
34.5	16.7	R (E)	**Route 269** in Hamilton (map p. 167)
40.2	5.7		Corvallis: conv. store
54.4	14.2	R (E)	**East Side Highway** (Route 203) in Stevensville (p. 168)
66.3	11.9	R (N)	**Route 93** in Florence: supermarket, restaurant
75.1	8.8	St (N)	intersection Route 12 in Lolo (p. 168); turn left/west here to skip Missoula
82.0	6.9		Route 93 at Old Hwy. 93 in Missoula (map p. 169)

Route 200 Shortcut

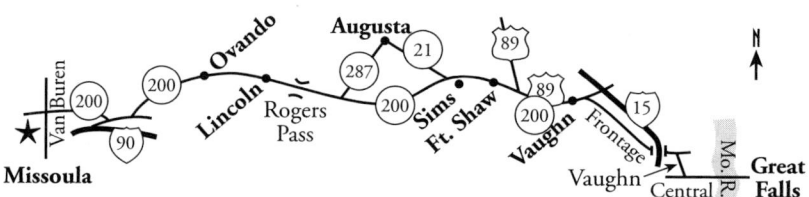

Mostly flat with long gentle hills for first 32 miles. Then 3,200 feet in a series of long steep hills and a final climb to Roger's Pass. Mostly downhill with occasional moderate hills for 90 miles to Missoula.

Cum	Leg	Dir	Road
0.0		West	**1st Ave. North** from Bike Trail in Great Falls (map p. 139)
0.1	0.1		cross Missouri River on Central Ave. Bridge
1.3	1.2	R (N)	**Vaughn Rd.**
2.2	0.9	L	**Frontage Rd.** at T (n/s, RR parallel on left)
3.4	1.2	St (W)	Frontage Rd., passing under I-15
11.6	8.2	L	**Route 200**

Cum	Leg	Dir	Road
12.0	0.4		Vaughn: conv. store, restaurant
19.3	7.3	St (W)	Route 200 towards Sun River
20.4	1.1		Sun River: conv. store
25.2	4.8		Fort Shaw: no services
31.1	5.9		Simms on left: no services
31.5	0.4	St (W)	Route 200
49.7	18.2	St (W)	Route 200 at intersection Route 287; saloon (4,240 ft)
68.8	19.1		Roger's Pass (5,610 ft)
80.0	11.2		Aspen Grove NFS CG: .5 mi. left on river, pretty, private, shade, tables, water, pit toilets
87.1	7.1		Lincoln (map p. 172)
112.4	26.3		Ovando .5 mi. off to left (p. 173)
122.9	9.5		Russell Gates NFS CG: nice sites on river, tables, shade, water, pit toilets
126.6	3.7		Larry's Clearwater Inn: motel, café, rest area
158.9	32.3	R (W)	Frontage Rd. just before entering I-90
164.5	5.6		Van Buren and Visitor Center in Missoula (map p. 169)

mile 2253

RESUME: MAIN ROUTE

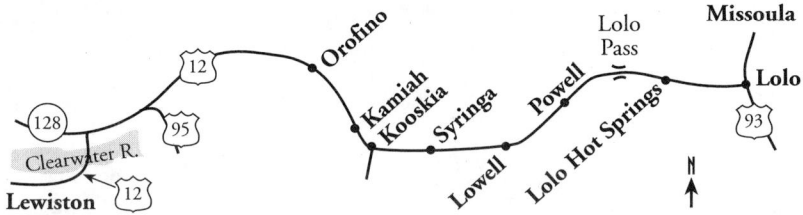

From Lolo to Lolo Hot Springs is 25 miles of steady moderate hill (1,000 feet). Then 7.4 miles of steep climbing (1,100 feet) to Lolo Pass. This is followed by over 100 miles of the most glorious downhill riding along raging rivers and a final 60 miles of mostly descending gentle hills beside a growing river to Lewiston.

Cum	Leg	Dir	Road
0.0		South	**Route 93** from Old Hwy. 93 in Missoula (map p. 169)
6.9	6.9	R (W)	**Route 12** in Lolo (map p. 168)
22.4	15.5		Lewis & Clark NFS CG
32.1	9.7		Lolo Hot Springs (p. 176)
33.5	1.4		Lee Creek NFS CG
39.5	6.0		Lolo Pass (5,235 ft.): visitor center
48.8	9.3		DeVoto Grove: beautiful rest stop, restrooms
50.4	1.6		White Sands NFS CG (1.5 mi., 200 ft down!)

Cum	Leg	Dir	Road
52.0	1.6		Powell (p. 177)
55.3	3.3		Whitehorse NFS CG (on river)
55.6	0.3		Wendover NFS CG (on river)
63.6	8.0		Jerry Johnson NFS CG (north side of road)
91.2	27.6		Wilderness Gateway NFS CG (across river)
109.7	18.5		Apgar NFS CG (on river)
116.6	6.9		Lowell (p. 178)
118.6	2.0		Wild Goose NFS CG (on river)
123.9	5.3		Syringa: café
138.7	14.8		Kooskia east access road (map p. 179)
140.0	1.3		Kooskia west access road
147.7	7.7		Kamiah (map p. 180)
162.4	14.7		Greer: café across river
170.0	7.6		Orofino bridge (map p. 181)
179.2	9.2		Peck Junction: café
185.8	6.6		Lenore: no services
186.3	0.5		Rest Area: water, rest rooms, tables, by river
203.2	16.9	BR	Route 12 (Nez Perce Visitor Center 1.8 mi. left)
206.8	3.6		cross Hatwai Creek
207.3	0.5	BL	**Bike Trail** on eastbound side of Route 12 (cross all 4 lanes carefully)
211.7	4.4		cross Clearwater River bridge on sidewalk on southbound side into Lewiston (map p. 183)

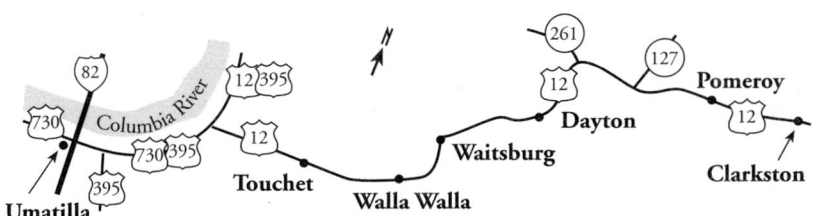

After 9 miles of flat riding along the river, there are 11 miles of steep climbing (2,200 feet) to Alpowa Summit. Then 1,500 feet of climbing shorter, but still steep, hills for 45 miles to Dayton. Only 800 feet of climbing fewer and easier hills for 32 miles to Walla Walla. It gets even easier down to the Columbia River (400 feet), and then a final 26 miles of shorter moderate hills along the river.

Cum	Leg	Dir	Road
0.0		West	**Route 12** from Visitor Center in Clarkston (map p. 183)
8.0	8.0		Chief Timothy State Park CG (p. 184)
20.4	12.4		Alpowa Summit
27.5	7.1		Pataha: no services
30.4	2.9		Pomeroy: Pioneer Motel, restaurants
43.0	12.6	L	Route 12

Cum	Leg	Dir	Road
66.4	23.4		Dayton at Courthouse (map p. 187)
71.7	5.3		Lewis & Clark Trail State Park CG (p. 187)
76.1	4.4	L (S)	Route 12 in Waitsburg (p. 188)
85.9	9.8		Dixie: small grocery
91.9	6.0	BR	Exit for Bus. Route 12, **Isaacs Ave.**
93.4	1.5	L	**Tausick**
93.7	0.3	R	**Bike Trail**
94.5	0.8	St	**Cambridge**
94.7	0.2	L	**Wilbur**
95.0	0.3	R	**Alder** in Walla Walla (map p. 188)
97.4	2.4	R	**12th**
97.5	0.1	L	**Rose**
98.7	1.2	R	**Wallula** (n/s, **watch mileage!**)
101.4	2.7	L	**Route 12**
103.4	2.0		Whitman Mission .8 mi. on left
108.9	5.5		Lowden: winery
113.1	4.2		Touchet: conv. store, café
121.5	8.4		Pierce's Green Valley CG (p. 189)
125.8	4.3	BL (S)	**Route 730** (Madam Dorion CG on right, water, pit toilet)
140.5	14.7		Sand Station CG (pit toilet, no water)
142.8	2.3		Hat Rock CG (p. 191)
149.2	6.4	R (N)	**Willamette**, follow right, down hill around dam
150.7	1.5	L (W)	**3rd St.** (n/s) near lower dam Visitor Center
152.1	1.4		Oregon Welcome Center in Umatilla (map p. 190)

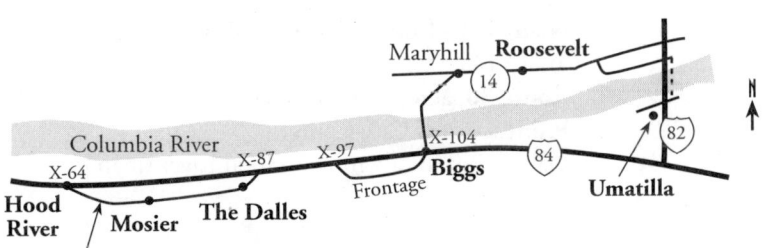

Historic Columbia River Hwy.

Route 14 is a series of long gentle and moderate hills, finally climbing a tough 500-foot hill to Maryhill. Then flat along the river to The Dalles. There is a long moderate hill to Rowena and a steep 600-foot climb up to Rowena Crest before dropping to Mosier. Then a steep 300-foot climb up to the Twin Tunnels.

0.0		East	**3rd St.** from Oregon Welcome Center under south end of I-82 bridge (map p. 190)
0.2	0.2	L (N)	**Bike Trail** up hill onto I-82 bridge

Cum	Leg	Dir	Road
0.9	0.7	BR	down Bike Trail at north end of I-82 bridge
1.1	0.2	R (W)	Bike Trail under I-82
2.0	0.9	L (W)	**Christy Rd.**
9.5	7.5	L (W)	**Route 14**
28.3	18.8		Crow Butte State Park CG (p. 191)
48.8	20.5		Roosevelt: café ?
49.7	0.9		Roosevelt Ferry: conv. store
74.8	25.1		John Day Dam
81.7	6.9	L (S)	**Route 97**, down hill, over bridge
84.3	2.6	R (W)	**Frontage Rd.** in Biggs Junction (p. 194)
86.4	2.1		Oregon Trail Marker on left (p. 194)
91.7	5.3	R	**under I-84**
91.8	0.1	L (W)	onto I-84
101.8	10.0	R	**Exit 87**
102.0	0.2	L (S)	**Route 197**, over I-84
102.3	0.3	R (W)	**Route 30** into The Dalles (map p. 195)
104.8	2.5		Visitor Center
105.6	0.8	L	**Webber** (Route 30) under I-84
105.7	0.1	R (W)	Route 30 (6th St.)
107.3	1.6	St (W)	Route 30 (Old Columbia River Highway)
108.7	1.4		Columbia Gorge Discovery Center on right
112.9	4.2		Rowena: no services
115.6	2.7		Rowena Crest
121.9	6.3		Mosier: conv. store
122.0	0.1	R	**Rock Creek Rd.** (n/s) to Historic Columbia River Highway (Hatfield Trail)
122.7	0.7	R	**Historic Columbia River Highway** (Hatfield Trail)
127.2	4.5		Trail Visitor Center
128.4	1.2	St (W)	**Route 30**, across Hood River
128.8	0.4	R	**Front** towards City Center
129.0	0.2		Oak at 2nd in downtown Hood River (map p. 197)

Cum	Leg	Dir	Road

Gentle hills along I-84, bike trails, and frontage roads for 34 miles. Then 1,400 feet of significant climbing and spectacular views on Historic Columbia River Highway before dropping back to Troutdale. Flat along Marine Drive.

Cum	Leg	Dir	Road
0.0		West	Oak from 2nd in Hood River (map p. 197)
1.9	1.9	L (W)	**I-84**
7.7	5.8		Viento State Park CG
16.3	8.6	R	**Exit 47** to Forest Lane and Herman Creek
16.6	0.3	L	under I-84
16.7	0.1	R	**Frontage Rd.** to Forest Lane and Cascade Locks
17.5	0.8	R	**Forest Lane** (n/s), over I-84
19.5	2.0	R (W)	**Wa Na Pa St.** (Route 30), into Cascade Locks (p. 199)
20.4	0.9	St (W)	**Bike Trail** next to road just under Bridge of the Gods
24.3	3.9	R	Under I-84 towards Bonneville Dam
24.4	0.1	L (W)	**I-84** at Bonneville Dam interchange (until Bike Trail is completed to Warrendale)
27.1	2.7	R	**Exit 37**, Warrendale Rd.
27.6	0.5	L	under I-84
27.7	0.1	R	**Frontage Rd.**
29.4	1.7	L	**Route 30**
29.7	0.3	L (W)	**Historic Columbia River Highway**
30.0	0.3		Ainsworth State Park CG (p. 199)
33.6	3.6		Multnomah Falls
36.6	3.0	BL	Historic Columbia River Highway
41.9	5.3		Crown Point
51.3	9.4	L	**across bridge into Troutdale** (p. 199)
52.2	0.9	R (N)	**257th St.,** down hill
52.6	0.4	L (W)	**Frontage Rd.** after going under I-84
52.9	0.3	BR	**Marine Drive**
60.6	7.7	L (S)	**Bike Trail**, just before I-205
60.7	0.1	R	**I-205 Bike Trail** northbound at Airport Way (p. 204)

mile 2748

Cum	Leg	Dir	Road

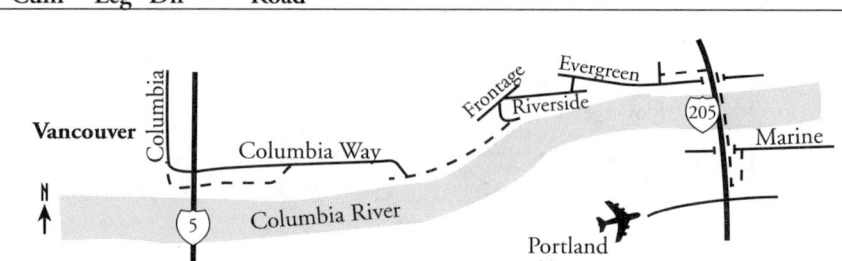

Moderate steady climb over the I-205 bridge and then flat along the river.

Cum	Leg	Dir	Road
0.0		North	**I-205 Bike Trail** from Airport Way (p. 204)
2.7	2.7	R (W)	**SW 23rd**
3.0	0.3	L (S)	**Ellsworth**
3.1	0.1	R (W)	**Evergreen Highway**
5.4	2.3	L (S)	**State**
5.5	0.1	R (W)	**Riverside**
5.8	0.3	L	**Frontage Rd.** (n/s)
5.8	0.0	L (S)	**Columbia Way**, down hill, over RR
6.0	0.2	R (S)	**Bike Trail**
6.9	0.9		Water Resources Education Center
7.2	0.3	BR (W)	**follow park road** out to Columbia Way
8.9	1.7	St (W)	pick up Bike Trail on left side of Columbia Way
9.6	0.7	St (W)	under I-5 bridge
9.7	0.1	St (N)	Columbia in Vancouver (map p. 202)

Cum	Leg	Dir	Road

Mostly flat with a little climb to the St. John's Bridge. Then occasional gentle and moderate hills along the river to Rainier and a final short steep climb over the bridge to Longview.

Cum	Leg	Dir	Road
0.0		South	**Bike Trail** on west side of I-5 bridge at foot of Columbia in Vancouver (map p. 202)
0.9	0.9		follow Bike Trail under I-5
1.0	0.1	L (S)	around cloverleaf onto I-5 Bike Trail on east side of I-5
1.7	0.7	L (W)	back under I-5; follow Bike Trail carefully towards Expo Center and along Marine Drive
2.9	1.2	L	Bike Trail next to **Portland Rd.** at traffic light
4.6	1.7	R (W)	Cloverleaf access to **Columbia Blvd.**/Rivergate/ St. John's Bridge
4.8	0.2	L (E)	**Columbia Blvd.**, across Portland and RR
5.0	0.2	R (S)	**Bike Trail**
6.1	1.1	St	**Carey**
6.2	0.1	R	**Willamette**
7.2	1.0	R	up **Philadelphia**, after going under bridge
7.3	0.1	R	U-turn onto St. **John's Bridge**
8.0	0.7	R (N)	**Route 30** after bridge, down hill
8.4	0.4	L (N)	Route 30
22.0	13.6		Scappoose at Columbia Ave.
23.5	1.5		Airport Park CG (.5 mi. right on West Lane)
29.6	6.1		St. Helens: lots of shopping/restaurants
32.1	2.5		Columbia City
35.3	3.2		Deer Island: conv. store
47.9	12.6		Rainier (p. 205)
49.3	1.4	R (N)	**Route 433** (Lewis & Clark Bridge approach; walk on sidewalk on northbound side!)

Cum	Leg	Dir	Road
51.2	1.9	St (N)	Oregon Way
52.2	1.0	St (N)	15th
53.0	0.8	BL (N)	**Olympia Way**
53.1	0.1		Chamber of Commerce & R.A. Long Square (map p. 205)

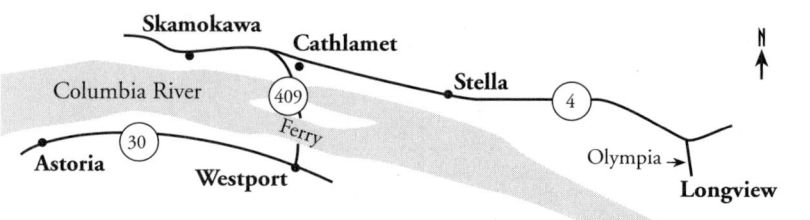

Long gentle to moderate hills to Cathlamet. Tough 640-foot climb to Clatsop Crest from Westport, and then several moderate and significant hills to Astoria.

0.0		North	**Olympia Way** from R.A. Long Square (map p. 205)
0.6	0.6	ML (W)	**Ocean Beach Hwy.** (Route 4)
9.8	9.2		Stella: general store
14.9	5.1		County Line Park CG (rough ground, shade, beach on river, good restroom, no shower)
24.7	9.8	L (S)	**Main St.** (Route 409) in Cathlamet (map p. 207)
28.6	3.9		Cathlamet Ferry Landing (every hour on the hour)
28.6	0.0	St (S)	Route 409 from Westport Ferry Landing
29.0	0.4	R (W)	**Route 30** in Westport (p. 209)
33.2	4.2		Clatsop Crest (656 feet)
40.4	7.2		Knappa: restaurant, conv. store
44.1	3.7		Svensen: restaurant, conv. store
49.8	5.7		John Day City Park: rest rooms, water
55.3	5.5		Astoria Visitor Center (map p. 209)

DETAILED DIRECTIONS — EASTBOUND

Cum	Leg	Dir	Road

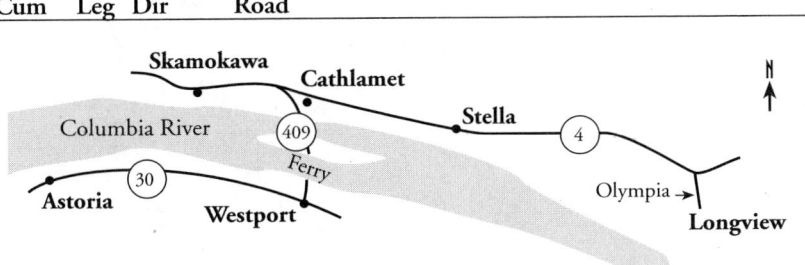

Several moderate to significant hills with one final tough 600-foot climb just before Westport. Long gentle to moderate hills from Cathlamet to Longview.

Cum	Leg	Dir	Road
0.0		East	**Route 30** from Astoria Visitor Center (map p. 209)
11.2	11.2		Svensen: restaurant, conv. store
14.9	3.7		Knappa: restaurant, conv. store
22.1	7.2		Clatsop Crest (656 ft elevation)
26.3	4.2	L (N)	**Route 409** in Westport (p. 209)
26.7	0.4		Westport Ferry Landing (every hour at 15 past)
26.7	0.0	St (N)	Route 409 from Cathlamet Ferry Landing
30.6	3.9	R (E)	**Route 4** in Cathlamet (map p. 207)
40.4	9.8		County Line Park CG (rough ground, shade, beach on river, good br, no shower)
45.5	5.1		Stella: general store
54.7	9.2	BR	**Olympia Way**
55.3	0.6		RA Long Square in Longview (map p. 205)

mile 2927

Cum	Leg	Dir	Road

Vancouver

Columbia River

Hayden Island

5

N

Longview

Lewis & Clark Bridge

Marine

Portland

Columbia Blvd.

Willamette River

Rainier

Columbia City

St. Helens

Scappoose

Willamette

Carey

Portland

St. John's Bridge

30

Occasional gentle to moderate hills with short steep climb to St. John's Bridge.

Cum	Leg	Dir	Road
0.0		South	**Olympia Way** from Chamber of Commerce & R.A. Long Square in Longview (map p. 205)
0.1	0.1	BR (W)	15th, becomes Oregon Way
1.9	1.8	St (W)	Route 433 over Lewis & Clark Bridge (WALK on sidewalk on northbound side)
4.0	2.1	MR (S)	**Route 30**
5.6	1.6		Rainier (p. 205)
18.2	12.6		Deer Island: conv. store
21.4	3.2		Columbia City
23.9	2.5		St. Helens: lots of shopping/restaurants
30.0	6.1		Airport Park CG (.5 mi. left on West Lane)
31.5	1.5		Scappoose at Columbia Ave.
45.1	13.6	R	up hill to **St. John's Bridge**
45.5	0.4	L	over St. John's Bridge
46.2	0.7	R	U-turn onto **Philadelphia** at end of bridge, down hill
46.3	0.1	L	**Willamette**
47.3	1.0	L	**Carey**, after RR bridge
47.4	0.1	St	Bike Trail
48.5	1.1	L	**Columbia Blvd.** (n/s), over RR and Portland Rd.
48.7	0.2	R	Cloverleaf access to **Portland Rd.**
48.9	0.2	L (N)	Portland Rd.
50.1	1.2		jog R onto Bike Trail
50.6	0.5	R (E)	Bike Trail on far side of **Marine Dr.** at traffic light
51.8	1.2		follow Bike Trail carefully, L (E) under I-5, loop right onto east side of I-5 northbound
52.5	0.7		follow Bike Trail around cloverleaf, L under I-5, loop around left onto west side of I-5 northbound
53.5	1.0	R	**Columbia** in Vancouver (map p. 202)

Cum	Leg	Dir	Road

Flat with two short steep climbs before I-205 bridge.

Cum	Leg	Dir	Road
0.0		South	onto Bike Trail from Columbia in Vancouver (map p. 202)
0.1	0.1	St (E)	under I-5 bridge
0.8	0.7	St (E)	**Columbia Way** (don't BR on Bike Trail)
2.5	1.7	BR	on Bike Trail into Park
2.8	0.3		Water Resources Education Center
3.7	0.9	L (W)	Columbia Way (n/s), over RR, up hill
3.9	0.2	R (E)	**Frontage Rd.** (n/s)
3.9	0.0	R (E)	**Riverside** (n/s)
4.4	0.5	L (N)	**Chelsea**
4.5	0.1	R (E)	**Evergreen**
6.6	2.1	L (N)	**Ellsworth**
6.7	0.1	R (E)	**23rd**
7.0	0.3	L	**I-205 Bike Trail** southbound
9.7	2.7	L (E)	**Airport Way** Exit

mile 2819

Cum	Leg	Dir	Road

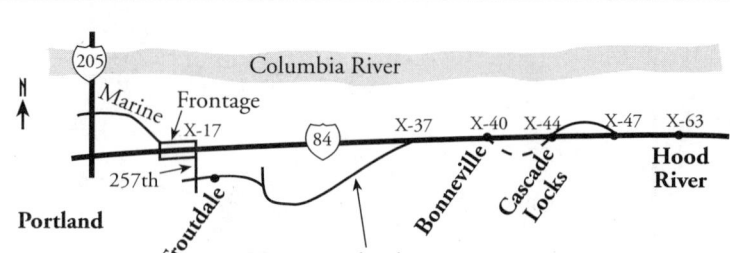

Flat to Troutdale, then long climb to crest. Gentle hills for 34 miles along I-84.

Cum	Leg	Dir	Road
0.0		L (E)	**Airport Way** Exit from I-205 Bike Trail
0.1	0.1	L (N)	Bike Trail to Marine Drive
0.2	0.1	R (E)	**Marine Drive**
7.9	7.7	St (S)	under I-84
8.1	0.2	L (E)	**Frontage Rd.**
8.4	0.3	R (S)	**257th St.**, up hill
8.6	0.2	L (E)	**Columbia River Highway** through Troutdale (p. 199)
9.5	0.9	R	follow Historic Columbia River Highway up hill
19.0	9.5		Crown Point
27.3	8.3		Multnomah Falls
30.9	3.6		Ainsworth State Park CG (p. 199)
31.2	0.3	R (E)	**Route 30**, I-84
31.5	0.3	R	**Frontage Rd.** before entry to I-84
33.5	2.0	St (E)	onto **I-84** (until Bike Trail is completed to Bonneville)
36.2	2.7	R (E)	Exit 40, Bonneville Dam
36.4	0.2	St (E)	on bike trail beside eastbound ramp to I-84
40.3	3.9	St (E)	**Route 30** (Wa Na Pa St.) at Bridge of the Gods
40.6	0.3		Cascade Locks (p. 199)
41.1	0.5	L	**Forest Lane**
43.1	2.0	L (E)	**Frontage Rd.**, after crossing I-84
44.0	0.9	St (E)	onto **I-84**
52.9	8.9		Viento State Park CG on left
58.5	5.6	R	Exit 62 onto **Route 30** in W Hood River
58.7	0.2	R	**Cascade Ave.**
59.8	1.1	St	**Oak**
60.5	0.7		downtown Hood River at 2nd (map p. 197)

Cum	Leg	Dir	Road

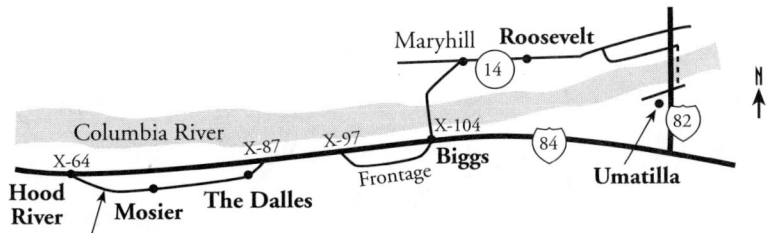

Historic Columbia River Hwy.

Steep 300-foot climb out of Hood River plus 600-foot from Mosier. Spectacular views. One gentle hill out of Rowena, and then flat to Biggs. Steep 500 foot climb out of Biggs, and then Route 14 is a series of long moderate hills.

Cum	Leg	Dir	Road
0.0		St (E)	**Oak** at 2nd in Hood River (map p. 197)
0.2	0.2	L (E)	**State**
0.6	0.4	St	**Old Columbia River Drive**
1.8	1.2	St	**Hatfield Trail** at Visitor Center
6.3	4.5	ML	access road at Eastern Trail Head, down hill
7.0	0.7	L (E)	**Old Columbia River Highway** (Route 30) in Mosier
7.2	0.2		Mosier: conv. store
13.5	6.3		Rowena Crest
16.2	2.7		Rowena: no services
20.4	4.2		Columbia Gorge Discovery Center on left
23.4	3.0	L	**Webber** (Route 30) under I-84
23.5	0.1	R (E)	**2nd** (Route 30)
24.3	0.8		Visitor Center in The Dalles (map p. 195)
26.9	2.6	L (N)	**Route 197**
27.2	0.3	R (E)	**I-84**
37.2	10.0	R (E)	Exit 97 onto **Frontage Rd.**
42.5	5.3		Oregon Trail Marker on right
44.6	2.1	L (N)	**Route 97** in Biggs Junction (p. 194), over bridge, up hill
47.2	2.6	R (E)	**Route 14**
54.1	6.9		John Day Dam
79.2	25.1		Roosevelt Ferry: conv. store
80.1	0.9		Roosevelt: café
100.6	20.5		Crow Butte State Park CG (p. 191)
119.4	18.8	R (S)	**Christy Rd.**
126.9	7.5	R (E)	dead end paved road
127.8	0.9		under I-82
127.9	0.1	L	up **Bike Trail**, south on northbound span of I-82 bridge
128.8	0.9	BL	down hill on Bike Trail
128.9	0.1	R	**3rd St.** (n/s)
129.0	0.1		Oregon Welcome Center in Umatilla (map p. 190)

mile 2748

Cum	Leg	Dir	Road

After 55 miles of gentle to moderate hills to Walla Walla, hills become significant, with 2,000 feet of climbing in 32 miles to Dayton and another 3,500 feet in 45 miles to Alpowa Summit before cruising downhill and flat into Clarkston.

Cum	Leg	Dir	Road
0.0		East	**3rd** from Oregon Welcome Center, Umatilla (map p. 190)
0.1	0.1		under I-82 bridge
1.4	1.3	R (S)	at T near lower dam Visitor Center, up hill, L,R,L, becomes Willamette
2.9	1.5	L (E)	**Route 730**
9.3	6.4		Hat Rock CG (p. 190)
11.6	2.3		Sand Station CG
26.3	14.7	BR (E)	**Route 12** (Madam Dorion CG on left)
30.6	4.3		Pierce's Green Valley CG (p. 189)
39.0	8.4		Touchet: conv. store, café
43.2	4.2		Lowden: winery
48.7	5.5		Whitman Mission .8 mi. on right
50.7	2.0	R	**Wallula**
53.4	2.7	L	**Rose** (n/s), after RR
54.6	1.2	R	**12th** in Walla Walla (map p. 188)
54.7	0.1	L	**Alder**
55.7	1.0	St	around Carnegie Art Center onto Alder
57.1	1.4	L	**Wilbur**
57.4	0.3	R	**Cambridge**
57.6	0.2	St	**Bike Trail**
58.4	0.8	L	**Tausick**
58.7	0.3	R	**Isaacs**
59.6	0.9	MR	**Route 12**
66.2	6.6		Dixie: small grocery
76.0	9.8	R (E)	Route 12 in Waitsburg (p. 188)
80.4	4.4		Lewis & Clark Trail State Park CG (p. 187)
85.7	5.3		Dayton at Courthouse (map p. 187)
109.1	23.4	BR (E)	Route 12
121.7	12.6		Pomeroy: Pioneer Motel, restaurants

Cum	Leg	Dir	Road
124.6	2.9		Pataha: no services
131.7	7.1		Alpowa summit
144.1	12.4		Chief Timothy State Park CG (p. 184)
152.1	8.0		Visitor Center in Clarkston (map p. 183)

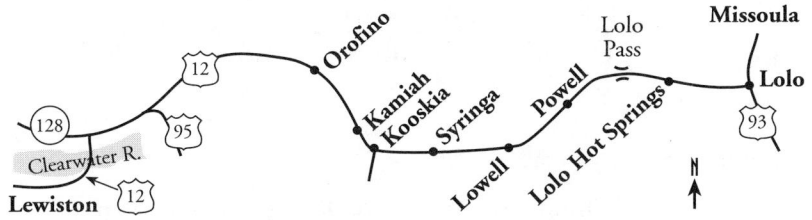

It's 72 miles of long gentle hills along the river to Kooskia. There's 4,000 feet of steady climbing in the next 100 miles to Lolo Pass, starting out easy and getting steeper towards the end. Then it's all downhill to Lolo.

Cum	Leg	Dir	Road
0.0		East	**Bike Trail** on north side of Clearwater River, Lewiston
4.4	4.4	MR (E)	**Route 12**
7.8	3.4	BR (E)	Route 12 (Nez Perce Visitor Center 1.8 mi. right)
25.4	17.6		Rest Area: water, rest rooms, tables, by river
32.5	7.1		Peck Junction: café
41.7	9.2		Orofino bridge (map p. 181)
49.3	7.6		Greer: café
64.0	14.7		Kamiah (map p. 180)
71.7	7.7		Kooskia west access road (map p. 179)
87.8	16.1		Syringa: café
93.1	5.3		Wild Goose NFS CG (on river)
95.1	2.0		Lowell: (p. 178)
102.0	6.9		Apgar NFS CG (on river)
120.5	18.5		Wilderness Gateway NFS CG (across river)
148.1	27.6		Jerry Johnson NFS CG (north side of road)
156.1	8.0		Wendover NFS CG (on river)
156.4	0.3		Whitehorse NFS CG (on river)
159.7	3.3		Powell (p. 177)
161.3	1.6		White Sands NFS CG (1.5 mi., 200 ft down!)
162.9	1.6		DeVoto Grove
172.2	9.3		Lolo Pass (5,235 feet)
178.2	6.0		Lee Creek NFS CG
179.6	1.4		Lolo Hot Springs (p. 176)
189.3	9.7		Lewis & Clark NFS CG
204.8	15.5	L (N)	**Route 93** in Lolo (map p. 168)
			Turn R (S) to skip Missoula.
211.7	6.9	L (N)	**Old Hwy. 93** in Missoula (map p. 169)

mile 2465

Cum	Leg	Dir	Road

LEMHI PASS AND BIG HOLE ROUTES

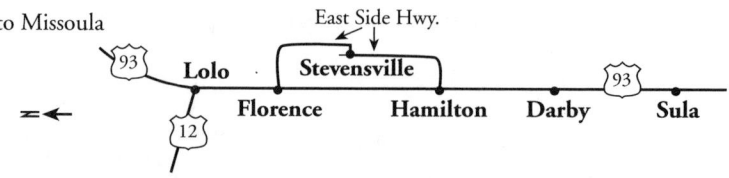

Up gentle hills all the way to Sula.

0.0		South	**Route 93** at Old Hwy. 93 in Missoula (map p. 169)
6.9	6.9	St (S)	intersection Route 12 in Lolo (p. 168)
15.7	8.8	L (E)	**East Side Highway** (Route 203) in Florence: supermarket, restaurant
27.6	11.9	L (S)	**Main St.** (Route 269) in Stevensville (p. 168)
41.8	14.2		Corvallis: conv. store
47.5	5.7	L (S)	**Route 93** in Hamilton (map p. 167)
64.2	16.7		Darby (p. 166)
79.1	14.9		Spring Gulch NFS CG (166)
82.0	2.9		Sula (p. 165)

BIG HOLE ROUTE

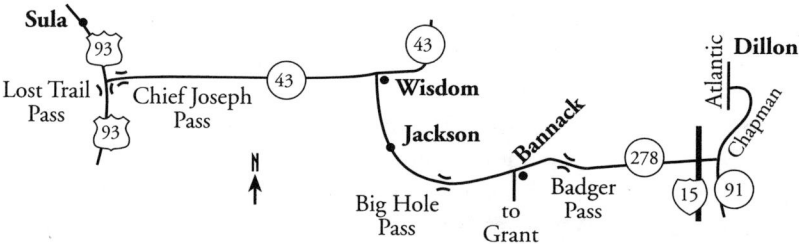

After a tough 3,000-foot climb in 14 miles to Chief Joseph Pass, it's 25 miles of gorgeous downhill to Wisdom, except for one short climb up to the Big Hole National Battlefield. After a gentle 400-foot climb to Jackson, there is 1,400 feet of serious climbing to Big Hole Pass, a long downhill, and a final 900-foot push to Badger Pass, before the long downhill to Dillon.

0.0		South	**Route 93** from Sula (p. 165)
6.2	6.2		Lost Trail Hot Springs (p. 165)
12.6	6.4	L (E)	**Route 43** at Lost Trail Pass (7,000 ft)
13.7	1.1		Chief Joseph Pass (7,240 ft)
21.9	8.2		May Creek NFS Campground (p. 164)

Cum	Leg	Dir	Road
29.1	7.2		Big Hole National Battlefield (p. 165)
38.7	9.6	R (S)	**Route 278** in Wisdom (map p. 164)
56.6	17.9		Jackson (p. 163)
67.4	10.8		Big Hole Pass (7,360 ft)
82.4	15.0		intersection Bannack Rd. (p. 163)
86.0	3.6		Badger Pass (6,760 ft)
99.8	13.8	L (N)	**Frontage Rd**. (old Route 91) after passing under I-15
103.3	3.5	R	**Atlantic**, at Hospital
103.8	0.5	L	**Reeder** in Dillon (5,100 ft) (map p. 155)
			(Skip ahead to resume combined Routes in Dillon)

LEMHI PASS ROUTE

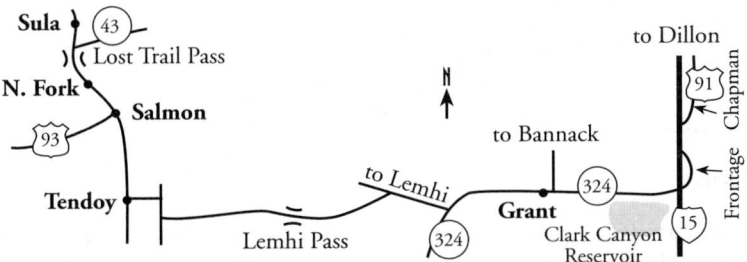

After a tough 2,700-foot climb to Lost Trail Pass in 13 miles, it's 24 miles of fast downhill to North Fork. There are gentle hills along the river to Salmon, and then 800 feet of gentle rise to Tendoy before starting the difficult 2,600 foot climb up to Lemhi Pass on rough dirt road. After 12 miles of fairly steep downhill on a better dirt road, it's paved and mostly level and down all the way to Dillon.

Cum	Leg	Dir	Road
0.0		South	**Route 93** from Sula (p. 165)
6.2	6.2		Lost Trail Hot Springs
12.6	6.4	St (S)	Route 93 at Lost Trail Pass (7,000 ft)
26.3	13.7		Gibbonsville, café, cabins
37.1	10.8		North Fork (3,630 ft) (p. 162)
57.9	20.8	L (S)	Route 93 over Salmon River in Salmon (map p. 160)
58.5	0.6	St (S)	**Route 28**, where Route 93 turns west
78.4	19.9	L (E)	**Tendoy Lane** (dirt road), at Post Office
78.5	0.1	R	**Agency Creek Rd.**
78.8	0.3	L (E)	Agency Creek Rd.
90.6	11.8	St	cross Lemhi Pass (7,373 ft); .2 mi. walk to Sacajawea Memorial at spring headwater of Missouri River
102.7	12.1	L	**Route 324** (paved road)
112.4	9.7		Grant (5,800 ft)(p. 158)

Cum	Leg	Dir	Road
124.7	12.3	St (N)	**Frontage Road**, after crossing I-15 (p. 157 for description and campgrounds)
131.6	6.9	St	**I-15**
136.2	4.6	BR	Exit 56 to Barretts
136.4	0.2	R,L (N)	**Frontage Rd.**
140.1	3.7	St	Frontage Rd.; becomes old Route 91 (n/s)
143.6	3.5	R	**Atlantic**, at Hospital
144.1	0.5	L	**Reeder** in Dillon (5,100 ft) (map p. 155)

RESUME COMBINED LEMHI PASS AND BIG HOLE ROUTES

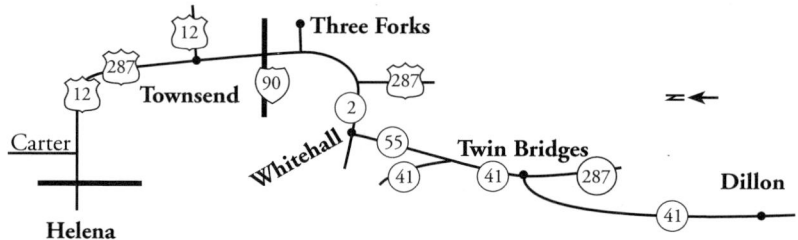

Long gentle to moderate, mostly down, hills to Cardwell. Shorter moderate and significant hills through the canyon to Three Forks. Long gentle to moderate, mostly up, hills to Helena.

0.0		North	**Montana Ave.** from Visitor Center in Dillon (map p. 155)
1.1	1.1	St	**Route 41** towards Twin Bridges
28.0	26.9	L (N)	**Route 55** in Twin Bridges (p. 153)
38.5	10.5		Silverstar (p. 153)
42.3	3.8	St	Route 55 towards Whitehall
54.4	12.1	MR (E)	**Main** at IGA store
54.8	0.4		Whitehall (p. 153)
62.2	7.4	L (E)	**Frontage Rd.** after crossing under I-90
62.5	0.3		Cardwell (p. 153)
69.6	7.1		Lewis & Clark State Park Caverns & CG (p. 151)
74.6	5.0	St (E)	**Route 287** at intersection
84.5	9.9	St (N)	Route 287 at Route 205 in Three Forks (map p. 151)
85.8	1.3		cross I-90: Wheat Mountain Bakery & Deli
116.2	30.4	St (N)	Route 12/287 in Townsend (p. 150)
128.6	12.4		Winston; conv. store
147.8	19.2		Route 12/287 at Carter Rd. in Helena (map p. 147)

Cum	Leg	Dir	Road

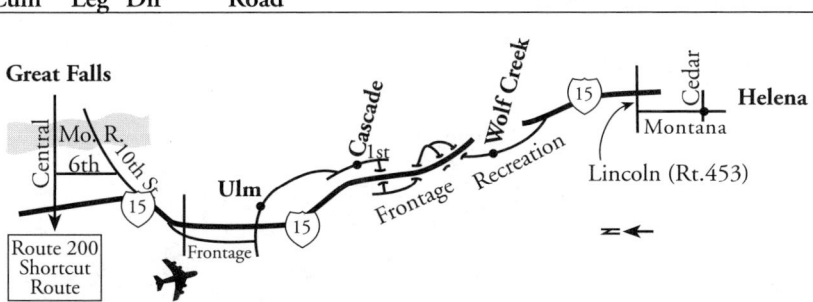

Immediately out of Helena is a long significant 1,200 foot climb over two hills. Although it's downhill overall from here to Great Falls, there are many moderate hills to Wolf Creek, a couple near Cascade, and a final 400-foot climb out of Ulm.

Cum	Leg	Dir	Road
0.0		North	**Montana Ave.** from Cedar in Helena (map p. 147)
6.7	6.7	R (E)	**Lincoln Rd.** (n/s)
7.1	0.4	L (N)	onto **I-15**
16.1	9.0		Exit 209 for Gates of the Mountains (p. 148)
25.9	9.8	R (N)	Exit 219: Spring Creek, **Recreation Rd.**
33.9	8.0		Wolf Creek (p. 147)
36.9	3.0		Wolf Creek NFS Campground (p. 147)
45.3	8.4		Stickney Creek NFS Campground (p. 147)
57.6	12.3	St	under I-15 onto **Frontage Rd.**
60.4	2.8	R	Frontage Rd. just before I-15
64.9	4.5	R	under I-15 onto Frontage Rd.
65.0	0.1	L	**Route 68** (1st St.) towards Cascade (p. 146)
66.2	1.2	BR	**Ulm Rd.** (n/s, at baseball field at north end of Cascade)
80.4	14.2		Ulm: conv. store, bar
80.6	0.2	R (N)	**Ulm-North Frontage Rd.** after passing under I-15
87.9	7.3	R	over I-15 at Airport
88.0	0.1	L	onto **I-15** towards Great Falls
89.0	1.0	R	Exit 278: **Route 89 S, 200 E, 10th Ave.**
90.0	1.0	L (N)	**6th St. SW**
91.3	1.3	R (E)	**Central Ave.**
91.7	0.4		cross Missouri River on Central Ave. Bridge
91.9	0.2		**1st Ave. North** at Bike Trail in Great Falls (map p. 139)

mile LP-92

Cum	Leg	Dir	Road

ROUTE 200 SHORTCUT

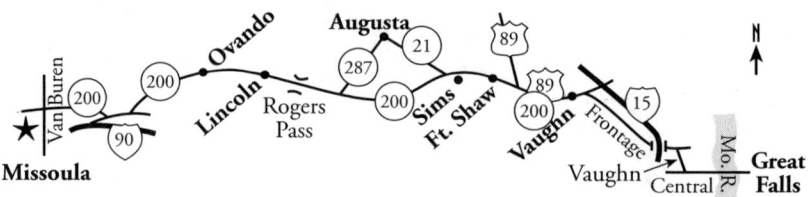

Long gentle to moderate hills as you climb 3,100 feet to Lincoln. The final 1,400 feet to Roger's Pass is significant. Although it's mostly downhill and level to Great Falls, there is about 1,500 feet of steep climbing in a series of big nasty hills before Simms.

Cum	Leg	Dir	Road
0.0		East	**Broadway** from Van Buren in Missoula (map p. 169)
5.6	5.6	L (E)	**Route 200**
6.4	0.8	BL	Route 200
37.9	31.5		Larry's Clearwater Inn: motel, café, rest area
41.6	3.7		Russell Gates CG: nice sites on river, tables, shade, water, pit toilets
50.6	9.0		Ovando .5 mi. off to right (p. 173)
77.4	26.8		Lincoln (map p. 172)
84.5	7.1		Aspen Grove NFS Campground, .5 mi. right on river, pretty, private, shade, tables, water, pit toilets
95.7	11.2		Roger's Pass (5,610 ft)
114.8	19.1	St (E)	Route 200 at intersection Route 287; saloon (4,240 ft)
133.0	18.2	St (E)	Route 200
133.4	0.4		Simms on right: no services
139.3	5.9		Fort Shaw: no services
144.0	4.7		Sun River: conv. store
152.4	8.4		Vaughn: conv. store, restaurant
152.8	0.4	R (E)	**Frontage Rd.** before I-15
162.3	9.5	R	**Vaughn Rd.** (n/s) towards City Center
163.2	0.9	L (E)	**Central Ave.**
164.3	1.1		cross Missouri River on Central Ave. Bridge
164.5	0.2		**1st Ave. N** at Bike Trail in Great Falls (map p. 139)

Cum	Leg	Dir	Road

RESUME: MAIN ROUTE

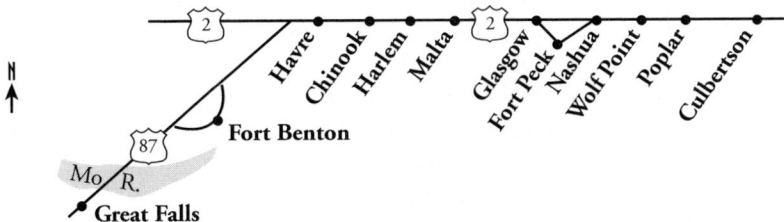

There is a big climb out of Great Falls to the plateau, and then long gentle to moderate hills to Havre. Fort Benton is 250 feet lower on the river. Route 2 varies from flat to long gentle and occasionally moderate hills. The Master Plan in Chapter 3 shows which segments are flatter and which are hillier.

Cum	Leg	Dir	Road
0.0		North	**Route 89**, 200 from River Edge Bike Trail at 9th St. across river in Great Falls; Bike Trail on southbound side of bridge (map p. 139)
0.5	0.5	St	up hill
1.4	0.9	L (N)	**Route 87**
24.9	23.5		Carter on right: no services
37.1	12.2	R (E)	**Route 386** down hill to Fort Benton
38.6	1.5	R (E)	**13th**
38.9	0.3	L	**Front St.** in Fort Benton (map p. 137)
39.5	0.6	L (N)	**21st St.**
39.9	0.4	R	**St. Charles St.**, up big hill
42.3	2.4	R	**Route 87**
51.1	8.8		Loma (p. 136)
78.0	26.9		Big Sandy (p. 136)
88.6	10.6		Box Elder: conv. store
109.6	21.0	R (E)	**Route 2**
112.9	3.3		Havre (map p. 135)
134.3	21.4		Chinook (map p. 133)
143.4	9.1		Zurich on left: conv. store ?
155.4	12.0		Harlem on left (p. 133)
158.9	3.5		Fort Belknap Agency: café, conv. store, rest area with restrooms and water
183.6	24.7		Dodson on right: small grocery store, café
201.1	17.5		Malta (map p. 132) (alternate route avoids Route 2 for 21 miles on rough pavement at same mileage; see p. 131 for description)
218.8	17.7		Intersection to Sleeping Buffalo Hot Springs (p. 131)

Cum	Leg	Dir	Road
228.6	9.8		Saco (p. 131)
242.1	13.5		Hinsdale on left: conv. store, small grocery, saloon
256.8	14.7		Rest Area: restrooms, water, shade, covered tables
270.8	14.0		Glasgow (map p. 129) (Fort Peck side trip: p. 130)
285.0	14.2		Nashua: Bergie's homemade ice cream! conv. store (alternate route avoids Route 2 for 25 miles on good pavement, but adds 5.4 miles; see p. 128 for description)
300.9	15.9		Frazer on left: no services
319.7	18.8		Wolf Point (map p. 128)
341.7	22.0	R	**5th Ave**. in Poplar (p. 127)
342.2	0.5	L (E)	paved road after tracks
355.2	13.0	L	**Brockton Rd**. into Brockton
355.3	0.1	R (E)	**Route 2**
374.1	18.8		Culbertson at Broadway (map p. 127)

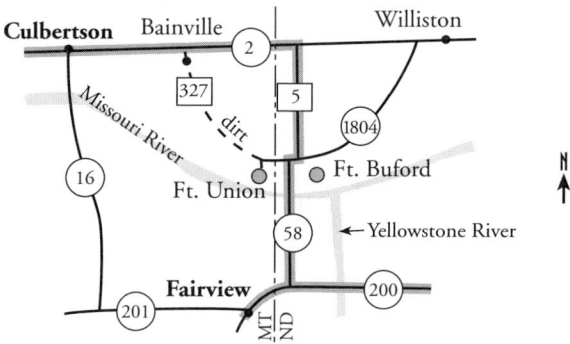

Route 2 is gentle to moderate up hill. Route 5 drops you down to flat Route 58

0.0		East	**Route 2** from Broadway in Culbertson (map p. 127)
14.4	14.4		Bainville on right
25.1	10.7	R (S)	**CR 5**
35.1	10.0	R (W)	**Route 1804**; Fort Union 2 mi. west (p. 125); Fort Buford on left (p. 125)
35.6	0.5	L (S)	**Route 58**
36.9	1.3		cross Missouri River
45.5	8.6	R (W)	**Route 200**
46.4	0.9		Route 200 at Route 201 in Fairview (map p. 122)

Cum	Leg	Dir	Road

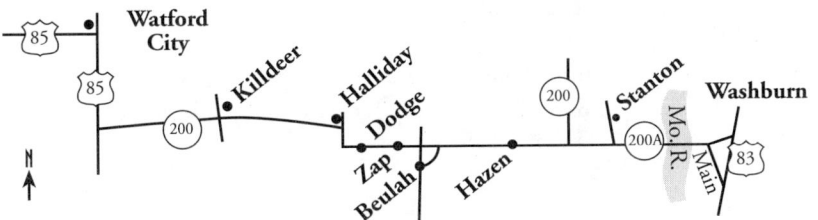

Long gentle to moderate hills all the way.

Cum	Leg	Dir	Road
0.0		North	**Route 200** from Route 201 in Fairview (map p. 122)
0.9	0.9	St (E)	Route 200 at intersection with Route 58
4.0	3.1		cross Yellowstone River
19.1	15.1	R (S)	**Route 85/200**
21.5	2.4		Alexander (p. 122)
24.1	2.6	St (E)	Route 85/200
33.9	9.8		Arnegard on left
41.1	7.2		Route 85/200 at Route 23 in Watford City (map p. 121)

mile 1366

After a big drop to Roosevelt Park, there is a long tough climb back out. Hilly to Killdeer, but mostly down. Moderate hills to Stanton, and then easy riding.

Cum	Leg	Dir	Road
0.0		South	**Route 85/200** in Watford City (map p. 121)
15.0	15.0		Theodore Roosevelt National Park (p. 120)
15.5	0.5		cross Little Missouri River
15.7	0.2		National Grasslands CG (p. 120)
29.5	13.8		Grassy Butte on right: conv. store
34.1	4.6	L (E)	**Route 200**
54.3	20.2	St (E)	Route 200; Killdeer (p. 119) 1 mi. on left
60.9	6.6		Dunn Center on left
74.3	13.4		Halliday (p. 119) 1.0 mi. on left
82.5	8.2		Dodge
88.8	6.3		Golden Valley .4 mi. on right (p. 118)
89.3	0.5		Golden Valley (east access road)
95.4	6.1		Zap .3 mi. on right (p. 118)
96.2	0.8		Zap (east access road)

Cum	Leg	Dir	Road
102.4	6.2		Beulah 2.5 mi. R (S) on Route 49 (map p. 118)
103.4	1.0		Beulah (east access road)
109.0	5.6		Main St. in Hazen (map p. 117)
110.5	1.5		4th Ave. in Hazen
116.5	6.0	St (E)	**Route 200A** at intersection of Route 200 turning L (N)
121.3	4.8		Stanton 1.2 mi. L (N) on Route 31 (p. 117)
141.4	20.1	R (S)	Main St. into Washburn (map p. 114)

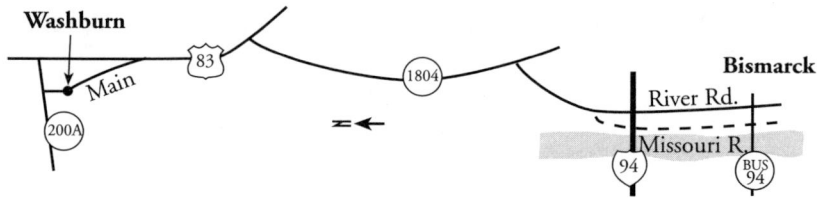

Gentle hills along the river with occasional moderate hill.

0.0		MR (S)	**Route 83** from Main in Washburn (map p. 114)
5.1	5.1	R (S)	**Route 1804**
31.2	26.1	R (S)	**River Rd.**
35.3	4.1	R (S)	into Pioneer Park and onto **Bike Trail**
37.0	1.7		River Rd. at Main Ave. (Bus. 94) in Bismarck (map p. 109)

Cum	Leg	Dir	Road

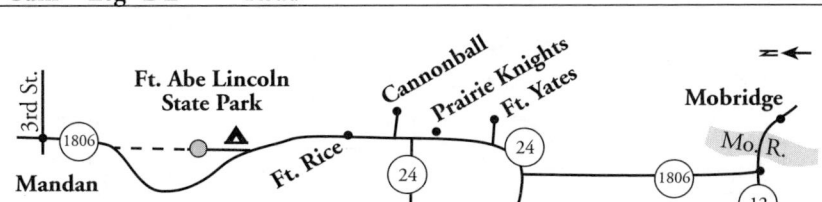

Long moderate hills with occasional short steep climbs.

Cum	Leg	Dir	Road
0.0		South	**Route 1806** from 3rd St. in Mandan (map p. 109)
2.5	2.5	L (S)	**Fort Lincoln Rd.**, continue through barrier
4.5	2.0		Fort Abraham Lincoln Visitor Center (p. 111), Campground; continue straight (south) on park road
5.5	1.0	ML (S)	Route 1806
18.7	13.2		Huff: no services
26.3	7.6		Fort Rice: conv. store
37.3	11.0		Cannonball 2 mi. on left: conv. store
38.3	1.0	St (S)	**Route 24/1806**
45.1	6.8		Prairie Knights Casino/Hotel
58.6	13.5		Fort Yates 2 mi. to left: Headquarters for Standing Rock Nation; bar, restaurant
61.0	2.4	L (S)	**Route 1806**
80.1	19.1		Kenel: conv. store
102.2	22.1	L (E)	**Route 12** over bridge into Mobridge (map p. 106)

mile 1146

Cum	Leg	Dir	Road

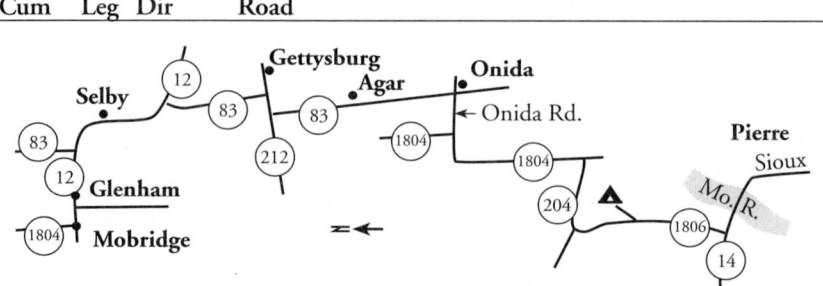

Big hill before Glenham. Long gentle to moderate hills with stretches of flat riding.

Cum	Leg	Dir	Road
0.0		East	**Route 12** from Route 1804 in Mobridge (map p. 106)
3.9	3.9	St (E)	Route 12 at 1804 South intersection
7.5	3.6		Glenham
17.4	9.9	St (E)	Route 12/83 at Route 12 intersection
20.1	2.7		Selby on left (p. 105)
24.0	3.9	R (S)	**Route 83**
54.6	30.6	R (W)	**Route 212**; Gettysburg (map p. 104) 5.2 mi. east
55.5	0.9	St (S)	**Route 83**
67.4	11.9		Agar on left: bar/restaurant
76.4	9.0	R (W)	**Onida Rd**. towards airport; Onida on left (p. 103)
88.4	12.0	St (W)	Onida Rd. (Route 1804 goes North)
94.4	6.0	L (S)	**Route 1804**
113.4	19.0	R (W)	**Route 204** across dam at Oahe Dam Visitor Center: water, restroom, exhibits
115.5	2.1	St (S)	**Route 1806**
120.6	5.1	L (E)	**Route 34**
121.2	0.6	R (S)	**Sale Barn Rd.**
121.6	0.4	L (E)	**Stanley**
121.8	0.2	L	Bike Path on far side of main road; over bridge
122.7	0.9		Pierre (map p. 100)

Cum	Leg	Dir	Road

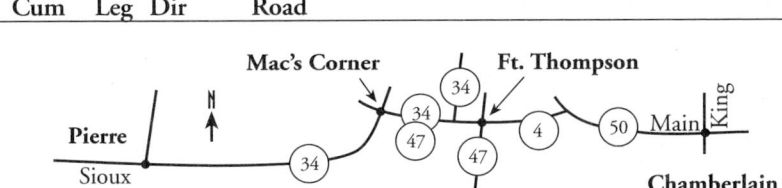

Long moderate hills to Mac's Corner. Long easier hills south with one big climb after turning onto Route 50.

0.0		East	**Route 34** (Wells Ave.) at Route 14 in Pierre (map p. 100)
1.9	1.9		Farm Island Recreation Area (p. 100)
45.2	43.3	R (S)	**Route 34/47** at Mac's Corner: conv. store
57.5	12.3	St (S)	**Route 47**
58.1	0.6	St (S)	**Route 4** in Fort Thompson (p. 100)
65.7	7.6	R (S)	**Route 50**
79.8	14.1		American Creek CG
80.4	0.6		King St. in Chamberlain (map p. 98)

mile 910

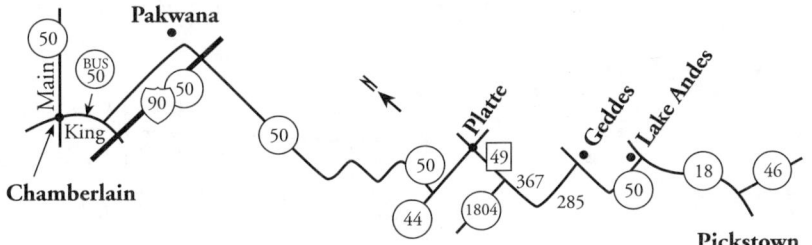

Many long moderate hills through dry farm country away from river

0.0		L (E)	**King St.** (Route 50) from Main up hill in Chamberlain (map p. 98)
3.2	3.2	L (E)	**Pukwana Rd.** (n/s) .2 mi. before I-90
9.5	6.3	BR (S)	main road (n/s)
10.9	1.4	St (S)	**Route 50** across I-90
35.9	25.0		Academy: no services
42.5	6.6	L (E)	**Route 44/50**
44.5	2.0	St	Route 44/50 at Route 1804 intersection
52.5	8.0	R (S)	**Main** (CR 49) in Platte (Map. p 98)
61.5	9.0	L (E)	**285th St**
68.4	6.9	R (S)	**374th Ave.** (Route 50); Geddes to left: bar, café
82.8	14.4	R (S)	to **Route 18/281** just before Lake Andes (p. 97)
83.1	0.3	MR (S)	Route 18/281
87.9	4.8		entrance to North Point Recreation Area CG
88.8	0.9		Route 46 in Pickstown (map p. 96)

Cum	Leg	Dir	Road

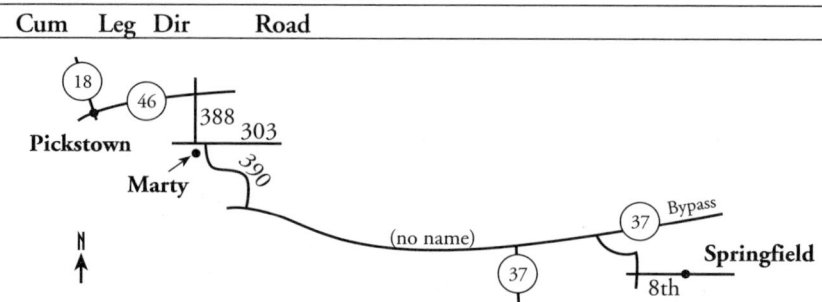

After a big climb out of Pickstown, gentle to moderate rolling country.

Cum	Leg	Dir	Road
0.0		L (E)	**Route 46** up hill from Pickstown (map p. 96)
2.8	2.8		Fort Randall Casino/Hotel/Restaurant
5.3	2.5	R (S)	**388th Ave.** (CR 21)
11.4	6.1	L (E)	**303rd St**. at Marty Indian School
11.5	0.1	R (S)	**390th Ave.**
18.4	6.9	L (E)	at T (n/s) in Greenwood: abandoned town
38.1	19.7	St (E)	across CR 18 (Avon Rd.)
41.1	3.0	St (E)	**Route 37**
45.3	4.2	St (E)	Route 37 at west access road to Springfield (map p. 95)

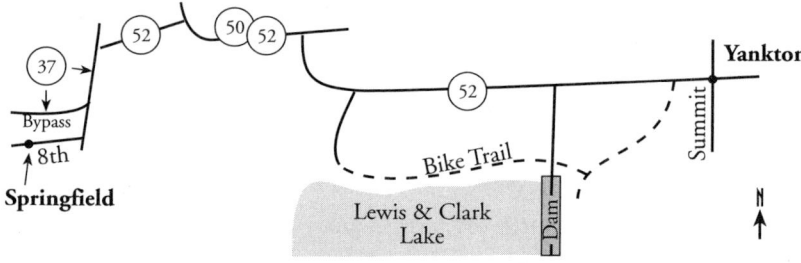

Long gentle to moderate hills, mostly up for 20 miles from Springfield.

Cum	Leg	Dir	Road
46.4	1.1	L (N)	**Route 37** at east access road to Springfield
49.1	2.7	R (E)	**Route 52**
61.3	12.2	R (E)	**Route 50/52**
66.2	4.9	R (S)	**Route 52** down big hill
69.7	3.5	R (S)	**Gavins Pt. Rd.** down hill to swim beach
70.4	0.7	L (E)	Follow **bike path** east, hugging lake. Several excellent picnic areas and campgrounds (see Yankton p. 90)
73.8	3.4	St	pass restaurant, marina
74.2	0.4	St	across dam road on Bike Trail down earth dam and left (East) at bottom. A side trip right (south) across dam takes you up hill to Visitor Center.
75.0	0.8	MR (E)	Bike Trail along Route 52
78.5	3.5		8th St. (Route 52) at Summit in Yankton (map p. 90)

Cum	Leg	Dir	Road

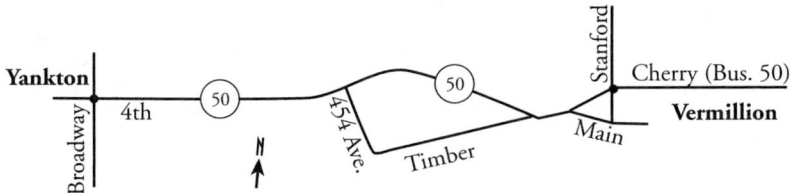

Flat bottomland with short moderate hill into Vermillion.

0.0		East	**4th St.** (Route 50) from Broadway in Yankton (map p. 90)
14.4	14.4	R (S)	**454th Ave.**
19.4	5.0	L (E)	**Timber** (n/s), follow pavement
27.7	8.3	R	**Bus. Route 50**
28.1	0.4	BL	Bus. Route 50, becomes Cherry
28.7	0.6		Cherry at Stanford in Vermillion (map p. 88)

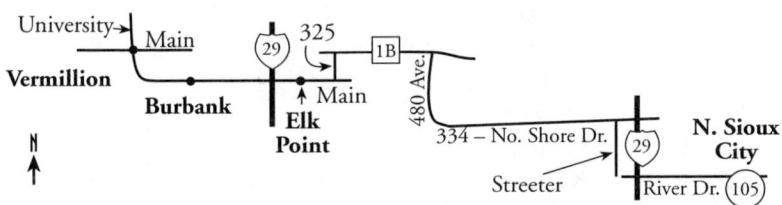

All flat bottomland.

0.0		South	**University** from Main St. in Vermillion (map p. 88)
6.2	6.2		Burbank: bar
14.6	8.4		Elk Point (p. 88)
15.8	1.2	L	**325th St**
15.9	0.1	R (E)	**CR 1B**
20.0	4.1	R (S)	**480 Ave.**
20.6	0.6	St	cross I-29
22.1	1.5	St	cross 330th St. (CR 6)
26.1	4.0	L (E)	**334th St.**, becomes North Shore Drive
30.2	4.1	St	Bike Trail along North Shore Drive after school
31.0	0.8	R (S)	**Streeter** (frontage rd.) along I-29
33.1	2.1	L (E)	**Route 105**, under I-29
34.1	1.0	R	**Military Rd.**
34.5	0.4	R (S)	**Riverside Blvd.**
35.9	1.4	R	into Riverside Park, through parking lot to bike path east along river
39.4	3.5		Sgt. Floyd Visitor Center in Sioux City (map p. 85)

mile 662

Cum	Leg	Dir	Road

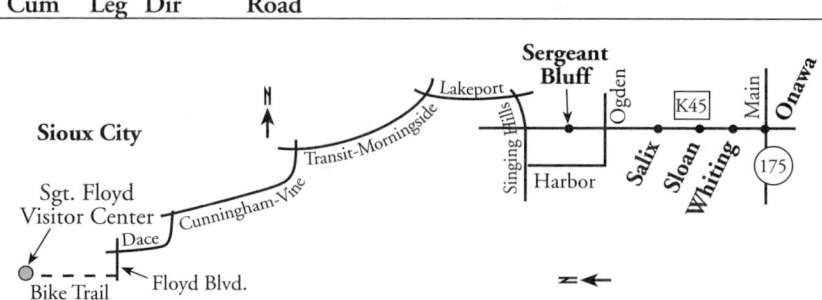

After moderate 300-foot hill up to Morningside, it's downhill and all flat.

		East	**River Bike Trail** from Sgt. Floyd Visitor (map p. 85)
1.4	1.4	L	at traffic circle, under I-29, onto **Floyd Blvd.**
1.7	0.3	R	**Dace**, over Sgt. Floyd River
2.1	0.4	R	**Cunningham** (n/s), pass stockyards
2.9	0.8	St	under Route 75
3.0	0.1	R	**Transit**, up hill, becomes Morningside
4.9	1.9	R	**S Lakeport**
7.2	2.3	R	**Singing Hills** (n/s): motels
8.4	1.2	St	across Lewis Blvd. (K45, Old 75): motels
8.9	0.5	L	**Harbor**
11.4	2.5	L	**Ogden**: motels
12.2	0.8	R	**K45**
19.5	7.3		Salix on left: bar
25.5	6.0		Sloan: bar, café, small market
33.7	8.2		Whiting on left: conv. store, bar, café, small market
41.4	7.7		K45 (10th St.) at Main St. in Onawa (map p. 83)

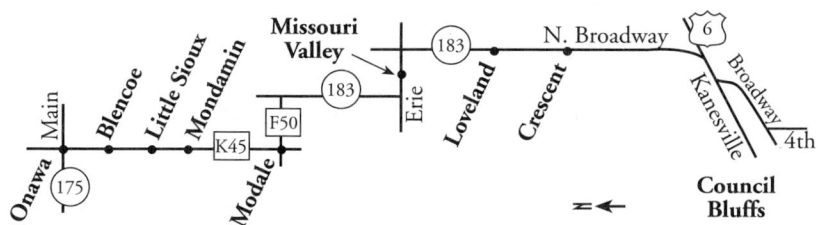

Flat bottomland to Crescent. Moderate Loess hills for last 8 miles.

		South	**10th St.** (K45) from Main St. in Onawa (map p. 83)
0.0		South	**10th St.** (K45) from Main St. in Onawa (map p. 83)
6.8	6.8		Blencoe: small bar/restaurant, conv. store
16.2	9.4		Little Sioux: no services
22.8	6.6		Mondamin: conv. store, bar, grill
29.7	6.9	L (E)	**Martin** (Route 300, becomes Route F50) in Modale: small restaurant, conv. store

Cum	Leg	Dir	Road
35.8	6.1	R (S)	**Route 183**
40.0	4.2	L (E)	**Erie** (Route 30,183) in Missouri Valley (map p. 82) (See map p. 82 for detour to DeSoto National Wildlife Refuge and Wilson Island State Park and Campground)
40.3	0.3	R (S)	**Route 183** from Erie St. in Missouri Valley
44.4	4.1		Intersection G14 to Wilson Island CG 7 mi. west
44.6	0.2		Loveland: café
55.2	10.6		Crescent: 3 small restaurants, conv. store
62.2	7.0	MR (W)	**Kanesville** in Council Bluffs (map p. 76)

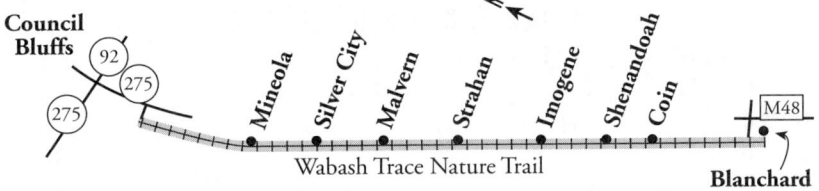

Mostly flat with some long gentle ups and downs on this former railroad. Hard-packed crushed limestone surface.

0.0		South	**Route 275** from Route 275/92 in Council Bluffs (map p. 76)
.4	0.4	R	into school parking lot and south on **Wabash Trace Nature Trail**
10.0	9.6		Mineola
15.6	5.6		Silver City
24.2	8.6		Malvern
30.0	5.8		Strahan
36.2	6.2		Imogene
45.2	9.0		Shenandoah (map p. 74)
56.2	11.0		Coin
61.8	5.6	L	first dirt road in Blanchard
62.0	0.2	R (S)	**M48** in Blanchard

mile 513

Cum	Leg	Dir	Road

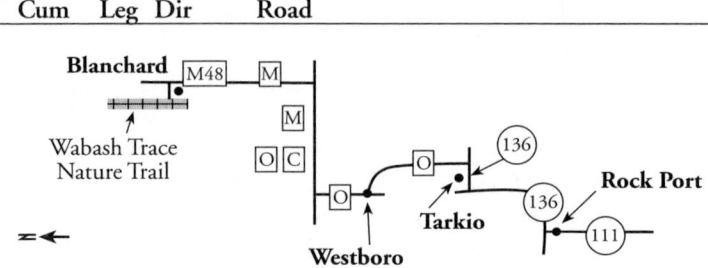

Lots of short steep ups and downs through rich farm country.

Cum	Leg	Dir	Road
0.0		R (S)	**M48** in Blanchard
0.2	0.2	St	**M** (n/s), across stop sign and Missouri state line
3.1	2.9	R (W)	**C/M**
3.9	0.8	St	**C**
8.0	4.1	St	C/O
8.2	0.2	L (S)	O
8.4	0.2	L (E)	O
17.8	9.4	R (W)	**Route 136**
18.8	1.0	L (W)	Route 136 in Tarkio (p. 74)
20.2	1.4	St	Route 136
26.6	6.4		Route 136 at Route 111 in Rock Port (map p. 72)

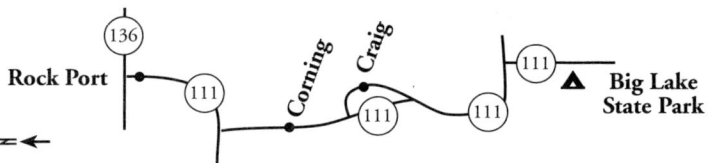

Gentle descent for 3 miles to flat bottomland.

Cum	Leg	Dir	Road
0.0		L (S)	**Route 111** from Route 136 in Rock Port (map p. 72) (St to Brownville; see p. 73 for map and description)
3.9	3.9	L (S)	Route 111 after crossing I-29
13.8	9.9		Corning: no services
21.6	7.8	BR	Route 111; Craig .2 mi. on left: café
22.0	0.4	MR	Route 111
28.2	6.2	R (S)	Route 111 (at Route 118 intersection)
30.3	2.1		Big Lake State Park (p. 72)

Cum	Leg	Dir	Road

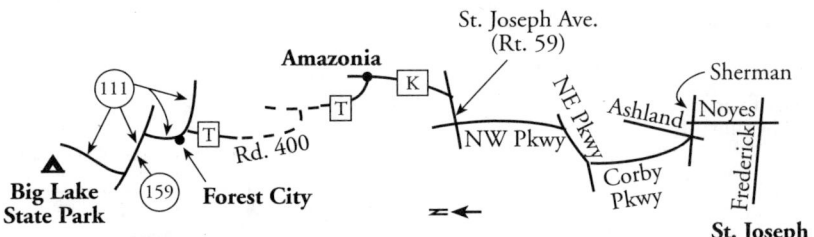

Flat bottomland, except for 6 short (60 ft) nuisance hills on dirt Road 400 after Forest City. Last 6 miles has moderate hills approaching St. Joseph.

0.0		South	**Route 111** from Big Lake State Park (p. 72)
2.4	2.4	L (E)	Route 111/159
7.8	5.4	R (S)	Route 111
12.9	5.1		Forest City: bar, diner
13.2	0.3	R (S)	**Route T**
23.7	10.5	St (S)	pavement ends
27.6	3.9	R (S)	Route T
27.7	0.1	St (S)	Pavement resumes in Nodaway
32.2	4.5	R	**Route K** in Amazonia: covered picnic tables, water
38.2	6.0	MR	**St. Joseph Ave.** (Route 59)
39.3	1.1	L	**Northwest Parkway**
40.8	1.5	MR	**Northeast Parkway**
40.9	0.1	BL	**Corby Parkway**
41.4	0.5	St	Sherman
41.4	0.0	R	**Noyes**
41.6	0.2		Noyes at Frederick in St. Joseph (map p. 69)

mile 370

Cum	Leg	Dir	Road

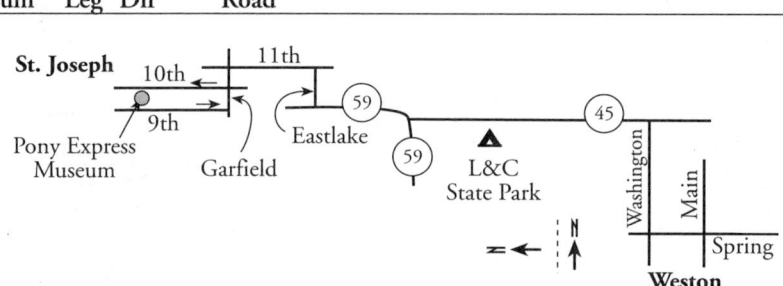

Flat bottomland ending with gentle hills into Weston.

Cum	Leg	Dir	Road
0.0		South	**9th** from Pony Express Museum in St. Joseph (map p. 69)
0.9	0.9	L (E)	**Garfield**
1.1	0.2	R (S)	**11th**
1.6	0.5	R (W)	**Eastlake**
2.0	0.4	L (S)	**King Hill Ave.** (Route 59)
2.6	0.6	BR	Route 59
3.8	1.2	St (S)	Route 59 across Route 752
18.4	14.6	St (S)	**Route 45** where Route 59 turns R (W)
19.5	1.1		Lewis & Clark State Park (p. 68)
31.1	11.6	R	**Washington**
31.8	0.7	L	**Spring**
31.9	0.1		Spring at Main in Weston (map p. 67)

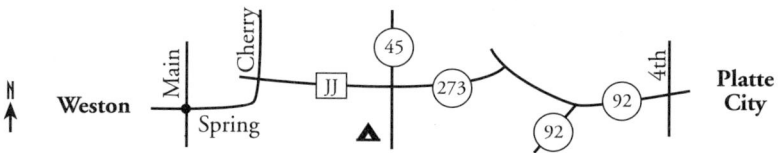

Rolling farm country with occasional short steep hills. Long climbs to Route 45 from both directions.

Cum	Leg	Dir	Road
0.0		East	**Spring** from Main in Weston (map p. 67)
0.2	0.2	L	**Cherry**
0.3	0.1	R (E)	**Walnut** (Route JJ)
2.3	2.0	St	**Route 273** (Weston Bend State Park & CG .4 mi. South)
6.2	3.9	R	to **Route 92**
6.5	0.3	St	Route 92
7.5	1.0	St	Route 92 at 4th St. in Platte City (map p. 66)

Cum	Leg	Dir	Road

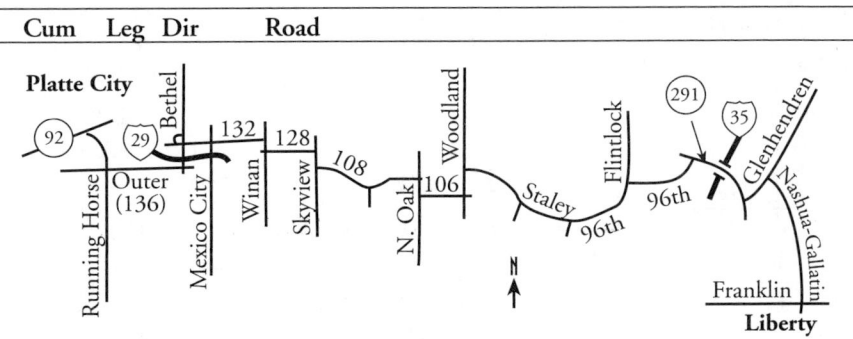

This whole section is moderately hilly with mostly short ups and downs through farm country and some suburban neighborhoods.

Cum	Leg	Dir	Road
0.0		R (S)	**Running Horse** from Route 92 in Platte City (map p. 66)
1.1	1.1	L (E)	**136th**, cross over I-435, becomes Outer
2.6	1.5	L (N)	**Bethel** (across I-435)
2.8	0.2	L,L (E)	**Outer Rd.**
4.3	1.5	St (E)	across Mexico City Rd. (n/s) onto 132nd (n/s); airport 2 mi. south on Mexico City Rd.
5.1	0.8	R (S)	**Winan**
5.6	0.5	L (E)	**128th**
7.1	1.5	St (E)	across Interurban Rd.
8.1	1.0	R (S)	**Skyview**
9.1	1.0	St (S)	Skyview
10.6	1.5	L (E)	**108th**
11.8	1.2	BL (E)	108th (n/s)
14.2	2.4	St	across Route 169
14.7	0.5	R (S)	**North Oak**
15.0	0.3	L (E)	**106th**
16.0	1.0	L (N)	**Woodland**
16.2	0.2	R (E)	**Staley**
18.2	2.0	BL	Staley
19.2	1.0	BL	**96th**
19.7	0.5	St (E)	cross over I-435
22.3	2.6	R (E)	96th
22.9	0.6	R (E)	**LP Cookingham** (Route 291)
23.4	0.5	L (E)	**Glenhendren**
23.7	0.3	R (E)	**Nashua** (becomes Gallatin)
25.8	2.1	L (E)	Gallatin at Kansas in Liberty (map p. 60)

mile 288

Cum	Leg	Dir	Road

Spur Route to Independence

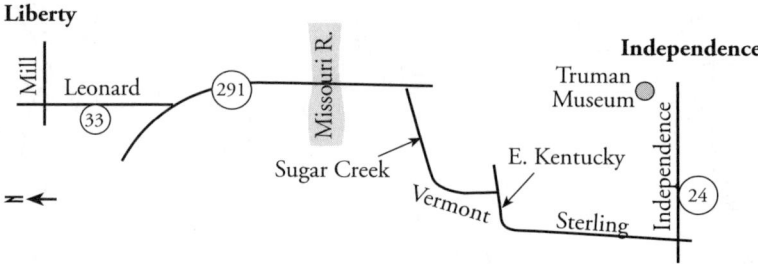

Long gentle hills, big road, and light traffic to river. Quiet back road with long significant hill up to Independence.

Cum	Leg	Dir	Road
0.0		South	**Leonard** from Mill in Liberty (map p. 60)
.7	.7	ML	**Route 291**, bike trail on west side
6.1	5.4	R	**Sugar Creek**, becomes Vermont
10.0	3.9	R	**E Kentucky**
10.2	.2	L	**Sterling**
11.4	1.2	L	**Independence Ave.** (Route 24)
12.6	1.2		Truman Museum on left

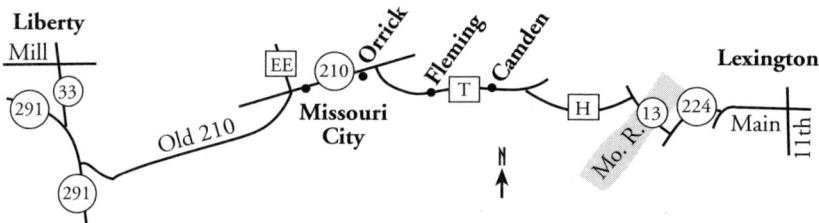

Flat 10 miles, then short hills and traffic through Missouri City. Light traffic with few short hills through Camden. Flat bottomland with final climb to Lexington.

Cum	Leg	Dir	Road
0.0		South	**Leonard** (Route 33) from Mill in Liberty (map p. 60)
0.6	0.6	ML	**Route 291** (bike trail and frontage road on west side)
3.0	2.4	L	**Old 210 Highway**
8.6	5.6	R	**Route 210** (n/s)
10.0	1.4		Missouri City: no services
19.2	9.2		Orrick .5 mi. off to right
20.2	1.0	R (S)	**Route T**
23.0	2.8		Fleming: no services
25.5	2.5		Camden: no services
26.9	1.4	R	**Route H**
31.6	4.7	R (S)	**Route 13** in Henrietta: café, covered picnic tables, water

Cum	Leg	Dir	Road
36.1	4.5	L (E)	**Route 224** after crossing Missouri River on narrow .6 mi. bridge
36.5	0.4	ML	**Main**
36.7	0.2		Main at 11th in Lexington (map p. 59)

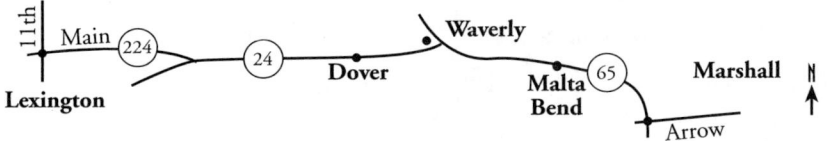

Gentle to moderate short hills through rolling farm country.

0.0		East	**Main St.** from 11th in Lexington (map p. 59)
2.1	2.1	ML (E)	**Route 24**
10.5	8.4		Dover: conv. store
20.5	10.0	R (S)	**Route 65** in Waverly: small store, restaurant
24.4	3.9		Grand Pass
28.9	4.5		Malta Bend: conv. store
39.0	10.1	L (E)	**Arrow** (Route 20) in Marshall (map p. 58)

mile 225

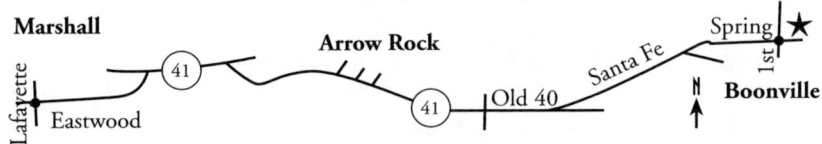

Gentle to moderate short hills through rolling farm country.

0.0		R (E)	**Eastwood** from Jefferson in Marshall (map p. 58)
2.5	2.5	R (E)	**Route 41**
4.3	1.8	R (S)	Route 41
14.6	10.3		Arrow Rock on left (map p. 56)
14.8	0.2		Arrow Rock State Historical Site Museum on left
15.1	0.3		Arrow Rock State Historical Site Campground on left
27.4	12.3	St (E)	**Old Route 40**
27.8	0.4	BL	**Santa Fe Rd.**
33.6	5.8	BL	**Spring**
33.9	0.3		Spring St. at Visitor Center in Boonville (map p. 53)

Cum	Leg	Dir	Road

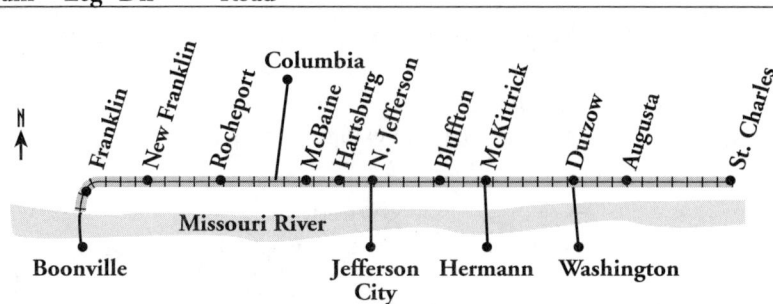

Scenic flat riding on hard-packed crushed limestone rail trail.

Cum	Leg	Dir	Road
0.0		North	**Main St**. across Missouri River from Boonville (map p. 53)
0.7	0.7	L	**Katy Trail** at north end of bridge
2.7	2.0		Franklin: Katy Roundhouse Campground, restaurant (p. 52)
3.5	.8		New Franklin (p. 52)
13.4	9.9		Rocheport (map p. 50)
22.2	8.8		McBaine: 9-mile spur to Columbia (p. 50)
34.3	12.1		Wilton (water, restroom)
38.1	3.8		Hartsburg (p. 49)
48.5	10.4		N Jefferson: 2-mile spur to Jefferson City (p. 48)
60.5	12.0		Tebbetts: restroom, Mrs. Turner's Store
75.8	15.3		Portland (café, bar)
80.8	5.0		Bluffton (p. 48)
90.9	10.1		McKittrick: 3-mile spur to Hermann (map p. 46)
114.0	23.1		Marthasville: bike shop, restrooms, water, restaurants
117.7	3.7		Dutzow: conv. store, 4-mile spur to Washington (p. 45)
125.4	7.7		Augusta (p. 44)
131.1	5.7		Matson (restroom)
135.7	4.6		Weldon Springs (restroom)
146.0	10.3		Greens Bottom Rd. (restroom)
152.2	6.2		Katy Trail at Frontier Park in St. Charles (map p. 42)

Cum	Leg	Dir	Road

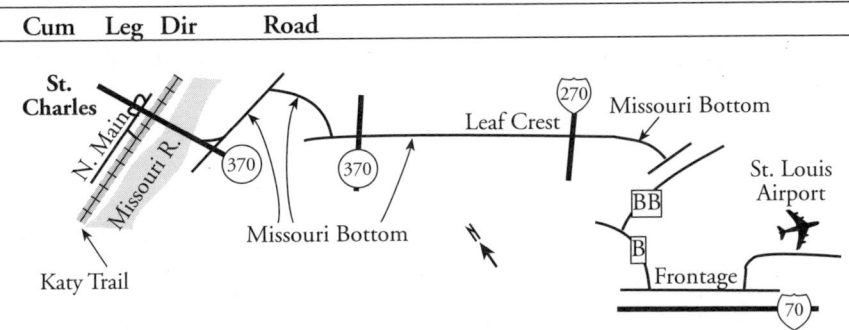

Flat with one moderate climb up to Leaf Crest. Heavy traffic near airport.

Cum	Leg	Dir	Road
0.0		East	**Katy Trail** from Frontier Park in St. Charles (map p. 42)
0.1	0.1		Lewis & Clark Center (Perry St. on left)
0.3	0.2		Visitor's Bureau on left
1.8	1.5	R,L	onto **N Main** just before RR and 370 bridge overhead
1.9	0.1	L	up **Bike Trail** onto Route 370 Bridge eastbound
2.1	0.2	MR (S)	Route 370 bridge over Missouri River
3.2	1.1	BR	Exit for Earth City Expressway
3.4	0.2	L	**Missouri Bottom**
4.7	1.3	R	Missouri Bottom
6.1	1.4	L	Missouri Bottom at T
6.6	0.5	St	**Leaf Crest**
6.9	0.3	St	Missouri Bottom, over I-270
8.8	1.9	St	across 50 ft. of grass at traffic light at end of Missouri Bottom towards 1st runway
8.9	0.1	R	**Route BB** around airport
9.2	0.3	L	**Route B** at light
9.8	0.6	L	**Frontage Rd.**
10.9	1.1	L	into Main Terminal at Airport (map p. 41)

mile 0

6

APPENDICES

Dinner on the hoof.
The Corps of Discovery were especially fond of buffalo tongue.

APPENDIX A — SUGGESTED BICYCLE PREPARATION

MAJOR items that should be done by bicycle shop. These are big things that can wreak havoc with a bike trip. If you do them early (February or March), the bike shop will have more time to do them carefully and schedule them easily. If you wait until April or May, bike shops get busy, less experienced people may do the work, it takes longer, etc:

1. Hubs, Bottom Bracket, Headset — Check bearings; replace if necessary. Most bicycles now have sealed bearings that should last 5–15 years, depending on how much water, dirt, and salt gets in them.

2. Check front and rear racks. Pull at them from different angles to stress them. I once broke a weld this way and had it fixed. It's much easier to do this at home than in the middle of North Dakota.

MINOR items that can be done by a bicycle shop or by yourself. These are things that can cause either major or minor inconveniences on a bike trip. They are much easier to fix at home when you have both time and nearby resources:

3. New chain (should last 1–3 years, depending on mileage, water, and dirt). I used to use very basic cheap chains and change them more often. However, since shifting "systems" have become more complicated and finicky, I now ask for advice at the bicycle shop to assure compatibility before buying a new chain.

4. Check freewheel (should last 2–5 years). If a new chain skips (especially in high gears), your freewheel is worn and you need a new one.

5. Replace brake and derailleur cables and housing every 2–5 years, depending on usage and mileage. I like the housing with teflon inserts for smooth action. Check brake lever hoods. These are easy and cheap to replace when you replace cables, but very difficult to replace at other times.

6. Check brake pads. Replace if necessary. Pay a couple of dollars extra to get higher performance pads; this is cheap insurance.

7. Check tires and replace them if you have any doubts. Tires last 2,000–10,000 miles, depending on type, quality, weight, and usage. Flats are a real nuisance, and they can be dangerous on fast downhills. Tires that wear out on a trip are much worse than a nuisance; bicycle shops in small towns (and even small cities) often don't carry good quality tires for touring. I strongly recommend the biggest and strongest Kevlar-belted tires that will fit on your rims and frame. With Kevlar-belted tires I average one flat tire every 5,000 miles; I have a friend who averages one flat every 500 miles on lightweight tires.

8. Replace tubes every 2–3 years, or when you get 2–3 patches on them. There are new tubes out that claim superior flat prevention, but I don't know how true it is. I use basic tubes.

9. Handlebar tape or padding is a matter of personal preference.

10. Saddles are a matter of personal preference. Ideally, you're searching for comfort; realistically, you're trying to minimize discomfort. Beware of claims that saddles will "wear in" and become comfortable! If a saddle is not comfortable immediately, try another one.

11. Check pedals. If they are "clipless" and you are having any problem getting in or out, deal with the problem before your tour. If you use toe clips and straps, check them for wear.

Appendix B —Suggested Equipment List

See also discussion of equipment in Chapter 2 — Philosophy (p. 15)

A. Bicycle Equipment

1. heavy duty rear rack (Blackburn, Beckman, Gordon); 4-point attachment is stronger and more stable than 3-point attachment
2. heavy duty front low–rider rack (keeping weight low, especially on the front wheel, improves stability and safety)
3. front and rear panniers, preferably in high visibility color or rain covers
4. 2 or 3 large (27oz) water bottles and cages and/or "backpack hydration system"
5. cycle computer (optional)
6. spare tube + patch kit
7. small handlebar bag is optional (although handy, they distribute weight too high and create wind resistance)
8. clipless pedals or toe clips (even when loose, they keep your feet positioned for efficient cycling)
9. tools (see philosophy of tools on page 15)
   critical: tire levers, chain tool, hex wrenches, small adjustable wrench, spoke wrench to fit your spokes, bottle opener, corkscrew
   optional: cable cutter, metric wrench set, screwdrivers, freewheel puller
10. pump

B. Camping Equipment

1. sleeping bag (recommend synthetic, lightweight; put on clothes to keep warm on 10% of the nights when it is cold)
2. sleeping pad (Therm–a–rest is industry standard. Get shortest and thinnest model that is comfortable for you.)
3. Therm-a-rest chair (your sleeping pad fits inside of the frame)
4. pillow/case (personal preference; try for light and small!) I use a small piece of foam rubber with a homemade pillowcase.

C. Bicycle Clothes

1. bike shorts (recommend synthetic crotch liner) I take them in the shower with me and wash them out each night.
2. bike shirt in high visibility color
3. "touring" bike shoes (stiff sole, comfortable for walking too)
4. tights
5. polypro shirt (long sleeve; I like zip turtleneck for temperature flexibility)

6. rain parka (should be waterproof; breathable waterproof fabric is nice, but not necessary; visible color and lots of ventilation; use for windbreaker and extra warmth as well as rain)

7. helmet (some kind of mirror recommended for bike or helmet) I'm probably alive today because my helmet split instead of my head.

8. sunglasses (for eye protection, comfort, and prescription if needed)

9. polypro gloves

10. balaclava (provides warmth, even under a helmet)

11. riding socks

D. Evening Clothes

1. slacks (recommend lightweight and small to pack—jeans are heavy)

2. short sleeve shirt

3. turtleneck shirt (I like zip turtleneck for flexibility)

4. sweater (wool or polar fleece for warmth, light weight, packable)

5. underwear

6. small light shoes (comfortable for lounging and walking)

7. light shorts

8. evening socks?

9. pajamas?

E. Personal Stuff

1. toothbrush, toothpaste (carry in self-seal plastic bag rather than fancy travel kit)

2. small towel + washcloth

3. soap + soap carrier

4. any medication you need

5. small flashlight (recommend Mini–Mag Light)

6. camera, film, mailers

7. wallet (recommend self-seal plastic bag)

8. small light fanny pack for wallet, camera, flashlight

F. First Aid Kit

1. various sizes of band-aids, non-adhering dressings, gauze pads, and adhesive tape. Abrasions are the most common type of injury.

2. anti-bacterial ointment

3. your choice of general pills for headache and muscle ache

4. any medications you may be taking

F. Common Equipment (when touring with a group)

1. tent	13. knife
2. groundcloth	14. cooking spoon
3. dining fly	15. dish towel
4. tarpaulin	16. dish soap + scrubber
5. tools	17. laundry soap
6. 2 pumps	18. juice jug
7. first aid kit	19. seasoning
8. 2+ stoves, matches	20. locks + cables
9. 2+ pans	21. ropes
10. plates	22. books, maps, papers
11. spoons	23. sun screen
12. cups	24. water filter?

General Suggestion for packing and planning

left rear:	evening clothes
right rear:	sleeping bag
left front:	bike clothes
right front:	common equipment
rack:	tent, sleep pad

Leave room for food that must be bought and carried each day!
Rear is for light/bulky (50%); front is for small/heavy (50%).
Keep weight low, close to center line, and between axles.

APPENDIX C — WEATHER DATA

There is a general discussion of weather in Chapter 2 (Philosophy) on page 11. The temperature and precipitation data below may provide some help in planning the timing of your tour(s), as well as help in managing your expectations! Keep in mind that "record" high temperatures are about 20–30° higher than the averages shown, and you should not be surprised by temperatures 10–15° higher. "Record" lows are about 20° below the averages shown, and you should not be surprised by temperatures 5–10° lower.

Average Daily High and Low Temperature

	Apr	May	Jun	Jul	Aug	Sep	Oct
St. Louis, MO	67	76	85	89	87	80	69
	46	56	66	79	68	61	48
Sioux City, IA	62	73	82	87	84	75	64
	38	50	60	65	62	52	40
Bismarck, ND	55	68	77	84	83	71	59
	31	42	52	56	54	43	33
Great Falls, MT	55	65	75	83	82	70	60
	32	41	49	53	52	44	36
Missoula, MT	58	66	74	83	82	71	57
	31	38	46	50	49	40	31
Lewiston, ID	62	70	80	89	88	77	63
	40	47	54	59	59	51	41
Walla Walla, WA	63	71	80	88	87	78	65
	43	49	56	61	61	53	44
Vancouver, WA	59	66	72	77	78	73	63
	39	44	49	52	52	47	41

Average Precipitation (inches)

	Apr	May	Jun	Jul	Aug	Sep	Oct
St. Louis, MO	3.5	4.0	3.7	3.9	2.9	3.1	2.7
Sioux City, IA	2.3	3.7	3.7	3.3	3.0	2.9	1.9
Bismarck, ND	1.7	2.2	2.7	2.1	1.7	1.5	0.9
Great Falls, MT	1.4	2.5	2.4	1.2	1.5	1.2	0.8
Missoula, MT	1.0	1.8	1.8	0.9	1.2	1.1	0.7
Lewiston, ID	1.1	1.3	1.3	0.7	0.8	0.8	0.9
Vancouver, WA	2.8	2.4	1.6	0.8	1.2	2.0	3.2

National Climactic Data Center

Appendix D — Recommended Books

Ambrose, Stephen. (1996). *Undaunted Courage: Meriwether Lewis, Thomas Jefferson, and the Opening of the American West.* Simon & Schuster: NY.

> This is history that reads more like an adventure novel. Even if you don't think you're interested in Lewis and Clark, you will be after you read this. There's a reason why this book has sold several million copies.

Dufur, Brett. (1999). *Katy Trail Guidebook, 5th edition.* Rocheport, MO: Pebble Publishing (www.pebblepublishing.com).

> 224-page guidebook devoted to the 245-mile Katy Trail written by a local journalist/historian. Lots of detailed history, places to stay, places to eat, and things to do along the way. This book is very helpful if you want to spend more than a few days traversing the 150 miles we use on this trail.

DeVoto, Bernard. (1953). *The Journals of Lewis and Clark.* New York, NY: Houghton Mifflin.

> Brief summary of their journals in a single volume.

Duncan, Dayton. (1987). *Out West.* New York, NY: Viking Penguin

> Wonderful stories about Duncan's trip in a Volkswagen camper following the general route of Lewis and Clark. Especially good descriptions of life in the mid-1980s in these areas.

Faneslow, Julie. (1994). *Traveler's Guide to the Lewis & Clark Trail.* Helena, MT: Falcon Press.

> Very good historical summaries and modern-day descriptions of the areas visited by Lewis and Clark. Since it was written for car travellers, it assumes you can travel far and fast to find places to stay and eat. It lacks the detailed information bicycle tourers would like to know to plan and execute a trip.

Fifer, Barbara and Soderburg, Vicky. (1998). *Along the Trail with Lewis & Clark,* Montana Magazine.

> Brief descriptions of the journey of Lewis and Clark with excellent large scale detailed maps and many quotes from their journals.

Moulton, Gary E. (1990). *The Journals of the Lewis & Clark Expedition.* Volumes 1–11, University of Nebraska Press: Lincoln, NE.

> Eleven volumes of the original journals—the real thing!

Olmsted, Gerald. (1986). *Fielding's Lewis & Clark Trail.* New York, NY: Fielding (WC Morrow).

> Although older (before the Katy Trail), this guide for car travellers provides good descriptions of towns and areas along the Trail. Also sketchy descriptions of what Lewis and Clark did at various places.

APPENDIX E — SOURCES OF ADDITIONAL INFORMATION

State Tourism Offices

Missouri Tourism Commission
Box 1055, Jefferson City, MO, 65102
800-877-1234, www.missouritourism.org

Kansas Department of Tourism
700 SW Harrison, Topeka, KS 66603
785-296-3487, www.kansascommerce.com

Iowa Department of Tourism
200 E Grand Ave., Des Moines, IA, 50309
800-345-4692, www.traveliowa.com

Nebraska Travel & Tourism
Box 98913, Lincoln, NE 68509-8913
800-228-4307, www.visitnebraska.org

South Dakota Department of Tourism
800-732-5682, www.travelsd.com

North Dakota Tourism
604 East Blvd., Bismarck, ND 58505-0825
800-435-5663, www.ndtourism.com

Travel **Montana**
Box 200533, Helena, MT 59620-0533
800-847-4868, www.visitmt.gov

Idaho Travel Council
Box 83720, Boise, ID 83720-0093
800-847-4843

Washington State Tourism
Box 42500, Olympia, WA 98504
800-544-1800, www.tourism.wa.gov

Travel **Oregon**
800-547-7842, www.traveloregon.com

Lewis & Clark Organizations

Lewis & Clark National Historic Trail (National Park Service)
    1709 Jackson St., Omaha, NE 68102
    402-221-3471, www.nps.gov/lecl

Lewis & Clark Trail Heritage Foundation
    Box 3434, Great Falls, MT 59403
    www.lewisandclark.org

Interpretive Centers and Museums

Museum of Westward Expansion
    11 N 4th Street, **St. Louis, MO** 63102
    314-655-1700

Lewis and Clark Center
    701 Riverside Drive, **St. Charles, MO** 83467
    636-947-3199, www.lewisandclarkcenter.org

National Frontier Trails Center
    318 W Pacific, **Independence, MO** 64050
    816-325-7575

Western Historic Trails Center
    3434 Richard Downing Ave., **Council Bluffs, IA** 51501
    712-366-4900, www.iowahistory.org

Lewis & Clark Interpretive Center
    Box 607, **Washburn, ND** 58577
    877-462-8535, www.fortmandan.com

Knife River Indian Villages National Historic Site
    Box 9, Stanton, ND 58571
    701-745-3309, www.nps.gov/knri

Lewis and Clark National Historic Trail Interpretive Center
    4201 Giant Springs Road, **Great Falls, MT** 59403
    406-727-8733, www.fs.fed.us/r1/lewisclark/lcic.htm

Big Hole National Battlefield
    Box 237, **Wisdom, MT** 59761
    406-689-3155, www.nps.gov/biho

Nez Perce National Historical Park
    Box 100, **Spalding, ID** 83450
    208-843-2261, www.nps.gov/nepe

Fort Clatsop National Memorial
    Route 3, Box 604-FC, **Astoria, OR** 97103
    503-861-2471, www.nps.gov/focl

Lewis and Clark Interpretive Center
    Fort Canby State Park, Box 488, **Ilwaco, WA** 98624
    360-642-3029

Other Parks

Katy Trail State Park
    Missouri Department of Natural Resources
    800-334-6946, www.katytrail.showmestate.com

Theodore Roosevelt National Park
    Box 7, Medora, ND 58645
    701-623-4466, www.nps.gov/thro

Other

Lewis & Clark Trail by Bicycle
    www.kcnet.com/~rex

APPENDIX F — PUBLIC TRANSPORTATION

The map below shows **train** and **bus** routes that may be useful for:

1. getting to and from the start and end of your tour

2. emergencies

3. combining portions of a Lewis & Clark tour with another tour

4. parts of your tour you may not want to ride because of time constraints; delays due to bad weather, equipment problems, etc.; or just preference to ride certain parts and avoid other parts

   In the town descriptions and maps in Chapter 4 I have included access to major **airports** in St. Louis (Mile 0), Kansas City, MO (Mile 286), Omaha, NE (Mile 500), and Portland, OR (Mile 2800).

   There is also very easy access to smaller airports in Pierre, SD (Mile 910), Bismarck, ND (Mile 1140), Great Falls, MT (Mile 1780), and Missoula, MT (Mile 2,200). The trade–off is that smaller airports have easier bicycle access, but more difficult airline connections.

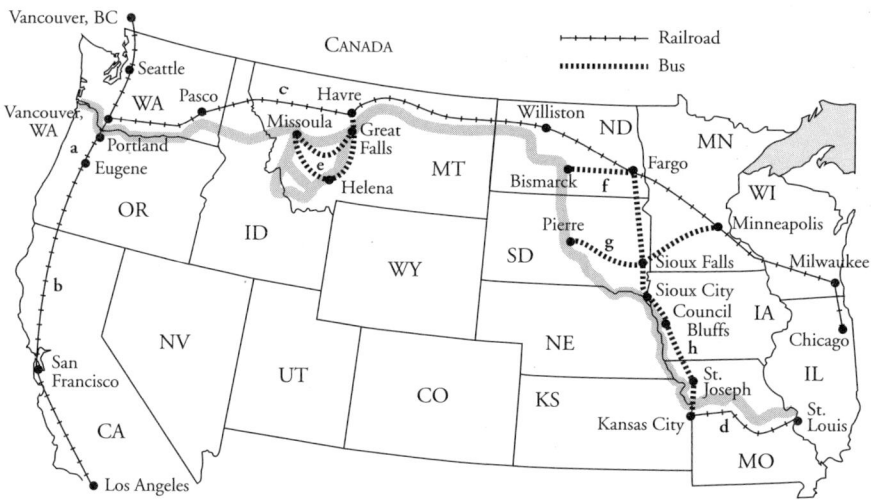

The map shows four AMTRAK daily passenger trains near our bicycle route. They generally require that bicycles be boxed, and boxes are usually available at stations. However, it's always a good idea to call in advance and ask about reservations and bicycles. (800-872-7245, www.amtrak.com)

a. AMTRAK Cascades runs modern trains between Vancouver, BC, and Eugene, OR, intersecting our route in Vancouver, WA, and Portland, OR.

b. AMTRAK Coast Starlight runs between Seattle, WA, and Los Angeles, CA, intersecting our route in Vancouver, WA, and Portland, OR.

c. AMTRAK Empire Builder runs parallel to our route between Portland, OR, and Minneapolis and Chicago, with many stops on or near our route in Vancouver, WA, The Dalles, OR, Pasco, WA, Whitefish, MT, Havre, MT, Malta, MT, Glasgow, MT, Wolf Point, MT, and Williston, ND.

d. AMTRAK Missouri runs across the state between St. Louis and Kansas City with several stops on or near our route in Independence, Jefferson City, Hermann, and Washington.

The map also shows several major bus routes that intersect our route. Bus companies generally require that bicycles be boxed. However, I have found that bus drivers are often willing to carry a bicycle with panniers in the luggage space below—if there is room. It helps if you are flexible!

e. Rimrock Trailways (800-225-7655) has multiple bus lines in western Montana between Great Falls, Helena, Three Forks, and Missoula. They also run up to Whitefish, Shelby, and Havre where they intersect with AMTRAK.

f. Greyhound runs between Bismarck and Fargo, and then on to Minneapolis. It also runs between Kansas City, St. Joseph, MO, Omaha/Council Bluffs, Sioux City, IA, and Sioux Falls, SD. (800-739-5020, www.greyhoundlines.com)

g. Jack Rabbit runs a daily bus between Pierre, SD, and Sioux Falls, SD, which then connects to a bus to Fargo and AMTRAK. At Sioux Falls you can also make connections on Greyhound to Sioux City, Omaha, St. Joseph, MO, and Kansas City. (800-444-6287, www.jackrabbitlines.com)

h. Jefferson Lines runs between Omaha, St. Joseph, MO, and Kansas City. (816-364-0486, www.jeffersonlines.com)

Index

If you like this book, please share this page with a friend—or give a book as a gift.

BICYCLE GUIDE TO THE LEWIS & CLARK TRAIL, by Tod Rodger

This 3,000 mile tour offers magnificent scenery, quiet roads, a variety of accommodations and food, and wonderful people. Ride your bicycle, your car, or your armchair to experience and appreciate our wonderful United States, as you follow in the footsteps of America's greatest explorers and learn about the opening of the west.

In addition to **85 route maps**, detailed directions, and touring hints you expect in a typical bicycle guide, this book offers:

- **Master Plan**, to help you design the tour that's best for you, depending on your preferences for distance per day and type of lodging

- **125 Town Descriptions** (75 with **Maps**) to help you find what you need in each town, such as lodging, camping, restaurants, food stores, bike shops, and museums.
  Plus, historical sketches of towns and stories of what Lewis and Clark did in the area

- Separate **Cue Sheets** (detailed directions) and **Maps** for both westbound and eastbound travellers which you can tear out and put in your pocket or handlebar bag

TOD RODGER has ridden over 125,000 miles and led adults and high school students on many one- to five-week bicycle tours, both camping and staying in B&Bs and motels. He knows what bicycle tourers want and need in a guide.

For more information, see: **www.deerfootpublications.com**

Order Form

Name_____

Street _____

Town_____State _____Zip _____

Email_____Phone_____

Ship to (if different from above)
Name_____

Street _____

Town_____State ___ _____Zip _____

	Price	Quantity	Total
Bicycle Guide to the Lewis & Clark Trail	$24.95	_____	_____
Sales tax (in Massachusetts, add 5%)			_____
Shipping			4.00
TOTAL			_____

Send with your check to:
Deerfoot Publications, 16 Deerfoot Trail, Harvard, MA 01451

Notes:

NOTES:

If you like this book, please share this page with a friend—or give a book as a gift.

BICYCLE GUIDE TO THE LEWIS & CLARK TRAIL, by Tod Rodger

This 3,000 mile tour offers magnificent scenery, quiet roads, a variety of accommodations and food, and wonderful people. Ride your bicycle, your car, or your armchair to experience and appreciate our wonderful United States, as you follow in the footsteps of America's greatest explorers and learn about the opening of the west.

In addition to **85 route maps**, detailed directions, and touring hints you expect in a typical bicycle guide, this book offers:

- **Master Plan**, to help you design the tour that's best for you, depending on your preferences for distance per day and type of lodging

- **125 Town Descriptions** (**75** with **Maps**) to help you find what you need in each town, such as lodging, camping, restaurants, food stores, bike shops, and museums.
  Plus, historical sketches of towns and stories of what Lewis and Clark did in the area

- Separate **Cue Sheets** (detailed directions) and **Maps** for both westbound and eastbound travellers which you can tear out and put in your pocket or handlebar bag

TOD RODGER has ridden over 125,000 miles and led adults and high school students on many one- to five-week bicycle tours, both camping and staying in B&Bs and motels. He knows what bicycle tourers want and need in a guide.

For more information, see: **www.deerfootpublications.com**

Order Form

Name_____

Street_____

Town_____State _____Zip _____

Email_____Phone_____

Ship to (if different from above)
Name_____

Street_____

Town_____State _____Zip _____

	Price	Quantity	Total
Bicycle Guide to the Lewis & Clark Trail	$24.95	_____	_____
Sales tax (in Massachusetts, add 5%)			_____
Shipping			4.00
TOTAL			_____

Send with your check to:
Deerfoot Publications, 16 Deerfoot Trail, Harvard, MA 01451